AMERICAN INDIAN STUDIES

AMERICAN INDIAN STUDIES
STUDIES
A BIBLIOGRAPHIC
GUIDE

Phillip M. White

Reference Librarian
Bibliographer for American Indian Studies
San Diego State University

1995
LIBRARIES UNLIMITED, INC.
Englewood, Colorado

To Pauline, Charlene, Harlan,
Leota, Paul, and W. D.

LIBRARIES UNLIMITED, INC.
P.O. Box 6633
Englewood, CO 80155-6633
1-800-237-6124

Project Editor: *Rebecca Morris*
Copy Editor: *Ramona Gault*
Design and Layout: *Pamela J. Getchell*
Proofreader: *Ann Marie Damian*
Artwork Designed by: *Joan Garner*

Library of Congress Cataloging-in-Publication Data

White, Phillip M.
    American Indian studies : a bibliographic guide / Phillip M. White.
        xi, 163 p. 17x25 cm.
    Includes bibliographical references and index.
    ISBN 1-56308-243-8
    1. Indians of North America--Bibliography.   2. Reference books--Indians of North America--Bibliography.   I. Title.
Z1209.W52   1995
[E77]
016.970004'97--dc20   94-24345
                                                          CIP

CONTENTS

5 Bibliographies *(Continued)*
Bibliography of Bibliographies *(Continued)*

INTRODUCTION

This book is intended to guide college students, librarians, and other researchers in utilizing library resources for information on American Indians, or Native Americans. Its primary focus is Indians of North America—the indigenous peoples of the contiguous United States, Canada, and Alaska. Some sources listed here also include Native Hawaiians, Indians of Mexico, and Indians of Central America and South America.

The study of American Indians touches on virtually every area of life and requires many subject disciplines, including history, anthropology, archaeology, sociology, social work, education, psychology, political science, public affairs, law, criminal justice, medicine, public health, religion, mythology, philosophy, folklore, business, economics, literature, music, and arts and crafts. Information on American Indians is voluminous and is found in books, encyclopedias, magazines, journals, newspapers, newsletters, government publications, travel guides, pamphlets, dissertations, theses, conference proceedings, atlases, and computer databases. The information may be current or historical, general or specialized, intended for the beginner or the in-depth researcher. This guide will alleviate confusion for the researcher by providing direction and organization in choosing and utilizing the best sources in the major disciplines for the study of American Indians.

This guide describes the major information sources available for American Indian research: encyclopedias, dictionaries, handbooks, ethnographic surveys, periodical and newspaper indexes and abstracts, computer databases, directories, statistical sources, bibliographies, book catalogs, biographical sources, dissertation sources, government publications, and microform collections.

Materials included are in English, and most were published in the United States between the early 1970s and 1993. The subject content ranges from ancient times to contemporary life and culture.

Entries are descriptively and critically annotated, and annotations range in length from 20 to 200 words, with longer annotations for the more important works. Materials are arranged within each section in order of importance, with some sources added just prior to publication to include important recently published titles. In chapter 6, subject disciplines are organized alphabetically.

Each of the 12 chapters represents a major type of information source available in libraries. These categories of materials are those commonly utilized by students when writing term papers and by researchers when surveying the literature for publication. The organization of the guide is meant to represent a research strategy useful for most researchers and most topics in American Indian studies.

Researchers may begin by searching for books on their topics. Then they should consult a guide to the literature for direction on further steps in the research process. Reference books such as encyclopedias, handbooks, and ethnographic surveys are important bridges for surveying the field of study. Dictionaries provide brief definitions and names of important individuals in the field. Directories are vital for specific information such as addresses, names, telephone numbers, statistics, and biographical summaries.

Bibliographies can save researchers the time and effort of having to "start from scratch" with a topic. Bibliographies pull together many sources on a subject, including books, periodical articles, and government publications, thus expanding the knowledge of materials available to researchers. Periodical and newspaper indexes, abstracts, and databases are major sources of information for most researchers for their coverage of narrow topics and for contemporary issues. The comprehensive researcher also will want to identify theses and dissertations available on his or her topic. Another major resource for research on American Indians is materials published by the U.S. government. Additional information may be found in biographies and in special microform collections.

The best search strategy for researchers in American Indian studies is determined by the topics under study, but the order of sources presented in this guide represents a logical approach to efficient research.

ACKNOWLEDGMENTS

I would like to thank the reference librarians at San Diego State University Library for providing assistance and suggestions with this project. Specifically, I want to thank Carolyn Fields for suggesting I create the book. I also thank Robert Carande, Bruce Harley, Pat Knobloch, Catherine Friedman, Greta Marlatt, Linda Muroi, and Doug Cargille for their ideas and assistance.

In the American Indian Studies Department of San Diego State University, I offer thanks to Richard Carrico and Dr. Linda Parker for their lectures and knowledge.

At the University of California, Riverside, I send many thanks to Dr. Cliff Trafzer for his encouragement.

I also want to thank Bonnie Biggs, Reference Librarian and American Indian Studies Bibliographer at California State University, San Marcos, for her continued support and information-sharing.

A very special thanks goes to Dr. G. Edward Evans of Loyola Marymount University for his many years of service offering critical reviews for the selection of reference materials in American Indian studies, and for his advice and suggestions.

At the University of Texas at Austin, Perry-Castaneda Library, I offer thanks to Glenn Gillespie, Ron Seeliger, Kathy McIver, John Tongate, and Robin Fradenburgh.

At Southwest Texas State University Library, I must thank Dr. Bill Mears, as well as Stephanie Langenkamp.

At the College of Wooster Library, I owe many thanks to Denise Monbarren for her continued support.

At the University of Nevada, Las Vegas, I thank Dr. Stephen Fitt for his mentoring role.

I also want to thank my good friend Cathy Reams Dow for teaching me about Indian arts and crafts of the Southwest.

I owe a debt of gratitude to the Diegueno/Kumeyaay, Luiseno, and Cupeno Indians of San Diego County for educating me through their powwows, meetings, and celebrations.

Thanks also goes to Joan Shelby and Joyce Green for their assistance in preparing the manuscript.

BOOKS

Thousands of books are available on American Indians, covering their histories, cultures, religions, languages, contemporary issues, legal battles, and so on. Most researchers want to find books on their specific topics when beginning their literature review. To determine whether these books exist or are available in libraries, they must check under the correct terms. Books are listed under controlled subject terms in the card catalogs and computerized catalogs of libraries. The first step in locating books is to make sure to use the correct subject terms.

Subject Headings

Subject headings are the words or phrases under which books are found in library catalogs. Although it may sound simple to look up books on a subject, it is often a difficult task to determine the correct terms to use. The Library of Congress in Washington, D.C., publishes a guide titled *Library of Congress Subject Headings* (Washington, D.C.: Library of Congress, 17th ed., 1994), which provides the correct subject terms to use when searching for books in most large libraries in the United States. In this guide, the main subject heading for American Indians is: Indians of North America. There are additional headings under other topics (e.g., Sun Dance) and under names of specific tribes and individuals. Researchers should always start their research for books by using the *Library of Congress Subject Headings* to determine the correct terms for the many topics in the field of American Indian studies. The four large, red-covered volumes of the *Library of Congress Subject Headings* are usually kept near the reference desks and by the online/card catalogs in libraries. Because of the importance of using the correct subject headings for researching books on American Indian topics, the appendix lists all the *Library of Congress Subject Headings* under "Indians of North America." All the cross-references are included for broader terms (BT), related terms (RT), and narrower terms (NT), as well as terms used for (UF) other terms, terms to USE instead of other terms, and see also (SA) references. This listing should be useful for all those searching for books in the field.

Classification Systems

Libraries use classification systems to place together materials on the same subjects. All knowledge is divided into major classes, then broken down into specific areas by combinations of letters and numbers. The two most common classification systems are the Library of Congress Classification System and the Dewey Decimal Classification System. Books and other materials are assigned call numbers based on these classification systems, and books are shelved in the book stacks by these call numbers.

The Dewey Decimal system is used primarily by smaller libraries, such as school libraries and smaller public libraries. Melvil Dewey divided all knowledge into nine classes (100-900), with a 10th class for general materials (000). From a base of 10, this offers 100 divisions of subject classes. Materials on American Indians fall into such class divisions as the following:

016.97	Bibliographies
299.7	Religion and Mythology
342	Legal Problems
398	Legends
497-498	Language
709.1	Art
810-811	Literature
920	Biography
970	General History of North America

Most university libraries and large public libraries in the United States use the Library of Congress Classification System, and this is the primary one with which researchers should become familiar for American Indian materials. The Library of Congress classification divides all knowledge into 21 classes (beginning with each letter of the alphabet except I, O, W, X, and Y) and uses a combination of letters and numbers for specific breakdowns of subject areas within these classes. With a base of 26 letters possible, this classification system allows for 676 subject divisions.

The following guide shows an overview of the major classes in the Library of Congress Classification System for books on American Indians:

Library of Congress Classes That Contain Books
on North American Indians

E51-E61	Pre-Columbian America. The Indians.
E71	North America (north of Mexico).
E73-E74	Mound Builders. Indians of North America.
E75	Periodicals. Societies. Collections.
E76	Congresses. Dictionaries. Directories. Guides to tribes. Study and teaching. Research. Historiography.
E77	General Works.
E78	Works by state, province, or region, A-Z. (For example, books on Indians of Arizona would have the call number E78.A7; books on Iowa Indians, E78.I6; Canada (general), E78.C2; British Columbia, E78.B9; Northwest coast of North America, E78.N78.)
E81-E83	Indian Wars.
E85-E87	Captivities.
E89	Biography (collective).
E90	Biography (individual).
E91	Government relations (general works).
E92	Government relations (Canada).
E93	Government relations (United States).
E94	Laws (collections). See also the K classes.
E95	Treaties (collections).
E97	Education.
E98	Other topics, A-Z, for example, art, E98.A7; children, E98.C5; games, E98.G2; religion, mythology, E98.R3; social life and customs, E98.S7; women, E98.W8.
E99	Tribes, A-Z (examples: Arapaho, E99.A7; Fox, E99.F7; Kwakiutl, E99.K9; Zuni, E99.Z9).
F1-F975	The United States local history class. Books on Indians of a specific locality may have an F classification.
F697-F698	Indian Territory history.
F1001-F1140	British America. Canada. Books on Canadian Indians, particularly by the early explorers, may have an F classification.
GN	The anthropology class. Indian books are in this class if they are part of an anthropology series or if the treatment is primarily anthropological.
HD231-HD234	Indian lands. (Older books on land transfers, leases, etc. may be here. The K and E classes are now more frequently used.)
KE*	The law of Canada class.
KE318.N3	Indian law students.
KE378.N3	Legal aid.
KE7701-KE7710	Native people.
KE7715	Land laws. Reserves and settlements.
KE7718	Claims.
KE7722	Other topics, A-Z. (For example, education, KE7722.E3; hunting and fishing rights, KE7722.H8.)

---

*The K classes were not fully developed until the 1960s, consequently many law libraries do not use the Library of Congress system or use it only for books published since that time.

KE7735	Indigenous legal systems—general works.
KE7739	Indigenous legal systems—special topics.
KE7742	Indigenous legal systems—administration.
KE7749	Indigenous legal systems—particular groups or topics, A-Z.
KE1044	Native people—Ontario.
KE1060	Native people—Quebec.
KF	The law of the United States class.
KF5660-KF5662	Indian lands.
KF8201-KF8228	Indian legal matters. (If the book is on Indian laws of a particular state, the KF will be followed by a third letter—KFC, California; KFN, New York.)
L	The education class.
LC2629	Education of Indians in Canada. (Most books on education are in the E97 class.)
M	The music class.
M1669	Indian vocal music.
ML3557	Writing on North American Indian music. (E59.M9 or E98.M9 may also have books on Indian music.)
N	The art class.
N8217.I5	Indians in art. (Used for Indians as subject matter—generally Indian art books are in E59.A7 or E98.A7.)
PE1127.I5	Indians of North America—juvenile literature (i.e., readers).
PM	The American Indian language class.
PM101-PM149	Indian languages, texts in Indian languages.
PM155-PM198	Indian literature, poetry, and its history and criticism; translations into English or other languages.
PM201-PM2711	Indian languages. (Dictionaries, grammars, etc.)
PN	The class for literary history and collections.
PN1995.9.I48	American Indians in motion pictures.
PN4883	Indian newspapers.
PN 6120.I6	Indians of North America—Drama.
PS	The American literature class.
PS153.I52	History and criticism of the fiction of Indian authors.
PS173.I6	Indians in literature—criticism.
PS508.I5	American Indian author collections.
PS591.I55	American Indian poetry.
R	The medicine class.
RA448.5.I5	Public health aspects concerning Indians.
RA801	Indians of North America—Health and Hygiene.
RA981.A35	Indian hospitals.
RC451.5.I5	Indian mental health.
Z	The bibliography class.
Z1208	American archaeology bibliography.
Z1209-Z1210	American Indian bibliography.
Z1229.I3	American Indian authors bibliography.
Z7116-Z7119	American Indian language bibliography.

Reprinted with permission from: Haas, Marilyn L. *Indians of North America: Methods and Sources for Library Research*. Hamden, CT: Library Professional Publications, 1983. ISBN 0-2080-1980-4.

GUIDES TO THE LITERATURE

Guides to the literature, or literature guides, are books that direct researchers in using the library for information in specific subject fields. They include the major types of information sources, such as bibliographies, dictionaries, encyclopedias, handbooks, periodical indexes, computer databases, and government publications. The general, all-purpose standard in the United States for the major reference sources in all subject fields is the *Guide to Reference Books* by Eugene P. Sheehy (Chicago: American Library Association, 10th ed., 1986). Pages 710-714 of this "librarian's Bible" present 37 of the most important reference sources published before 1986 on Native Americans. The supplement to Sheehy, *Guide to Reference Books Covering Reference Materials from 1985-1990, Supplement to the Tenth Edition*, edited by Robert Balay (Chicago: American Library Association, 1992) lists on pages 249-251 an additional 20 entries for Native American reference materials.

Two of these reference sources are guides to the literature, which are presented below. These are important starting points in understanding the structure of the study of American Indians and in identifying the principal reference materials and information sources available for research.

Another valuable source for researchers in determining what is available in the field is *American Reference Books Annual* (ARBA) (Englewood, CO: Libraries Unlimited, 1970-present, ISSN 0065-9959), which is an annual comprehensive review source for North American reference works.

1.   Haas, Marilyn L. **Indians of North America: Methods and Sources for Library Research.** Hamden, CT: Library Professional Publications, 1983. 163p. $29.50. LC 83-14007. ISBN 0-2080-1980-4.

Two guides to the literature serve researchers in the field of American Indian studies. Haas and Hirschfelder, Byler, and Dorris (entry 2) have created effective guides to a large body of literature, but with different emphases. Haas has organized her book as one would teach a library research course in the field. She begins by introducing subject headings, classification systems, and call numbers, with a listing of the Library of Congress classification for books on North American Indians. This is a practical guide to doing research but covers much more than the basic sources. Part 1 includes chapters on indexes, abstracts, and online databases, with descriptions of the coverage of each general and specific source, ranging from the *Readers' Guide to Periodical Literature* to the *List of Publications of the Bureau of American Ethnology with Index to Authors and Titles*. She compares current and retrospective sources and discusses the advantages of online database searching over manual searching. Other chapters cover such resources as library catalogs, handbooks, encyclopedias, directories, and government publications.

Part 2 of Haas is an annotated bibliography, primarily of books published since the 1970s, arranged by topics such as agriculture, alcohol, art, war, and women. A very useful feature of this section is the inclusion at the end of each annotation of the Library of Congress Subject Headings for the specific sources covered. This enables the researcher to check for additional books in his or her library to supplement the sources listed. The third section of the guide is an unannotated bibliography of books on major tribes.

This important guide serves college students and other researchers who need assistance in learning library research strategy and in learning about the myriad of sources for doing research and finding information on American Indians.

2. Hirschfelder, Arlene, Mary Gloyne Byler, and Michael A. Dorris. **Guide to Research on North American Indians**. Chicago: American Library Association, 1983. 330p. $32.50. LC 82-22787. ISBN 0-8389-0353-3.

This significant guide differs from Haas (entry 1) in its approach to the literature. It assumes a basic knowledge of library research skills and presents a summary of the major written literature in the field. It does not discuss computer databases, which are so important in research for current literature and for speed in searching. However, Hirschfelder, Byler, and Dorris impressively annotate approximately 1,100 English-language books, articles, and government publications of research importance in the field.

The guide is divided into four broad sections (introductory material, history and historical sources, economic and social aspects, and religion, arts, and literature), with 27 subfields of study covered extensively. Introductory essays explain the significance of materials on such topics as land tenure and resources, political organization, federal and state Indian relations, health, medicine, and disease, urban life, and music and dance.

This distinctive work should continue to be vital to researchers for many years, primarily for the older, important works in the field.

2a. Kibbee, Josephine Z. **Cultural Anthropology: A Guide to Reference and Information Sources**. Englewood, CO: Libraries Unlimited, 1991. 205p. (Reference Sources in the Social Sciences Series, no. 5). $47.50. LC 91-14042. ISBN 0-87287-739-6.

This guide includes cultural anthropology, but also materials in archaeology, physical anthropology, linguistics and other divisions within the field of anthropology. The annotations are separated into nine chapters: general and social science reference sources, general anthropology reference sources, anthropology bibliography, subfields of anthropology (physical, linguistic, applied, medical, psychological, cognitive, economic, political, urban, anthropology of education, anthropology of women), anthropology and the humanities, additional topics, area studies, periodicals, and supplemental resources. Some of the core materials for research on Native Americans are included.

3. Kuipers, Barbara J. **American Indian Reference Books for Children and Young Adults**. Englewood, CO: Libraries Unlimited, 1991. 176p. $32.50. LC 91-6880. ISBN 0-87287-745-0.

Kuipers's book serves as a guide to historically and culturally accurate reference books and nonreference books on American Indians for children and young adults. The first part of the book discusses evaluation criteria for the selection of culturally sensitive materials on American Indians by librarians, educators, and parents. Such criteria as qualifications of the author, scope of the book, and, of course, accuracy and objectivity in treatment of the subject matter are emphasized. Kuipers does an excellent job of summarizing traditional Indian values and identifies the typical problems of cultural ethnocentrism as reflected in the lack of authenticity and objectivity in the mainstream literature concerning Indians. She includes a list of reference sources and a list of American Indian bibliographies useful for materials in overcoming these stereotypes.

Part 2 is a most impressive annotated bibliography of American Indian books of reference value for use with children and young people. These books were selected from a listing of 6,923 titles in other bibliographies, based on accuracy of coverage and reading level of the intended students. The resulting 200 titles are extensively annotated and arranged by Dewey Decimal classification into broad subject areas (e.g., religion, social sciences, literature). This is a unique guide of importance to all librarians and educators concerned with teaching children accurately about American Indians.

4. Vane, Sylvia Brakke, and Lowell John Bean, eds. **California Indians: A Guide to Manuscripts, Artifacts, Documents, Serials, Music and Illustrations**. 2d ed. Menlo Park, CA: Ballena Press, 1990. 366p. (Ballena Press Anthropological Papers, No.36). $45.00; $33.00pa. LC 90-40604. ISBN 0-87919-119-8; ISBN 0-87919-118-Xpa.

This is a guide to known primary sources about native Californians, with suggestions about where to look for materials pertaining to California Indians. The emphasis is on ethnography and ethnohistory sources, but linguistic and archaeological sources are included. Also listed are many historical materials concerning California before the 1860s, when the state's Indian population was large. Because the information presented is designed primarily for the scholar, this guide omits the sources that are typically consulted in libraries, such as those covered by Haas and Hirschfelder, et al. (entries 1 and 2). The emphasis here is on primary source materials, such as manuscripts, pictures, and documents, which are difficult to locate through periodical indexes and databases. The bulk of the guide is devoted to a survey of important collections in counties. Listed are university libraries, government agency collections, public libraries, private libraries, State of California collections, Indian tribal museums, and historical societies that hold manuscripts, archival material, photographs, maps, newspapers, periodicals, pamphlets, artifacts, recordings, or other special collections of interest to the scholar in American Indian studies. A section on publications serves as a directory of periodicals, publishers, and audiovisual materials specifically on California Indians. For the serious researcher on California Indians, this substantial work complements the available mainstream library resources.

DIRECTORIES

Directories are listings of organizations, people, and other information arranged by subjects and alphabetical order. They include addresses, phone numbers, biographical information, numerical data, and other miscellaneous information. Directories are vital for locating current information on Indian schools, reservations, tribal councils, and organizations.

5.   Furtaw, Julia C., ed. **Native Americans Information Directory**. Detroit: Gale Research, 1993. 371p. $75.00. ISBN 0-8103-8854-5. ISSN 1063-9632.
    This is the newest comprehensive directory of all aspects of contemporary Native American life and culture. One volume contains more than 4,500 listings of resources concerning the cultures, heritage, education, politics, social concerns, employment, and media of American Indians and Native Hawaiians. This extremely attractive and well-printed directory compares with Klein (entry 6) in the types of information presented, but the two guides are organized differently. Furtaw divides her guide into sections on American Indians, Alaska Natives (including Eskimos and Aleuts), Native Hawaiians, and Aboriginal Canadians (Indians, Metis, and Inuits).
    Included in each category are tribal communities; national, regional, state/provincial, and local organizations; federal government agencies; federal domestic assistance programs; state/provincial and local government agencies; library collections; museum collections; research centers; education programs and services; Native American studies programs; scholarships, fellowships, and loans for Indian students; print and broadcast media (directories, journals and magazines, newsletters, Indian newspapers); publishers of Indian materials; and videos of importance. Entries are well annotated for materials covered, and full addresses, phone numbers, and contact people are included for all organizations, agencies, tribal councils, and schools. This is a must for all libraries providing information on

American Indians. Though Klein (entry 6) covers most of the same organizations and agencies, this guide should be in every library as well for its ease of use and its inclusion of Native Hawaiian information. A section on general resources on Native Americans concludes the guide, listing broad-based resources for minorities and culturally disadvantaged groups. This section is organized much like preceding sections of the guide, listing organizations (e.g., American Civil Liberties Union), governmental agencies (e.g., Minority Business Development Agency), financial aid sources, and videos on racism, prejudice, and minorities. No biographical information is provided on Indian leaders, however. And researchers will need to look elsewhere for direct information on powwows and other Indian celebrations and events. But most often, this wonderful guide will tell researchers whom to contact and where to write or call for further information on most topics.

6. Klein, Barry T., ed. **Reference Encyclopedia of the American Indian**. 6th ed. West Nyack, NY: Todd Publications, 1993. 679p. $125.00; $49.50pa. ISBN 0-915344-30-0; ISBN 0-915344-33-5pa.

Klein has added new listings and updated data in this new edition of a significant, standard reference work for contemporary Indian information. Like Furtaw (entry 5), this set comprises a thorough listing of Native American directory information. It is divided into four main sections: Section one, the most important, lists data on reservations; tribal councils; tribes; government agencies; Indian schools; Indian Health Services offices; national, state, and regional associations; radio and television stations and programs for Indians; museums, monuments, and parks; libraries specializing in Indian collections; audiovisual media about Indians; periodicals important for Indian information; and a new section on arts and crafts shops specializing in Indian materials.

Section two lists Canadian reserves and bands, associations, museums, libraries, periodicals, colleges, and radio and television communications.

The third section is an unannotated bibliography of approximately 4,500 books about American Indians that are still in print. A broad subject and tribal classification is tagged onto this section to categorize the books listed.

The fourth section is an excellent source on contemporary Indians. Over 2,500 biographical sketches of prominent contemporary American Indians and non-Indians are given. Many fields are covered, including business, the professions, the arts, and politics. Non-Indians are those active in Indian affairs, especially in anthropology, archaeology, history, and art.

Researchers can find important directory information on American Indian reservations, tribes, organizations, agencies, associations, colleges, and museums in this guide and in Furtaw (entry 5).

6a. Champagne, Duane. **The Native North American Almanac; A Reference Work on Native North Americans in the United States and Canada**. Detroit: Gale Research, 1994. 1,274p. $95.00. ISBN 0-8103-8865-0.

This monumental work will be of lasting value for many years. The field of American Indian studies has been recently blessed with several new directories, such as Furtaw (entry 5), Klein (entry 6), and Hirschfelder (entry 7), that provide an enormous amount of valuable reference information in single volumes. Researchers will use Champagne's volume for historical and contemporary information about the

Indians of North America, including a chronology (pages 1-187), chapters on demography, major culture areas, languages, law and legislation, administration, activism, environment, urbanization, religion, arts, literature, media, health, education, economy, and biographies. Many knowledgeable contributors made this task possible. Maps, pictures, tables, and bibliographies for each chapter add to the usefulness of the guide. Directory information accompanies the articles in each chapter, providing addresses and telephone numbers for reservations, powwows, schools and colleges, organizations, museums and research centers, and Indian media contacts.

7. Hirschfelder, Arlene, and Martha Kreipe de Montano. **The Native American Almanac; A Portrait of Native America Today**. New York: Prentice Hall, 1993. 341p. $25.00. LC 93-1057. ISBN 0-671-85012-1.

Not as comprehensive as Furtaw (entry 5) or Klein (entry 6) for directory information, Hirschfelder's book nevertheless is chock-full of useful information on the history and traditions of Native Americans. *The Native American Almanac* is unique in its coverage of many aspects of Indian life today combined with historical coverage of important events and issues. It also includes directory information, such as reservations, landmarks, museums, and cultural centers.

The first 35 pages provide an excellent historical overview of relations between Native Americans and nonnatives in the United States, with statistics, tables, charts, and maps. Subsequent chapters are titled "Native Americans Today," "Supreme Court Decisions Affecting Native Americans," "Treaties," "The Bureau of Indian Affairs and the Indian Health Service," "Tribal Governments," "Languages," "Education," "Religion," "Games and Sports," "Artists," "Film and Video Arts," "Employment, Income, and Economic Development," and "Native Americans and Military Service." These chapters are well written, well illustrated, concise, and current, and filled with directory information and statistics. For example, in the chapter on education, researchers will discover directory information on Indian-controlled postsecondary schools, the Bureau of Indian Affairs postsecondary schools, education organizations and programs, and regional resource and evaluation centers.

The Native American Almanac is especially strong on providing summaries of laws, treaties, and court cases historically affecting American Indians and statistics on Indian populations. It would make a good textbook for university classes in American Indian studies.

The appendixes list Native American tribes by state, reservations, rancherias, colonies, and historic Indian areas; a chronology of Indian treaties 1778-1868; and a general chronology covering 1492-1992. Most of the information from the appendixes duplicates that in Furtaw and Klein (entries 5 and 6), but *The Native American Almanac* includes information difficult to locate elsewhere, such as endangered sacred lands (p. 113), inductees into the American Indian Athletic Hall of Fame (pp. 132-39), Native American actors (pp. 180-82), non-Indian actors as Indians (p. 179), Indians receiving Medals of Honor (p. 229), and American naval fighting ships with Indian names (pp. 235-36). This quick and convenient reference tool will serve researchers for many years.

Another directory similar to *The Native American Almanac* and to the *Reference Encyclopedia of the American Indian* (entry 6) is the *Native American Directory* (Tucson, AZ: Native American Co-op), with a 1994 edition coming soon. Although not as comprehensive as the two directories above, this volume lists powwows and celebrations, as well as organizations, schools, museums, crafts guilds, Indian culture centers, urban health centers, performing artists, trading posts, and other important directory information on American Indian interests. For a more comprehensive listing of powwows covering 1993-1997, use *Pow Wow* by Fred Snyder (San Carlos, AZ: National Native American Co-Op, 1993. $5.00).

7a. Frazier, George W., ed. **The American Indian Index**. Denver, CO: Arrowstar, 1985. 325p. $21.45. LC 85-20155. ISBN 0-935151-39-7.

This directory provides more than 6,000 contacts for researchers and librarians who need addresses and telephone numbers for tribal offices, powwows, Indian organizations, federal and state offices, museums and libraries, programs for employment, health services and housing, Indian publications and periodicals, arts and crafts centers, and census information. A new edition will benefit those seeking a quick reference guide to directory information. Another somewhat dated directory providing information on Indian-owned businesses and statistics of businesses in which Indians have been involved is *The Red Pages: Businesses Across Indian America* (Toppenish, WA: LaCourse Communications, 1985. 282p.).

8. Eagle/Walking Turtle. **Indian America: A Traveler's Companion**. 3d ed. Santa Fe, NM: John Muir Publications, 1993. 432p. $17.95pa. ISBN 1-56261-110-0.

Indian America is useful as a directory as well as a guide to Indian reservations in the United States. Tribal councils' addresses and telephone numbers are listed, with directions to the reservations from major highways. Organized by major geographic regions (the Great Plains, Mountain and Plateau, the North, the Northeast, the Northwest, the South, the Southeast, the Southwest, and the West), the directory lists states within each region and major tribes in each state that allow visitors onto their reservations. Visitor information is given for powwows, ceremonies, and other public events, as well as the arts and crafts available. Brief histories of the tribes are provided. Black-and-white photographs of historically important Indian leaders enhance the guide, and line-drawing maps indicate locations of reservations. The appendix is especially useful for listings of Indian Moons, a powwow calendar for North America, Indian arts and crafts shows, Navajo rug auctions, and Indian stores, museums, and rodeos. A detailed index also makes this guide valuable for travelers and researchers seeking quick facts.

9. Shanks, Ralph, and Lisa Woo Shanks, eds. **The North American Indian Travel Guide**. Petaluma, CA: Costano Books, 1986. 278p. $14.95pa. LC 86-70680. ISBN 0-930268-07-5.

Similar to Eagle/Walking Turtle (entry 8), this travel guide is most useful to researchers as a directory for addresses and phone numbers of tribal councils, reservations, monuments, museums, parks, and ceremonies. The Shankses also provide summaries of what visitors can expect when visiting reservations and learning centers.

Tribes are listed by states for the United States and by provinces for Canada. Brief histories of the tribes and many photographs within the text make this an attractive guide and a useful directory for tribal information.

Another traveler's guide that complements Eagle/Walking Turtle (entry 8) as well as *The North American Indian Travel Guide* is *North American Indian Landmarks: A Traveler's Guide,* by George Cantor (Detroit: Visible Ink, 3d ed., 1993). This source is a guide to over 300 Indian sites relevant to American Indian history and culture, listing maps, locations, hours open, and useful histories of the landmark sites.

An older guide that contains much useful information on the histories, cultures, traditions, and ceremonies of Indians, and is still useful for travelers to Indian lands, is *A Guide to America's Indians, Ceremonies, Reservations, and Museums* by Arnold Marquis (Norman, OK: University of Oklahoma, 1974. 280p. $17.75pa. ISBN 0-8061-1148-8).

Other national travel guides for directory information on American Indian reservations, sites, monuments, and campgrounds are *Native America* by John Gattuso (New York: Prentice Hall General Reference, 1991. 389p. Insight Guides. $19.95pa. ISBN 0-13-467119-8), *Fodor's Indian America* by Jamake Highwater (New York: Fodor's Travel Publications, 1975), and *Discover Indian Reservations USA: A Visitors' Welcome Guide* by Veronica E. Tiller (Denver, CO: Council Publications, 1992. 402p. $19.95pa. LC 92-071259. ISBN 0-9632580-0-1). Regional Indian travel guides include *The Earth Is Our Mother, A Guide to the Indians of California, Their Locales and Historic Sites*, 3d ed., by Dolan H. Eargle, Jr. (San Francisco: Trees Company, 1993. 194p. $12.95pa. LC 86-50411. ISBN 0-937401-09-9), *Traveler's Guide to Native America: The Southwest Region* by Allen Hayward (Minocqua, WI: Northword, 1993. $16.95pa. ISBN 1-55971-158-2), and *Traveler's Guide to Native America, The Great Lakes Region* by Allen Hayward (Minocqua, WI: Northword, 1992. 192p. $16.95. LC 92-9426. ISBN 1-55971-139-6).

9a. Folsom, Franklin, and Mary Elting Folsom. **America's Ancient Treasures, A Guide to Archaeological Sites and Museums in the United States and Canada**. Albuquerque: University of New Mexico, 1993. 459p. $37.50; $19.95pa. LC 92-32120. ISBN 0-8263-1424-4; ISBN 0-8263-1450-3/pa.

This illustrated guide to prehistoric Indian life leads researchers and travelers to museums, exhibits, and archaeological sites in the United States and Canada. The authors have done an excellent job of summarizing what there is to see and discover at these sites and collections, as well as the directions to get there and the telephone numbers and addresses. The guide is divided into large regions of the United States and Canada (e.g., Southwest, Great Plains) and then by states and provinces, with a detailed index included. The scholar and researcher will gain more substantive information on the history and cultures of pre-Columbian Indians of North America here than they will in Eagle/Walking Turtle (entry 8), Shanks (entry 9), or the other travel guides mentioned within entry 9.

ENCYCLOPEDIC SOURCES

4

Specialized encyclopedias, dictionaries, handbooks, and ethnographic surveys are important tools for researchers in American Indian studies. These encyclopedic volumes represent a wide variety of types and styles of reference sources that are consulted for specific information, such as definitions, facts, or dates, and for historical, background, or summary information on specific topics. Encyclopedias, handbooks, dictionaries, and ethnologies vary in their content and length of coverage of topics, from brief definitions to long essays or chapters. There are specific language dictionaries for many Indian tongues, such as *Chemehuevi: A Grammar and Lexicon* by Margaret L. Press (Berkeley, CA: University of California, 1979. $54.90. LC 78-62874. ISBN 0-520-09600-2), and *The Navajo Language: A Grammar and Colloquial Dictionary* by Robert W. Young, and William Morgan (Albuquerque: University of New Mexico, 1980. $35.00. LC 79-56812. ISBN 0-8263-0536-9). And there are dictionaries and handbooks on specific topics such as ethnobotany: James A. Duke's *Handbook of Northeastern Indian Medicinal Plants* (Lincoln, NE: Quarterman, 1986. LC 85-62814. ISBN 0-88000-142-9) is one example. But the dictionaries, handbooks, and encyclopedias included in this guide are ones that explain many aspects of American Indian cultures and histories or that focus on one broad topic (e.g., *The Encyclopedia of Native American Religions* [entry 21]). Most provide information on people, places, and events which are well established in the field of study and therefore do not represent new information or contemporary research. Some atlases present surveys of Indian-nonnative relations along with illustrations and maps. These sources will assist researchers in defining terms, understanding historical events and cultural traits, surveying background information, and obtaining brief summaries of people associated with events under study.

Increasing numbers of electronic editions of encyclopedias are appearing, such as *The American Indian: A Multimedia Encyclopedia* (New York: Facts on File, 1993, $295.00. ISBN 0-8160-2835-4) produced on CD-ROM. This and other titles on video disc and compact disc are especially useful for public school students and the general public.

Encyclopedias, Handbooks, and Dictionaries

10.   Sturtevant, William C., ed. **Handbook of North American Indians**. Washington, DC: Smithsonian Institution, 1978-. 20v. (in progress). LC 77-17162.

> Volume   4. **History of Indian-White Relations**. Wilcomb E. Washburn, ed. 1988. 838p. $47.00. ISBN 0-16-004583-5;
>
> Volume   5. **Arctic**. David Damas, ed. 1984. 845p. $29.00. ISBN 0-16-004580-0;
>
> Volume   6. **Subarctic.** June Helm, ed. 1981. 853p. $25.00. ISBN 0-16-004578-9;
>
> Volume   7. **Northwest Coast**. Wayne Suttles, ed. 1990. 793p. $38.00. ISBN 0-16-020390-2;
>
> Volume   8. **California**. Robert F. Heizer, ed. 1978. 800p. $25.00. ISBN 0-16-004574-6;
>
> Volume   9. **Southwest,** Pt. 1. Alfonso Ortiz, ed. 1979. 701p. $23.00. ISBN 0-16-004577-0;
>
> Volume 10. **Southwest,** Pt. 2. Alfonso Ortiz, ed. 1983. 884p. $25.00. ISBN 0-16-004579-7;
>
> Volume 11. **Great Basin**. Warren L. D'Azevedo, ed. 1986. 863p. $27.00. ISBN 0-16-004581-9;
>
> Volume 15. **Northeast**. Bruce G. Trigger, ed. 1978. 942p. $27.00. ISBN 0-16-004575-4.

Nine of the proposed 20 volumes have been completed in this monumental set that gives "an encyclopedic summary of what is known about the prehistory, history, and cultures of the aboriginal peoples of North America north of the urban civilizations of central Mexico," as stated in the preface. This is a definitive source produced by scholars for anthropological research. Each volume is written and edited with clarity and thoroughness and at a level understandable by college students and useful for the specialist as well. Most volumes are organized by geographical regions and include introductory overviews and chapters on topics such as the environments in which the Indians lived, their languages and linguistics, histories and prehistories, histories of research in the field, summaries of individual tribes and culturally and linguistically related peoples, the arts, religious beliefs and practices, contemporary concerns, and other cultural aspects of the tribes. Each volume is well illustrated with black-and-white photographs, maps, and drawings. Chapters list sources, which refer to the extensive bibliographies at the end of each volume. Detailed indexes for each volume allow researchers to quickly locate specific topics.

Of unique value to college student researchers is volume 4, *History of Indian-White Relations*. Topics include the national policies of the United States, Britain, France, Canada, Spain, Mexico, and other countries toward Indians; military policies; political and legal relations; economic relations; religious relations; and conceptual relations. Also discussed are such subjects as the history of the legal status of American Indians and the portrayal of Indians in the movies.

No other encyclopedia compares with this set in its comprehensive coverage of historical and contemporary topics. These volumes should be consulted first in researching any topic or tribe in American Indian studies. Because the series is printed by the U.S. Government Printing Office, the prices are extremely low for the quantity and quality of material.

Forthcoming volumes include the following: volume 1, *Introduction*; volume 2, *Indians in Contemporary Society;* volume 3, *Environment, Origins, and Population*; volume 12, *Plateau;* volume 13, *Plains*; volume 14, *Southeast*; volume 16, *Technology and Visual Arts;* volume 17, *Languages*; volume 18, *Biographical Dictionary*; volume 19, *Biographical Dictionary;* and volume 20, *Index.*

10a. Davis, Mary B., ed. **Native America in the Twentieth Century, an Encyclopedia**. New York: Garland, 1994. 787p. (Garland Reference Library of Social Science, Vol. 452). $95.00. LC 94-768. ISBN 0-8240-4846-6.

This much-needed encyclopedia highlights American Indians and Native Alaskans in the twentieth century, covering art, communications, daily activities, economic development, education, government policy, health, land, languages, law, museums, race relations, social issues, sports, tribal government, population, and urbanization issues. Several hundred contributors wrote the articles, ranging in length from a page to several pages. This unique and timely source provides overviews of research topics as diverse as the Navajo-Hopi land controversy, the Indian alcohol metabolism myth, allotment, the American Indian Movement, the American Indian Religious Freedom Act, the BIA schools, the Indian Health Service, the Indian Shaker Church, religion, urbanization, pottery, and tribal information. It is illustrated with 20 maps and 75 photographs and contains valuable bibliographic references at the end of each topic.

10b. John, Michael G. **The Native Tribes of North America, a Concise Encyclopedia**. New York: Macmillan, 1994. 210p. $70.00. LC 93-23429. ISBN 0-02-897189-2.

Organized by geographical regions and by languages within regions, more than 300 Native tribes in the United States and Canada are covered in short articles. Brief historical, cultural, and geographical information is presented on each tribe, with contemporary information for currently performed cultural activities, population statistics, and economic status of the tribes. This is a quick guide for brief tribal information, illustrated with maps, photographs, and color plates.

11. Waldman, Harry, ed. **Encyclopedia of Indians of the Americas**. St. Clair Shores, MI: Scholarly Press, 1981. 7v. $59.00/vol. LC 75-170347. ISBN 0-403-03586-4.

Originally published in 1975, this incomplete set begins with A and ends with Manzanita. Entries range in length from one sentence (Jackson Rancheria) to 43 pages (Language). Included are the native peoples of North America, Central America, South America, the Caribbean islands, and the Arctic region.

All the volumes are illustrated with many pictures, drawings, and maps. Volume 1 is an overview of broad subjects (e.g., "American Indian Art," "History of the Indians of the Americas," "Religion and Philosophy") and was written by authorities such as Frederick Dockstader and Vine Deloria, Jr. Several Indians participated in writing the chapters and consulting with the authors of the various sections. Volume 1 also includes a chronology spanning 25,000 B.C. to A.D. 1974 and covering pages 181-450. The scope of this set must be commended; it has proven to be of lasting value to researchers. The alphabetical arrangement of volumes two through seven makes them easy to use, whether one is searching broad topics or specific subjects. However, the lack of bibliographic references decreases the set's usefulness to researchers desiring to delve further.

11a. Terrell, John Upton. **American Indian Almanac**. New York: World, 1971. 494p. LC 70-142135.

This book is not an almanac, but is a compilation of articles about the history and prehistory of American Indian tribes. A vast amount of information is contained in these pages such as maps, Indian place names, archaeological sites, population estimates of tribes, significant dates, cultural information on the tribes, migration patterns, and tales from early explorers. The book is divided into ten major geographical sections, with a glossary and index included. Even though it was first published in 1971, this book is still uniquely useful for the prehistoric information and interesting reading.

12. Waldman, Carl. **Encyclopedia of Native American Tribes**. New York: Facts on File, 1988. 293p. $45.00. ISBN 0-8160-1421-3.

Articles covering over 150 tribes summarize the historical records, geographic locations, migrations, lifeways, languages, subsistence patterns, dwellings, clothing, tools, arts, legends, rituals, and other cultural facets of American Indians. Illustrated with over 250 color pictures and 11 maps, the articles are arranged alphabetically and are easy for beginning researchers to use.

13. Spicer, Edward H. "American Indians." In *Harvard Encyclopedia of American Ethnic Groups*, edited by Stephan Thernstrom. 58-114. Cambridge, MA: Harvard University Press, 1980. 1,076p. $95.00. LC 80-17756. ISBN 0-674-37512-2.

An excellent overview of American Indians in the United States from ancient to contemporary times. Tribes are arranged within regions (e.g., Peoples of the Atlantic Coast, the Western Great Lakes Country, the Mississippi Valley, Oklahoma, the Northern Plains), and the histories of the tribes are summarized chronologically. Annotated bibliographies are given after each section. Statistics on population bring the researcher up through the 1970s. A good article on federal government policy toward American Indians complements the chapter. This chapter condenses important historical information on Indian tribes in a readable format, highlighting important influences on the tribes.

14. Curtis, Edward S. **The North American Indian, Being a Series of Volumes Picturing and Describing the Indians of the United States and Alaska**. Washington, DC: Smithsonian Institution, 1907-1930: repr., New York: Johnson Reprint, 1970. 20v. and 4v. supplement. ISBN 0-384-10395-2.

Edward S. Curtis spent 30 years taking photographs of Indians in the United States, British Columbia, and Mexico. In his attempt to create a definitive pictorial record of Native North Americans, Curtis took over 40,000 photographs from 80 different tribes, including many well-known tribal leaders. More than 2,000 of these fascinating pictures of Indians in the United States in the early twentieth century are reproduced here. The accompanying text describes traditional cultures, customs, and activities among the tribes of that day. Topics include daily activities, dwellings, hunting, gathering, agriculture, foods and cooking, religion, mythology and creation myths, medicine and medicine men, dances, arts and crafts, population, dress, languages, and ceremonies. Volumes are arranged by geographic areas and then by tribes, with an index in the back of each of the 20 volumes. However, there is no cumulative index, so researchers must look through each volume's table of contents for their tribes or topics. The four large supplemental volumes contain excellent 9½ by 7 inch black-and-white photographs of Indian people and scenes, arranged to complement the first 20 volumes. Curtis has been criticized for posing and staging the people and scenes he photographed, but his work was comprehensive and professional and provides a valuable contribution to the understanding of American Indians and their traditional cultures and lives.

15.   Levinson, David, and Timothy J. O'Leary, eds. **Encyclopedia of World Cultures**. Vol. 1: **North America.** Boston: Human Relations Area Files, 1991. 424p. $100.00. LC 90-49123. ISBN 0-8161-1808-6.
      The first of a 10-volume set describing the cultures of the world, this impressive volume covers the cultural groups of the United States, Canada, and Greenland, excluding extinct cultures. Nearly 1,000 contributors have written the summaries that are the heart of the set. Included are 223 Native American cultures, mostly those in the western United States. The Native American entries are arranged alphabetically among other cultural groups. Specific tribes are analyzed (e.g., Lipan Apache), as well as linguistically or culturally related tribes (e.g., Pueblo Indians). Seventy of the Native American groups are described in three- to four-page summaries, 99 in half-page summaries, and 54 in mentions (short paragraph). The long summaries were written to represent a full range of cultural variation among all Native American cultures for the past and present. Each entry covers ethnonyms (for variations in tribal names), history and cultural relations, historical locations, demographic summaries for past and present, settlements, economy, kinship, marriage and family relations, sociopolitical organization, and religion and expressive culture. Short bibliographical references of important sources are included for each entry. Pages 417-424 contain an ethnonym index for identification of alternative names and names of major subgroups of cultures in the volume. This is an excellent beginning point for research on tribes.

16.   **Dictionary of Daily Life of Indians of the Americas, A-Z**. Newport Beach, CA: American Indian, 1981. 2v. $165.00. ISBN 0-937862-26-6.
      The introduction to this title explains the long history of cultural diversity among Indians of the Americas. Hundreds of languages were spoken, and many styles of social organization and social institutions existed. The concentration here is on pre-Columbian cultures, their habitations and construction, technology, clothing, narcotics, and myths and legends. This alphabetically arranged dictionary attempts to summarize major cultural elements in short articles. Included are such topics as agriculture, alcoholic beverages, athletics, basketry, concepts of beauty, burial customs, childbirth customs, child rearing, courtship, dance, domesticated plants and animals, education, music, mutilations and deformations, petroglyphs, prayer sticks, rock art, shamanism, totem poles, and weapons. Entries range in length from a paragraph to several pages. No bibliographic references are provided, however, and the student is

left to wonder where to look for more information. A general index accompanies the second volume.

17.   **Dictionary of Indian Tribes of the Americas**. 2d ed. Newport Beach, CA: American Indian, 1993. 3v. $375.00/set. ISBN 0-937862-28-2.

An alphabetically arranged encyclopedia of tribes, this set ranges from the Aleuts of the Arctic regions to the Onas near the Antarctic. Historians and anthropologists wrote the articles on 1,158 tribes of the western hemisphere from ancient times to the present, summarizing their cultural traits, geographic areas, religious beliefs, histories, relations with governments, and arts and crafts. This revised edition of the 1980 original contains 652 new entries and revisions of earlier entries, but more important, it provides bibliographic references. It also contains maps and drawings and a detailed index at the end of volume 3, making it useful for beginning researchers.

17a.   **Chronology of the American Indian**. 3d ed. Newport Beach, CA: American Indian Publishers, 1994. 298p. (American Indian Dictionary Series). $85.00. ISBN 0-403-09949-8.

This chronology attempts to summarize major events in the prehistory and history of Indians of the Americas. It is useful to students in providing an overview of important topics. Illustrations are scattered throughout. An older, but handy, volume for quick research is *The American Indian 1492-1970: A Chronology and Fact Book*, 2d ed., by Henry C. Dennis (Dobbs Ferry, NY: Oceana, 1976. 177p. $8.50. LC 76-116066. ISBN 0-379-00526-3).

18.   Leitch, Barbara A. **A Concise Dictionary of Indian Tribes of North America**. Algonac, MI: Reference Publications, 1979. 646p. LC 78-21347. ISBN 0-917256-09-3. (Revised edition due in late 1994, $75.00).

An excellent dictionary of the major tribes of the United States and Canada presented in alphabetical order, this work is easy to use, with an easy-to-read typeface. Students especially like the one- to three-page summaries of the locations, cultures, histories, and languages of tribes. About 200 pictures along with maps of tribal locations liven up the text. Brief bibliographic references are cited for further research. A detailed index of about 8,500 entries makes it possible to locate specific topics within the essays. This dictionary is useful for brief information.

19.   Confederation of American Indians, comp. **Indian Reservations: A State and Federal Handbook**. Jefferson, NC: McFarland, 1986. 329p. $45.00. LC 85-43573. ISBN 0-89950-200-8.

Information on the reservations and lands controlled by Indian tribes is arranged by state and reservation. This unique source lists the land status of reservations (the amount of acres owned by tribes, individual allotments, and other legal land status), brief histories of the tribes and their cultures, and other tribal data concerning their economies, populations, transportation, and communities.

20.   Ruby, Robert H., and John A. Brown. **A Guide to the Indian Tribes of the Pacific Northwest**. Norman: University of Oklahoma Press, 1986. 289p. (The Civilization of the American Indian Series, Vol. 173). $19.95pa. LC 85-22470; 1992. ISBN 0-8061-2479-2.

One- to three-page descriptions are provided of 150 Indian tribes that occupy or formerly occupied the states of the Pacific Northwest: Oregon, Washington, Idaho, and Montana. Entries are alphabetic and include information on tribal languages, alternative names, dwellings, diets, populations through the years, legal claims against the federal government, histories, contact with nonnatives, leaders of tribes (with some photographs), and major migrations and settlements. This is a good source for concise information on a variety of tribal topics. References to articles and books accompany each entry for more information.

21.   Hirschfelder, Arlene, and Paulette Molin. **The Encyclopedia of Native American Religions**. New York: Facts on File, 1992. 367p. $45.00. LC 91-21145. ISBN 0-8160-2017-5.

This encyclopedia focuses on the spiritual traditions of native peoples in the United States and Canada from ancient times to the present. In articles ranging from a few sentences to a few pages, Hirschfelder and Molin condense and explain the basic published information on religious beliefs, ceremonies, and practices, such as the Native American Church, sand painting, the Pueblo Eagle Dance, Hopi Kachinas, and the Iroquois False Face Society. The authors also discuss laws and court cases affecting Indian religious concerns, such as repatriation (National Museum of the American Indian Act and the Native American Grave Protection and Repatriation Act) and the peyote religion (People v. Woody and Employment Division, Department of Human Resources of Oregon, et al. v. Smith et al.). Much of the volume comprises biographies of Native American religious leaders and practitioners such as Wovoka and Black Elk, as well as Catholic and Protestant missionaries who influenced Indian religious traditions, such as Junipero Serra and Andrew White. Excellent indexes group entries under tribes and under broad subjects such as ceremonies (rain ceremonies, masked ceremonies, new fire ceremonies, etc.), court cases (court cases involving religious practices, court cases involving sacred objects, etc.), missionaries by denomination (Anglican missionaries, Baptist missionaries, etc.), and native religious leaders by theme (Ghost Dance of 1890, peyote, Sun Dance, etc.). A list of known sacred sites also is provided in the index. The lengthy bibliography of further readings is valuable for the researcher, who will just get the basics in this resource of lasting value.

22.   Gill, Sam D., and Irene F. Sullivan. **Dictionary of Native American Mythology**. Santa Barbara, CA: ABC-CLIO, 1992. 425p. $65.00. LC 92-27053. ISBN 0-87436-621-6.

Gill and Sullivan have created a valuable guide to the stories, rituals, songs, ceremonies, and creatures that reflect the qualities and characteristics of Native American cultures. Presented alphabetically, the paragraph-length summaries tell of ancient beings, deities, the beginning of creation, spiritual influences on daily life, important ceremonies to restore harmony and cure illnesses, and stories to teach lessons and morals as well as to entertain. The Indian names are used, and many cross-references are given for alternate or related stories. Bibliographic references for each entry provide valuable leads to more information. And the index by tribe guides researchers to the primary myths attributed to those tribes as well as to the bibliography of books, articles, proceedings, and Smithsonian Institution reports for more in-depth information.

This title complements Hirschfelder and Molin (entry 21) by concentrating on specific ancient myths and legends and not as much on whole religious systems or spiritual leaders.

22a. Patterson, Lotsee, and Mary Ellen Snodgrass. **Indian Terms of the Americas**. Englewood, CO: Libraries Unlimited, 1994. 275p. $30.00pa. LC 93-47170. ISBN 1-56308-133-4.

This unique dictionary describes objects, methods of doing things, and names of significant people, places and events associated with Native Americans. These terms represent everyday living tasks, ceremonies, and Indian tribes and people, such as Wilma Mankiller, Buffalo Soldiers, Anasazi, and Wakan Tanka. Along with the brief definitions are examples from the literature on use of the terms.

23. Moss, Joyce, and George Wilson, eds. **Peoples of the World: North Americans**. Detroit, MI: Gale Research, 1991. 441p. $39.95. ISBN 0-8103-7768-3.

For a good encyclopedic overview of the histories and cultures of some of the major American Indian tribes, the beginning researcher would do well to start here. This contains 10-page summaries of the populations, languages, geographic locations, historical backgrounds and major events, and contemporary issues of some of the most influential American Indian groups. Included are the Anasazi, Mound Builders, Thule, Aleuts, Cherokees, Cheyenne, Dakota, Hopi, Micmac, Navajo, Netsilik, Nez Perce, Seminoles, Seneca, and Western Apache. Basic references to further readings are provided for each tribal group. Although limited in scope, this work covers well the most important historical and contemporary events concerning the tribes included. Illustrated with maps and pictures.

24. Cayton, Mary Kupiec, Elliot J. Gorn, and Peter W. Williams, eds. **Encyclopedia of American Social History**. New York: Charles Scribner's Sons, 1993. 3v. $280.00. ISBN 0-684-19246-2.

Good overviews of the histories of American Indians are presented in four chapters: "Native Peoples Prior to European Arrival," by Olive Patricia Dickason (vol.1, pp. 3-14); "Native Peoples and Early European Contacts," by William R. Swagerty (vol.1, pp. 15-36); "American Indians of the East," by Daniel H. Usner, Jr. (vol.2, pp. 655-65); and "American Indians of the West," by Peter Iverson (vol.2, pp. 667-80). Each section has useful bibliographies listing important books, periodicals, articles, and U.S. government publications. Iverson includes a map (vol.2, p. 673) titled "Change in Western Indian Reservation Lands: 1885 to 1935," which is helpful for the study of that period of Indian history. He brings the history up to contemporary times in his section titled "Since 1970."

The Bureau of American Ethnology

The Smithsonian Institution is a trust establishment of the United States funded by the federal government and privately endowed monies. It is dedicated to learning and has many remarkable achievements attached to its name. It also has a long history of administering museums (e.g., the National Museum of American History), overseeing research bureaus and galleries, and publishing in widely divergent fields.

The Bureau of American Ethnology existed as a unique organization within the Smithsonian Institution from 1879-1965. It sponsored and published an amazing amount of ethnological and anthropological information about American Indians, primarily through its 200 Bulletins and 48 Annual Reports, and also through the Publications of the Institute of Social Anthropology, the Contributions to North

American Ethnology, the Introductions, the Miscellaneous Publications, and other series. In 1964, the Bureau of American Ethnology and the Department of Anthropology of the Museum of Natural History combined to form the new Smithsonian Office of Anthropology. This consolidated the work and resources of the Smithsonian in modern programs in ethnology, archaeology, and physical anthropology but terminated the bureau as a separate entity.

The distinguished Bulletins (ranging in length from 32 to 1,000 pages each and written between 1880 and 1940) and Annual Reports (averaging around 800 pages each and produced from 1881 to 1932) collected a massive amount of research in many phases of anthropology, including ethnology, archaeology, and linguistics, regarding American Indian cultures. For example, many reports cover the languages, literature, myths, legends, ceremonials, and songs of American Indians. The essays were written by a large number of authors and contributors (165 authors and coauthors are named in the first 48 Annual Reports). The reports received worldwide recognition and have excellent pictures, photographs, drawings, maps, and other illustrations. For example, the Second Annual Report of the Bureau of American Ethnology contained a report by Frank Hamilton Cushing on Zuni fetishes that remains the definitive report on the subject and is reprinted and widely available today. Other Smithsonian reports, which have been reprinted for sale, include the Indian music reports by Frances Densmore, such as *Mandan and Hidatsa Music* (Bulletin 80), *Menominee Music* (Bulletin 102), *Music of Acoma, Isleta, Cochiti and Zuni Pueblos* (Bulletin 165), *Nootka and Quileute Music* (Bulletin 124), *Northern Ute Music* (Bulletin 75), *Papago Music* (Bulletin 90), *Pawnee Music* (Bulletin 93), *Seminole Music* (Bulletin 161), *Teton Sioux Music* (Bulletin 61), *Yuman and Yaqui Music* (Bulletin 110), and *Handbook of American Indian Languages* by Frank Boas (Bulletin 40). Researchers on specific topics in American Indian studies should consult the indexes for the Bulletins and the Annual Reports to determine if their topics are covered. A treasure chest of information is hidden in these volumes.

Similar sets of primary source materials concentrating on California Indians are the University of California Publications in American Archaeology and Ethnology (1903-1964) and the Anthropological Record Series (1937-1972) from the University of California, Berkeley.

25.   Smithsonian Institution. Bureau of American Ethnology. **List of Publications of the Bureau of American Ethnology, with Index to Authors and Titles**. Washington, DC: Smithsonian Institution Press, 1914; repr., Scholarly Publishing, 1971. 134p. $49.50. ISBN 0-403-03633-X.

This is Bulletin 200, the last of the Bulletins. It lists the contents of the Bureau of American Ethnology Annual Reports, Bulletins, Publications of the Institute of Social Anthropology, Contributions of North American Ethnology, Introductions, and miscellaneous publications. The first half of the index simply lists the reports numerically with the titles and authors of the contributors within. The second half is an index to authors and titles with the various publications. The researcher must look through this section carefully to find the topics covered. For more detailed indexing, check *The 48th Annual Report of the Bureau of American Ethnology* (entry 26).

26. Smithsonian Institution. Bureau of American Ethnology. **The 48th Annual Report of the Bureau of American Ethnology.** Washington, DC: U.S. Government Printing Office, 1933. 1,220p.

This detailed subject index to the first 47 annual reports of the Bureau of American Ethnology provides all topics with subdivisions, tribes, and people covered in the set. Entries give volumes and page numbers after topics.

27. Hodge, Frederick Webb, ed. **Handbook of American Indians North of Mexico, 1910.** Repr., St. Clair Shores, MI: Scholarly Press. (Bureau of American Ethnology Bulletin, No. 30). 2,193p. $250.00/set. ISBN 0-403-00355-5.

This classic work serves as a dictionary, encyclopedia, and ethnographic overview of Indian tribes and their customs, arts, people, villages, and languages, as well as topics of all varieties concerning Indians in the United States, Canada, and Alaska. Alphabetically arranged entries range from brief definitions to essays of several pages and include some photographs and drawings. Topics are both broad and specialized (e.g., agency system, agriculture, agua caliente, dreams and visions, missions, pueblos, Sitting Bull). Of interest to researchers seeking in-depth studies are the references following each entry, which lead to the bibliography at the end of volume 2. These bibliographic references form the basis of American Indian scholarship at the beginning of the twentieth century and can be used to trace books, periodical articles, and proceedings from the eighteenth and nineteenth centuries.

"Synonymy," a valuable section at the back of volume 2, provides synonyms and various spellings of Indian names, tribes, and people and serves further as an index to the alphabetical section.

This source should be consulted by graduate students and others doing extensive research who need materials from past centuries, but it is useful to beginning researchers also for definitions and overviews.

The material on Canadian Indians from Hodge's work was extracted and published in 1913 as the *Handbook of Indians of Canada.* For Indians of the Americas south of the United States, use the *Handbook of South American Indians* (Bureau of American Ethnology Bulletin, No. 143) and the *Handbook of Middle American Indians* (Robert Wauchope, ed. Austin: University of Texas Press, 1964-1976, 16v.), and *Supplement to the Handbook of Middle American Indians* (Victoria R. Bricker, gen. ed. Austin: University of Texas Press, 1981-1992, 5v.).

28. Kroeber, A. L. **Handbook of the Indians of California.** Repr., New York: Dover, 1976. (Bureau of American Ethnology Bulletin, No. 78). 995p. $16.95pa. LC 76-19514. ISBN 0-486-23368-5.

Written by the early twentieth century's foremost scholar on California Indians, this enormous work is the outcome of 17 years of work with Indians by ethnologists, archaeologists, and educators. Some California Indians have criticized the information as inaccurate. Nevertheless, much work went into gathering and summarizing many aspects of the histories and cultures of over 50 Indian tribes and cultural groups such as the Yurok, Hupa, Pomo, Modoc, Washo, Cupeno, Cahuilla, and Diegueno. Topics covered include population, land, civilization, material culture, law, religion, the arts, politics, and geography. Many illustrations, drawings, and maps accompany the text. A bibliography of 415 books, articles, government reports, and other materials leads primarily to important nineteenth-century scholarship. A classified subject index and a general index provide detailed access to the volume. Scholars seeking the most important studies on California Indians before 1925 will benefit from starting with this ethnographic survey.

29. Powers, Stephen. **Tribes of California**. 1877; repr., Berkeley, CA: University of California Press, 1977. 635p. (Bureau of American Ethnology, Contributions to North American Ethnology, Vol. 3). $50.00. LC 75-13150. ISBN 0-520-03023-0.

Stephen Powers was a keen observer of the California Indians he studied in 1871-1872. He primarily published his articles on the habits, customs, legends, religious ideas, geographical boundaries, and other aspects of culture in the *Overland Monthly*, and later they were brought out in this book. He was not a trained anthropologist or ethnologist, and researchers must take whatever is useful from his observations. He recounts rituals such as the Karok Dance of Propitiation and the Pomo belief in a supreme being. His studies were a major influence on Kroeber's *Handbook of the Indians of California* (entry 28).

29a. Wright, Muriel H. **A Guide to the Indian Tribes of Oklahoma**. Norman, OK: University of Oklahoma, 1987. 300p. (Civilization of the American Indian Series, Vol. 33). LC 86-14678. ISBN 0-8061-0238-1.

This is a standard guide, first issued in 1951, describing the sixty-seven tribes in Oklahoma. The articles range from one page to more than 20 pages and are especially useful for historical research.

30. Swanton, John. **Indian Tribes of North America**. Washington, DC: U.S. Government Printing Office, 1952; repr., 1979. 726p. (Smithsonian Institution, Bureau of American Ethnology Bulletin, No. 145). $35.00pa. LC 52-61970. ISBN 0-87474-179-3.

Tribal names and geographic locations are presented in this standard work. Organized by the 49 states, Canada, the West Indies, and Mexico and Central America, Indian tribes are listed along with the meanings of the names, their linguistic connections, the history of the populations through the 1940s, and brief histories of the tribes. Each entry cites sources referring to the bibliography at the end. A detailed index lists tribal names and variant spellings. Useful for quickly locating tribes and their locations as determined through the mid-twentieth century.

31. Stoutenburgh, John L., Jr. **Dictionary of the American Indian**. New York: Philosophical Library, 1960; repr., Avenal, NJ: Outlet Book, 1990. 462p. $7.99. ISBN 0-517-69416-6.

This alphabetical dictionary describes tribes, leaders, settlements, geographic areas, ruins, monuments, material culture, languages, dialects, food, and other historical and cultural aspects of Indians of the United States. It is good for geographic locations of tribes and for Indian terms (e.g., *G'asdah bee gah*; Navajo term for the plant known as the owl's claw, used for making a yellow dye). The definitions are brief, varying from one sentence to a short paragraph. No bibliographic references are listed. This is strictly a dictionary for basic information.

32. Paterek, Josephine. **Encyclopedia of American Indian Costume**. Santa Barbara, CA: ABC-CLIO, 1993. 500p. $75.00. ISBN 0-87436-685-2.

This specialized encyclopedia presents the apparel and adornments of the Indian tribes of North America, as divided into 11 culture areas. The basic attire of each region is described, and important references are provided for further research. Some detailed information is given for specific tribes. Summaries of the authentic clothing of these tribes are given under categories such as "Women's Basic Dress," "Shaman or Special Costumes," and "Decorative Embellishment." A glossary of terms for garments and costumes is provided, along with a bibliography for each featured tribe. This is a unique source for researchers in American Indian studies. Researchers should note that the term regalia is used by Native Americans instead of costume for traditional attire for powwows and other celebrations.

33.   Waldman, Carl. **Atlas of the North American Indian**. New York: Facts on File, 1985. 276p. $29.95; $17.95pa. ISBN 0-87196-850-9. 1989. ISBN 0-8160-2136-8.

Much more than an atlas, this reference provides an overview of American Indian history and culture. It is arranged chronologically, with seven chapters centering on broad topics such as "Ancient Indians," "Ancient Civilizations," "Indian Lifeways," "Indians and Explorers," "Indian Wars," "Indian Land Cessions," and "Contemporary Indians." Each chapter is subdivided into detailed sections on civilizations, cultures, and histories. Excellent maps and drawings illustrate each section, such as the map on "Dominant Types of Shelter" in the section on "Shelter." The double-page map on pages 196-197 titled "Contemporary Indian Lands and Communities in the United States" well illustrates the locations of federal Indian reservations, state Indian reservations, and other Indian group lands. The appendix contains a chronology of North American Indian history from 50,000 B.C. through 1985; a list of tribes of the United States and Canada with historical and contemporary locations and reservations and trust areas; a dictionary of place names; a listing of museums, villages, and archaeological sites; and a detailed index by subjects, geographical names, historical people, tribes, and wars.

Another excellent atlas providing historical information on the Zuni Indians and the land they occupy is T. J. Ferguson and E. Richard Hart's *A Zuni Atlas* (Norman, OK: University of Oklahoma, 1990. 154p. [Civilization of the American Indian Series, Vol. 172]. $18.95pa. LC 85-40474. ISBN 0-8061-2287-0).

33a.   Coe, Michael, Dean Snow, and Elizabeth Benson. **Atlas of Ancient America**. New York: Facts on File, 1986. 240p. (Cultural Atlas Series). $45.00. LC 84-25999. ISBN 0-8160-1199-0.

Excellent pictures, photographs, and line drawings accompany the maps and text in this historical atlas of ancient America. Topics covered include native cultures and the environment, European discovery and conquest, the original settlement, culture areas, North America, Mesoamerica, and South America. Also included is illustrative material on topics such as Eskimo life, Hopi ritual drama, and life on the plains.

33b.   Tanner, Helen Hornbeck, ed. **Atlas of Great Lakes Indian History**. Norman, OK: University of Oklahoma, 1987. 224p. (Civilization of the American Indian Series, Vol. 174). $82.50; $45.00pa. LC 86-4353. ISBN 0-8061-1515-7; ISBN 0-8061-2056-8/pa.

This excellent atlas provides much more than maps for the time period (1640 to 1871) covered. This is a complex area of American Indian history, rich in a variety of tribes and cultures. Long articles cover the wars (Iroquois Wars of 1641 to 1701, the War of 1812, Pontiac's War, Black Hawk War of 1832), colonial time periods (the French era from 1720 to 1761), and historic topics (Indian villages and tribal distribution, Indian and colonial settlements around 1830, epidemics among Indians). A long bibliography of important sources is included.

34. Barnett, Franklin. **Dictionary of Prehistoric Indian Artifacts of the American Southwest**. Flagstaff, AZ: Northland Press, 1973. 130p. $12.95pa. LC 73-82865. ISBN 0-87358-120-2.

This dictionary is useful to beginning researchers in archaeology who are interested in artifacts. Illustrations, descriptions, and explanations of the uses of the many artifacts of the Indians of the prehistoric American Southwest are combined in one volume. Photographs depict the materials such as antler, bone, clay, shell, stone, and wood used in making tools, ornaments, and ceremonial objects. For example, under "Breastplate, Bone," a photograph of the bones with holes drilled at the ends accompanies the explanation of how breastplates were made.

35. Jelks, Edward B., and Juliet C. Jelks, eds. **Historical Dictionary of North American Archaeology**. Westport, CT: Greenwood, 1988. 760p. $105.00. LC 87-17581. ISBN 0-313-24307-7.

More than 1,800 significant archaeological sites of North America are described (out of "at least half a million archaeological sites recorded in North America," as stated in the preface), listing locations, archaeologists, dates of excavation, materials found, and contributions made to archaeological knowledge. This dictionary includes sites in Mexico, Canada, Alaska, and Greenland, yet concentrates on sites in the contiguous United States. Sources cited for each entry refer to the extensive list of references given at the end.

35a. Patterson, Alex. **A Field Guide to Rock Art Symbols of the Greater Southwest**. Boulder, CO: Johnson Books, 1992. 256p. $15.95pa. LC 92-883. ISBN 1-55566-091-6.

This attractive guide to petroglyphs and pictographs serves the novice as well as the experienced researcher, with materials quoted from almost 150 authors. Sections cover pictures of symbols with their ascribed meanings, alphabetical names with corresponding symbol descriptions, and a dictionary arrangement of subjects and their symbols and meanings. This is a well-illustrated guide throughout, with line drawings and photographs of the rock art. Also included are maps to the sites in Arizona, California, Nevada, Colorado, Utah, New Mexico, Texas, and Mexico, and a useful bibliography divided by rock art symbols.

35b. La Potin, Armand S., ed. **Native American Voluntary Organizations**. Westport, CT: Greenwood, 1987. 193p. (Ethnic American Voluntary Organizations). LC 86-25764. ISBN 0-313-23633-X.

More than 100 Indian and non-Indian volunteer organizations are summarized in this volume, including their histories, founding dates, publications, purposes, and leaders. These are historically important in understanding Indian-nonnative relations and Indian-government relations over the years. Two appendixes are very useful for researchers. These classify organizations by major functions (e.g., political-reformist, cultural-educational, social-fraternal, and professional) and by chronological listing with key historical events.

35c. Fritze, Ronald H. **Legend and Lore of the Americas Before 1492, an Encyclopedia of Visitors, Explorers, and Immigrants**. Santa Barbara, CA: ABC-CLIO, 1993. 319p. $50.00. LC 93-13367. ISBN 0-87436-664-X.

This unique encyclopedic volume serves researchers with brief articles on events and people in the Americas before Columbus. Topics covered include voyages to ancient America by the Chinese, the Scandinavians, the Libyans, and the Phoenicians; the Mormon beliefs of the visit of Jesus Christ in ancient America and the existence of *The Book of Mormon*; and the Vikings in Paraguay. Each topic includes bibliographic references to this fascinating reading.

Human Relations Area Files (HRAF)

The Human Relations Area Files, Inc. (address: P.O. Box 2054 Yale Station, New Haven, CT 06520, (203) 777-2334) is a consortium of over 300 colleges, universities, and libraries in 25 nations. HRAF was founded in 1949 as a private, nonprofit educational institution for the encouragement of cross-cultural study of human culture, society, and behavior. Information is compiled for teaching and research in the social and behavioral sciences, the humanities, and all other fields with an interest in human culture and behavior.

HRAF produces the HRAF Archive as well as several smaller subfiles and books for purchase. The HRAF Archive is a collection of information on the known cultures of the world. It is expanded and updated each year and now contains over 800,000 pages of information from 7,500 documents on more than 350 cultures. More than 1,500 cultures are represented so far, however, many American Indian peoples are not yet included in the HRAF files.

These materials were compiled from 1950 to the present but cover materials written from 1680-1990.

The collection comprises journal articles, dissertations, books, field notes, and other materials considered significant for cultural, anthropological, and linguistics research. Researchers will find mostly older materials analyzed. Libraries may have the HRAF collection in paper copy (5-by-8-inch paper slips) or on microfilm cards (3 by 5 inches). Beginning in 1994, the *Electronic HRAF* began publication, covering 75 cultures of the world with full-text documents on CD-ROM.

The data on the slips have been analyzed and annotated according to a system of 710 different category codes for cultural and natural information. Multiple copies of these slips allow cross-filing within each subject area file. Beginning researchers are often discouraged by the numbering system and often expect to find more information on their research topics than exists in the files. However, there is a massive amount of information to be retrieved from these files if researchers are patient enough to dig for the jewels therein.

Researchers will find information in the HRAF Archive on the following North American Indian tribes: Aleut, Arapaho, Bellacoola, Blackfoot (including the Blood and Piegan), Cherokee, Chipewyan, Comanche, Copper Eskimo, Creek (including the Alabama, Hitchiti, Koasati, and Yamasee), Crow, Delaware (including the Metoac), Dhegiha (including the Kansa, Omaha, Osage, Ponca, and Quapaw), Eastern Apache (including the Chiricahua, Gila, and Membreno), Fox, Gros Ventre, Hare, Hopi, Iroquois (including the Cayuga, Mohawk, Oneida, Onondaga, Seneca, and Tuscarora), Jicarilla, Klamath (including the Modoc), Mandan, Mescalero, Micmac, Mohave, Nahane (including the Kaska, Tahltan, and Tsetsaut), Navajo, Nootka (including the Makah), Northern Paiute (including the Eastern Mono, Surprise Valley Paiute of California, Atsakudokwa, Kidutokado, Kuyuidokado, Sawakudokwa, Tagotoka, Toedokado, Tunava, Wadadokado, and Wadatkuht), Ojibwa (including the Woodlands Ojibwas, Plains Ojibwas, Saulteaux and Chippewa, and Ottawa), Papago, Pawnee, Plateau Indians, Plateau Yumans (including the Havasupai, Keweyipaya, Southeastern Yavapai, Tolkepaya, Apachi-Mohave, Western Yavapai, Walapai, and Yavapai), Pomo, River Yumans (including the Cocopa, Halyikwami, Kohuana, Halchidhoma, Kaveltcadom, and Maricopa), Seminole, South Alaska Eskimo, Southeast Salish (including the Coeur d'Alene, Columbia, Chelan, Methow, Sinkaquaiius, Sinkiuse, Wenatchi, Pisquow, Kalispel, Pend d'Oreille, Semteuse, Lake, San Poil, Colville and Nespelem, Sinkaietk, and Spokan), Southern Paiute (including the Antarianunts, Chemehuevi, Kaibab, Las Vegas, Moapa, Panguitch, San Juan, and Shivwits), Taos (including the Picuris), Tewa (including the Hano, Nambe, Pojoaque, San Ildefonso, San Juan, Santa Clara, Tano, and Tesuque), Tlingit, Tubatulabal, Ute (including the Northern and Southern Ute, Moache, Moanunts, Pahvant, Taviwatsiu, Unitah, and Uncompahgre), Washo, Western Apache (including the Arivaipa, Carrizo, Cibecue, Pinaleno, San Carlos, Tonto, and White Mountain Apache), Western Shoshone (including the Beatty, Elko, Ely, Gosiute, Hamilton, Lida, Mahaguaduka, Wiyambituk, and Panamint), Winnebago, Yokuts (including the Wikchamni), Yurok, and Zuni.

Researchers should start with the *Outline of World Cultures* (entry 36) and the *Outline of Cultural Materials* (entry 37) when using the HRAF. These guides reveal whether the Indian tribe being researched is covered and how to pinpoint topics for research within the files.

For a list of all the sources included in the HRAF Archive, researchers can consult the *HRAF Source Bibliography* (New Haven, CT: Human Relations Area Files Press, 1976- [looseleaf for updating]).

36. Murdock, George P. **Outline of World Cultures**. 6th rev. ed. New Haven, CT: Human Relations Area Files Press, 1983. 259p. $25.00pa. LC 83-80510. ISBN 0-87536-664-3.

The *Outline of World Cultures* is the HRAF's organization and classification system for the known cultures of the world. The world is divided and subdivided, creating over 1,500 prehistoric, historic, and contemporary culture listings, each with a unique alphanumeric designation. For example, the designation for Cherokee Indians is NN8. This is the number in the HRAF files for materials on the Cherokee. Researchers can go directly to the files under this number, but to find the specific subject of research within the culture groups, the *Outline of Cultural Materials* (entry 37) is needed.

37. Murdock, George P., et al. **Outline of Cultural Materials**. 5th rev. ed. New Haven, CT: Human Relations Area Files Press, 1982. 247p. $25.00pa. LC 81-83836. ISBN 0-97536-654-6.

The *Outline of Cultural Materials* is the subject classification used by HRAF. It contains over 700 categories of topics for use in cross-cultural research. Categories and subcategories are assigned numbers to represent subject areas such as geography, demography, history and culture change, language, communication, food quest, agriculture, clothing, adornment, structures, settlements, marriage, kinship, family, war, religious practices, sex, education, and death. For example, within category 52 (recreation) is subcategory 524 (games).

A researcher could go to the HRAF Archive files, look under NN8 for the files on Cherokee, and go to the sequentially numbered sheets for number 524 to see if there are materials concerning games played by the Cherokee. HRAF also publishes the *Index to the Human Relations Area Files* (latest edition on microfiche, 1988), which is arranged by the *Outline of Cultural Materials* subject codes and enables researchers to determine the amount of coverage of specific topics in the culture files without first consulting the files themselves.

BIBLIOGRAPHIES

Bibliographies pull together citations to materials on topics. They may list periodical articles, books, government publications, theses and dissertations, conference proceedings, audiovisual materials, and other sources on particular topics. Bibliographies save researchers time by locating references together for materials on their topics. Sources cited in bibliographies might never be otherwise discovered by researchers if limited to their own libraries and access to available materials. The scope and content of bibliographies vary. They may be limited to materials of one type or materials published within specified time periods. Some contain annotations or descriptions of the sources, and others provide only bibliographic citations. Compilers of bibliographies must consider the nature of their subject and the intended users of the bibliography when deciding what types of materials to include and what time periods to cover. Some of the major bibliographies for American Indian studies are annotated here. Also cited are additional significant bibliographies that provide guidance to researchers working on major tribes and topics. Most include references to articles in journals, magazines, books, and U.S. government publications. Researchers should consult these bibliographies for older published materials on the historical, legal, and cultural aspects of American Indian studies.

One of the most significant sets of reference bibliographies included in this section is the Native American Bibliography Series, Jack W. Marken, general editor (Metuchen, NJ: Scarecrow Press, 1980-present).

These bibliographies are important for their comprehensive surveys of the literature on Indian tribes and topics. Each volume provides between 2,000 and 5,000 entries, listing periodical articles, newspaper articles, books, and government reports. Many of the important materials are annotated, and the volumes have good indexes by tribes and topics. Researchers will benefit greatly by discovering one of these bibliographies on their topic of interest.

Another series of bibliographies began in 1972, when the Newberry Library in Chicago established the Center for the History of the American Indian. This series was called the Newberry Library Center for the History of the American Indian Bibliographical Series, and 30 titles were published by Indiana University Press from 1976-1987 on Indian tribes, regions, and topics. These titles provide bibliographical essays with citations (averaging around 200 per volume) given in the text, focusing primarily on history rather than anthropological or ethnological coverage. In 1988, the orientation of the series changed, and publication was taken over by the University of Oklahoma Press under the title the D'Arcy McNickle Center Bibliographies in American Indian History Series. The focus now is on topical review essays and general bibliographies of recent literature from history, sociology, anthropology, literature, linguistics, and economics. They provide an overview of the bibliography in a discipline and cite important works for further research.

The arrangement of the bibliographies in this section is by tribes and topics, depending on the primary emphasis of the bibliography. If a bibliography deals with languages, for example, it is placed under languages, even if it is limited to a survey of a particular tribe. If a bibliography covers Indians within a state it is listed by state, but when it surveys more than one tribe or state, it is placed within a region, such as the Northeast. Within most categories, materials are listed alphabetically by author.

Bibliography of Bibliographies

American Indians (General)

38.   Murdock, George Peter, and Timothy J. O'Leary, comps. **Ethnographic Bibliography of North America**. 4th ed. New Haven, CT: Human Relations Area Files Press, 1975; **Volume 1, General North America; Volume 2, Arctic and Subarctic; Volume 3, Far West and Pacific Coast; Volume 4, Eastern United States; Volume 5, Plains and Southwest**. $35.00/vol. LC 75-17091.

38a. Martin, Marlene M., and Timothy J. O'Leary, comps. **Ethnographic Bibliography of North America: Supplement to the 4th Edition, 1973-1987**. New Haven, CT: Human Relations Area Files Press, 1990. 3v. $395.00/set. ISBN 0-87536-254-0.

This massive bibliography totals over 54,000 citations to articles, books, government reports, theses, dissertations, and ERIC documents concerning American Indian cultures and lifestyles, linguistics, archaeology, history, government relations, education, geography, urbanization, literature, and the arts. The five volumes in the 4th edition are arranged by broad geographic areas and subdivided by specific Indian groups. For example, volume 3, *Far West and Pacific Coast,* has divisions of Northwest Coast, Oregon Seaboard, California, Peninsula, Basin, and Plateau. Within each of these geographic divisions are 11 to 23 tribal groups. Some of the California tribes are in the California section, and some are in the Peninsula section. Researchers must scan the tables of contents of the volumes to locate the groups they are studying, because no subject indexes are available. Within each section, citations are arranged alphabetically by author.

The *Supplement to the 4th Edition* covers literature published between 1973 and 1987 and lists 25,058 citations to the same variety of materials (books, journal articles, U.S. government documents, theses, dissertations, and ERIC documents). The format is much improved in these three supplemental volumes, however. Volume 1,

Indexes, is divided into three main parts: author index, ethnic group index, and subject index. These provide reference numbers to volumes 2 and 3, making it possible to locate specific subjects and tribes within the volumes. This renowned bibliography will serve researchers in all areas of American Indian studies.

39. **International Bibliography of the Social Sciences: International Bibliography of Social and Cultural Anthropology**. New York: Routledge, 1955-. Annual. ISSN 0085-2074.

This important international bibliography serves as an index to over 700 journals, as well as books, technical reports, and conference papers, for social and cultural anthropology. Although arranged by categories of study within anthropology (e.g., morphological foundation, social organization and relationships, religion, magic and witchcraft), the researcher must rely on the excellent, detailed subject index in the back of each annual volume. There will be found references to scholarly research under Amerindians, tribal names, subjects dealing with Amerindians (e.g., horses— Amerindians), and geographic areas covering Amerindians (e.g., California—basketry). This standard bibliography has a time lag of three to four years from the date on the annual volume to its publication, but researchers doing comprehensive surveys of the literature should not miss this one.

40. **Bibliographic Guide to Anthropology and Archaeology**. Boston: G. K. Hall, 1988-. Annual. $200.00. ISSN 0896-8101.

This annual bibliography updates the *Author and Subject Catalogues of the Tozzer Library* (entry 208) since June 1986 for books, serials, microforms, maps, manuscripts, and audiovisual materials received in the Tozzer Library at Harvard University each year. Listings are by authors, titles, and subjects, using the Library of Congress Subject Headings. *Anthropological Literature* (entry 229) is created from analyzing the contents journals and collected works from the Tozzer Library collection.

41. Edmunds, R. David. **Kinsmen Through Time**. Metuchen, NJ: Scarecrow Press, 1987. 237p. (Native American Bibliography Series, No. 12). $27.50. LC 87-16679. ISBN 0-8108-2020-X.

42. Hand, Richard A. **A Bookman's Guide to the Indians of the Americas: A Compilation of Over 10,000 Catalogue Entries with Prices and Annotations, Both Bibliographical and Descriptive**. Metuchen, NJ: Scarecrow Press, 1989. 764p. $72.50. LC 88-38642. ISBN 0-8108-2182-6.

43. Harkins, Arthur M., et al. **Modern Native Americans: A Selective Bibliography**. Minneapolis: University of Minnesota, Training Center for Community Programs, 1971. 130p. LC 72-611467.

43a. Heard, J. Norman. **Handbook of the American Frontier: Four Centuries of Indian-White Relationships. Volume I: The Southeastern Woodlands. Volume II: The Northeastern Woodlands**. Metuchen, NJ: Scarecrow Press, 1987. LC 86-20326. (Vol. I, 407p. $39.50. ISBN 0-8108-1931-7); (Vol. II, 1990, 403p. $42.50. ISBN 0-8108-2324-1.).

Arranged alphabetically by people, places, battles, tribes, and events, this annotated bibliography guides researchers to materials on Indian and non-Indian relationships found in historical, ethnological, and biographical sources.

44. Hodge, William. **A Bibliography of Contemporary North American Indians**. New York: Interland, 1976. 310p. LC 75-21675. ISBN 0-8798-9102-5.

This bibliography and guide concentrates on contemporary Indians and their issues. Materials written about American Indians after 1875 are considered contemporary. The book begins with a "Study Guide for Indian Life Prior to 1875," which discusses significant books, articles, Smithsonian Institution reports, and other materials to guide students through time periods, subjects, and regional tribal histories. The contemporary bibliography of over 2,500 citations includes sections on Indian history, contemporary Indian images, material culture, social organization, population dynamics, reservations, languages, migration patterns, city living, economics, personality and culture, political organization, formal education, music and dance, social control, religion, and health. The author annotates some of the citations and marks the most important ones with asterisks. Sections are included on Canadian government documents, U.S. publications, current newspapers, newsletters, magazines, and maps. Indexes are given for subjects and authors.

45. Hoxie, Frederick E., and Harvey Markowitz. **Native Americans: An Annotated Bibliography.** Pasadena, CA: Salem Press, 1991. 325p. LC 91-16427. ISBN 0893566705.

46. Marken, Jack W. **The Indians and Eskimos of North America: A Bibliography of Books in Print Through 1972**. Vermillion, SD: Dakota Press, 1973. 200p. $5.00. ISBN 0-8824-9016-8.

47. Miller, Wayne Charles, et al. **A Comprehensive Bibliography for the Study of American Minorities**. New York: University Press, 1976. 1,380p. $266.00. LC 74-21636. ISBN 0-81475-373-6. (Pp. 783-909 cover Native Americans.)

48. O'Donnell, James H., III. **Southeastern Frontiers: Europeans, Africans, and American Indians, 1513-1840: A Critical Bibliography**. Bloomington: Indiana University Press, 1982. 118p. LC 81-48086. ISBN 0-2533-5398-X.

49. Perkins, David, and Norman Tanis, comps. **Native Americans of North America: A Bibliography Based on Collections in the Libraries of California State University, Northridge**. Metuchen, NJ: Scarecrow Press, 1975. 558p. repr. Northridge: California State University, 1975. $27.50. LC 75-623535. ISBN 0-8108-0878-1.

50. Smith, Dwight L., ed. **Indians of the United States and Canada: A Bibliography**. Santa Barbara, CA: ABC-CLIO, 1974 and 1983. 2v. (Clio Bibliography Series, Nos. 3 & 9). LC 73-87156. ISBN 0874361249 (v. 1). ISBN 0874361494 (v. 2).

These two volumes pull together more than 4,900 references on American Indians from the periodical index and database *America: History and Life,* written from 1954 through 1978. The volumes are divided into the following four sections: "Pre-Columbian Indian History," "Tribal History, 1492-1900," "General Indian History,

1492-1900," and "The Indian in the Twentieth Century." Each section is subdivided into regions and tribes. An excellent resource for historical sources, this book is also attractively printed and formatted. A practical subject index at the end further enhances its use.

51. Sorenson, John L. **Pre-Columbian Contact with the Americas Across the Oceans: An Annotated Bibliography.** Provo, UT: Research Press, 1990. 2v. 1,340p. $89.00/set. ISBN 0-934893-14-4.

52. Storck, Peter L. **A Preliminary Bibliography of Early Man in Eastern North America, 1839-1973**. Toronto: Royal Ontario Museum, 1975. 110p. $3.00. LC 76-364014. ISBN 0888541589.

53. Wolf, Carolyn E., and Nancy S. Chiang. **Indians of North and South America: A Bibliography Based on the Collection at the Willard E. Yager Library-Museum, Hartwick College, Oneonta, N.Y.** Metuchen, NJ: Scarecrow Press, 1988. 662p. $59.50. LC 88-6055. ISBN 0-8108-2127-3.
   More than 4,000 books, periodical articles, analyzed serial articles and essays, and newspaper clippings on American Indians published before 1976 are listed from the holdings of this library.

Agriculture

54. Harvey, Cecil. **Agriculture of the American Indian: A Select Bibliography.** Washington, DC: U.S. Department of Agriculture, Science and Education Administration, Technical Information Systems, 1979. 64p. (Bibliographies and Literature of Agriculture: no. 4). LC 80-601584.

Alcohol

55. Lobb, Michael L., and Thomas D. Watts. **Native American Youth and Alcohol: An Annotated Bibliography**. New York: Greenwood, 1989. 165p. (Bibliographies and Indexes in Sociology, No. 16). 210p. $52.95. ISBN 0-313-25618-7.

56. Mail, Patricia D., and David R. McDonald. **Tulapai to Tokay: A Bibliography of Alcohol Use and Abuse Among Native Americans of North America.** New Haven, CT: Human Relations Area Files Press, 1980. 372p. $25.00. LC 80-81243. ISBN 0-87536-253-2.

57. Street, Pamela B., Ronald C. Wood, and Rita C. Chowenhill, comps. **Alcohol Use Among Native Americans: A Selective Annotated Bibliography, Based Substantially on the Unpublished Work of Patricia Mail and Victoria Sears**. Berkeley, CA: University of California, School of Public Health, Social Research Group, 1976. 115p. LC 77-620503.

Aleut (Eskimo)

58. Hippler, Arthur E., and John Richard Wood. **The Alaska Eskimos: A Selected, Annotated Bibliography**. Fairbanks: University of Alaska, Institute of Social and Economic Research, 1977. 334p. (ISER Report Series, No. 45). $15.00. LC 77-620070. ISBN 0883530228.

59. Jones, Dorothy Miriam, and John R. Wood. **An Aleut Bibliography**. Fairbanks: University of Alaska, Institute of Social, Economic and Government Research, 1975. 195p. (ISEGR Report Series, No. 44). $15.00. LC 74-620054. ISBN 0883530163.

Apaches

60. Melody, Michael Edward. **The Apaches: A Critical Bibliography.** Bloomington: Indiana University Press, 1977. 86p. ISBN 0-2533-0764-3.

Arapaho

61. Salzmann, Zdenek. **The Arapaho Indians: A Research Guide and Bibliography.** New York: Greenwood, 1988. 113p. (Bibliographies and Indexes in Anthropology, No. 4). $47.95. LC 87-322274. ISBN 0-313-25354-4.

Archaeology

62. Anderson, Frank G. **Southwestern Archaeology: A Bibliography**. New York: Garland, 1982. 539p. ISBN 0824095545.

63. Bell, Robert Eugene. **Oklahoma Archaeology: An Annotated Bibliography**. 2d ed. Norman: University of Oklahoma Press, 1978. 155p. $8.95. ISBN 0806114975.

64. Milisauskas, Sarunas, Frances Pickin, and Charles Clark. **A Selected Bibliography of North American Archaeological Sites**. New Haven, CT: Human Relations Area Files Press, 1981. 393p. LC 81-178901.

Arts

65. Bradley, Ian L., and Patricia Bradley. **A Bibliography of Canadian Native Arts: Indian and Eskimo Arts, Craft, Dance and Music**. Agincourt, ON: GLC, 1977. 107p. $19.95. LC 78-320342. ISBN 0888740514.

66. Burt, Eugene C. **Native American Art: Five-Year Cumulative Bibliography, Mid-1983 Through 1988.** Seattle, WA: Data Arts, 1988. 157p. (EthnoArts Index, Supplemental Publication, No. 4). LC 90-192573.

67. Dawdy, Doris Ostrander. **Annotated Bibliography of American Indian Paintings**. New York: Museum of the American Indian, Heye Foundation, 1968. 27p. $2.50. LC 78-8195. ISBN 0-934490-05-8.

67a. Harding, Anne Dinsdale, and Patricia Bolling. **Bibliography of Articles and Papers on North American Indian Art**. Washington, DC: Department of the Interior, Indian Arts and Crafts Board, 1938, repr., New York: Gordon, 1980. 365p. $75.00. LC 39-26510. ISBN 0-8490-3115-X.

68. Minion, Robin. **Inuit Art and Artists**. Edmonton: University of Alberta, Boreal Institute for Northern Studies, 1986. 80p. (Boreal Institute for Northern Studies Bibliographical Series, No. 26). LC 87-209035. ISBN 0919058485.

69. Parezo, Nancy J., Ruth M. Perry, and Rebecca Allen. **Southwest Native American Visual Arts, Crafts and Material Culture: A Resource Guide**. New York: Garland, 1991. 2v. (Studies in Ethnic Art, Vols. 1 & 2). $165.00/set. LC 90-21395. ISBN 0-8240-7093-3.

70. Porter, Frank W., III. **Native American Basketry: An Annotated Bibliography.** New York: Greenwood, 1988. 256p. (The Art Reference Collection, No. 10). $45.00. LC 87-37570. ISBN 0-313-25363-3.

71. Wardwell, Allen. **Annotated Bibliography of Northwest Coast Indian Art**. New York: Museum of Primitive Art Library, 1970. 25p. (Primitive Art Bibliographies, No. 8). LC 79-26787.

Blackfoot

72. Dempsey, Hugh A., and Lindsay Moir. **Bibliography of the Blackfoot**. Metuchen, NJ: Scarecrow Press, 1989. 255p. (Native American Bibliography Series, No. 13). $27.50. LC 89-6444. ISBN 0-8108-2211-3.

72a. Johnson, Bryan R. **The Blackfeet: An Annotated Bibliography**. New York: Garland, 1988. 231p. (Garland Reference Library of Social Science, Vol. 441). $40.00. LC 87-32693. ISBN 0-8240-0941-X.

Cahuilla

73. Bean, Lowell J., and H. Lawton. **A Bibliography of the Cahuilla Indians**. Banning, CA: Malki Museum Press, 1967. 28p.

California

74.   Bleyhl, Norris Arthur. **Indian-White Relationships in Northern California, 1849-1920, in the Congressional Set of United States Public Documents.** Chico, CA: Association of Northern California Records and Research, 1978. 106p. $12.00. ISBN 0-686-38930-1.

75.   Heizer, Robert Fleming, and Albert B. Elsasser. **A Bibliography of California Indians: Archaeology, Ethnography, Indian History.** New York: Garland, 1977. 267p. (Garland Reference Library of Social Science, Vol. 48). $23.00. LC 76-52687. ISBN 0824098668.
      This bibliography covers two main periods: ancient California (prehistory, archaeology) and Indian history after 1542, when the Europeans discovered California. Emphasis is on materials published by associations but includes journal articles and books.

76.   Heizer, Robert F., Karen M. Nissen, and Edward D. Castillo. **California Indian History: A Classified and Annotated Guide to Source Materials.** Ramona, CA: Ballena Press, 1975. 90p. LC 75-325506.

77.   Heizer, Robert Fleming. **The Indians of California: A Critical Bibliography.** Bloomington: Indiana University Press, 1976. 68p. ISBN 0-2533-3001-7.

78.   Riddell, Francis A. **A Bibliography of the Indians of Central California.** Sacramento: State of California, Resources Agency, Department of Parks and Recreation, Division of Beaches and Parks, 1962.

Canada and Alaska (General)

79.   Abler, Thomas S., and Sally M. Weaver. **A Canadian Indian Bibliography 1960-1970.** Toronto: University of Toronto Press, 1974. 732p. $35.00. LC 75-300070. ISBN 0802020925.
      Listed are scholarly interest books, periodical articles, theses, and other materials that were written on the Canadian Indians and Metis between 1960 and 1970. Over 3,000 entries are annotated and arranged in a classified manner. A special section on pages 306-362 attempts to be a case law digest and pulls together all the case law related to Canadian Indian legal questions as decided in the courts since July 1867.

79a.   Corley, Nora T. **Resources for Native Peoples Studies.** Ottawa: National Library of Canada, 1984. 342p. (Research Collections in Canadian Libraries, Special Studies, No. 9). ISBN 0-660-52676-X.

79b.   Duff, Wilson, comp. **Selected List of Publications on the Indians of British Columbia.** Victoria: British Columbia Provincial Museum of Natural History and Anthropology, 1963. 32p.

79c. Harding, Jim, and Bruce Spence. **An Annotated Bibliography of Aboriginal-Controlled Justice Programs in Canada**. Regina, Sask.: Prairie Justice Research, School of Human Justice, University of Regina, 1991. 89p. (Aboriginal Justice Series, No. 3). $20.00pa. ISBN 0-7731-0190-X.

79d. Harding, Jim, and Beryl Forgay. **Breaking Down the Walls: A Bibliography on the Pursuit of Aboriginal Justice**. Regina, Sask.: Prairie Justice Research, School of Human Justice, University of Regina, 1991. 108p. (Aboriginal Justice Series, No. 2). $20.00pa. ISBN 0-7731-0191-8.

80. Helm, June. **The Indians of the Subarctic: A Critical Bibliography**. Bloomington: Indiana University Press, 1976. 91p. LC 76-12373. ISBN 0-2533-3004-1.

81. Helm, June, and Royce Kurtz. **Subarctic Athapascan Bibliography, 1984**. Iowa City: University of Iowa, Department of Anthropology, 1984. 515p. $5.00.

82. Hippler, Arthur E. **The Subarctic Athabascans: A Selected Annotated Bibliography**. Fairbanks: University of Alaska, Institute of Social, Economic, and Government Research, 1974. 331p. (ISEGR Report Series, No. 39). $15.00. LC 74-620010. ISBN 0883530120.

83. Hoover, Alan L. **A Selection of Publications on the Indians of British Columbia**. Victoria: British Columbia Provincial Museum, 1982. 50p. LC 82-190974. ISBN 0771883013.

84. Indian and Eskimo Affairs Program (Canada), Education Branch. **About Indians: A Listing of Books—Les Indiens: Une Liste de Livres a Leur Sujet**. 3d ed. Ottawa: Indian and Northern Affairs, 1975. 321p. LC 77-569751.

85. Krech, Shepard, III. **Native Canadian Anthropology and History: A Selected Bibliography**. Rev. ed. Norman: University of Oklahoma Press, 1993. 224p. $28.95. LC 93-037591. ISBN 0-8061-2617-5.

85a. Lochhead, Douglas, comp. **Bibliography of Canadian Bibliographies/ Bibliographie des Bibliographies Canadiennes**. 2d ed. Toronto: University of Toronto, 1972. 312p. LC 76-166933. ISBN 0-8020-1865-3.

85b. Maclean, John. **Canadian Savage Folk; the Native Tribes of Canada**. Toronto: Briggs, 1896. 641p.

86. Meiklejohn, C., and D. A. Rokala. **The Native Peoples of Canada: An Annotated Bibliography of Population Biology, Health, and Illness**. Ottawa: National Museums of Canada, 1986. 564p. $29.95. LC 87-164990. ISBN 0-660-10774-0.

86a. Peters, Evelyn J. **Aboriginal Self-Government in Canada: A Bibliography 1986**. Kingston, Ont.: Institute of Intergovernmental Relations, Queen's University, 1986. 112p. (Aboriginal Peoples and Constitutional Reform). $12.00. ISBN 0-88911-423-4.

86b. Peters, Evelyn J. **Aboriginal Self-Government in Canada: A Bibliography 1987-90**. Kingston, Ont.: Institute of Intergovernmental Relations, Queen's University, 1991. 58p. (Aboriginal Peoples and Constitutional Reform). $15.00. ISBN 0-88911-580-X.

86c. Proulx, Jean-Rene. **Bibliography of Guides and List of Archives**. Quebec: Consulting Services in Social Sciences Development and Cultural Change, Ministere Des Affaires Culturelles Du Quebec, 1985. 74p. (Review of Ethnohistorical Research on the Native Peoples of Quebec, Vol. 5). ISBN 2-5550-12262-3.

86d. Proulx, Jean-Rene. **Bibliography of Published Works**. Quebec: Consulting Services in Social Sciences Development and Cultural Change, Ministere Des Affaires Culturelles Du Quebec, 1985. 172p. (Review of Ethnohistorical Research on the Native Peoples of Quebec, Vol. 3). ISBN 2-5550-12263-1.

86e. Proulx, Jean-Rene. **Bibliography of Ethnohistorical Works 1960-1983**. Quebec: Consulting Services in Social Sciences Development and Cultural Change, Ministere Des Affaires Culturelles Du Quebec, 1985. 161p. (Review of Ethnohistorical Research on the Native Peoples of Quebec, Vol. 2). ISBN 2-5550-12261-5.

87. Smith, Dwight L. ed. **The History of Canada: An Annotated Bibliography.** Santa Barbara, CA: ABC-CLIO, 1983. 327p. $55.00. LC 82-24307. ISBN 0874360471.

87a. Verrall, Catherine. **Resource/Reading List 1987: Annotated Bibliography of Resources by and About Native People**. Toronto: Canadian Alliance in Solidarity with the Native Peoples, 1987. 111p. ISBN 0-92145-01-5.

87b. Verrall, Catherine, and Patricia McDowell. **Resource Reading List 1990: Annotated Bibliography of Resources by and About Native People**. Toronto: Canadian Alliance in Solidarity with the Native Peoples, 1990. 157p. ISBN 0-921425-03-1.

87c. Wai, Lokky. **Native Peoples of Canada in Contemporary Society: A Demographic and Socioeconomic Bibliography**. London, Ont.: Population Studies Centre, University of Western Ontario, 1989. 82p. $9.50pa. ISBN 0-7714-1060-3.

87d. Walcott, M. Alena. **A Selective Bibliography on the Indians of Eastern Canada**. Montreal: McGill University Library School, 1938. 4p.

88. Whiteside, Don. **Aboriginal People: A Selected Bibliography Concerning Canada's First People.** Ottawa: National Indian Brotherhood, 1973. 345p. LC 75-302032. ISBN 0919682022.
    This bibliography is unusual in that it concentrates on unpublished speeches and reports, conference proceedings, newspaper articles, and materials written by Canada's aboriginal people. It is arranged by subject classification, with indexes by authors and specific subjects.

Captivity

88a. **Narratives of Captivity Among the Indians of North America: A List of Books and Manuscripts on This Subject in the Edward E. Ayer Collection of the Newberry Library**. And **Supplement I**, by Clara A. Smith. Chicago: Newberry Library, 1912 and 1928; repr. Detroit: Omnigraphics, 1974. 120 + 49p. $35.00. LC 74-3100. ISBN 1-55888-193-X.

Catawba

89. Blumer, Thomas J. **Bibliography of the Catawba**. Metuchen, NJ: Scarecrow Press, 1987. 575p. (Native American Bibliography Series, No. 10). $59.50. LC 87-4389. ISBN 0-8108-1986-4.

Cherokee

90. Anderson, William L., and James A. Lewis. **A Guide to Cherokee Documents in Foreign Archives.** Metuchen, NJ: Scarecrow Press, 1983. 768p. (Native American Bibliography Series, No. 7). $40.00. LC 83-4636. ISBN 0-8108-1630-X.

91. Fogelson, Raymond D. **The Cherokees: A Critical Bibliography.** Bloomington: Indiana University Press, 1978. 98p. LC 78-3254. ISBN 0-2533-1346-5.

92. Eastern Band of Cherokee Indians Planning Board. **Bibliography: Eastern Band of Cherokee Indians.** Raleigh, NC: North Carolina Department of Natural and Economic Resources, Division of Community Services, 1974. 260p. LC 75-620768.

93. Kutsche, Paul. **A Guide to Cherokee Documents in the Northeastern United States**. Metuchen, NJ: Scarecrow Press, 1986. 541p. (Native American Bibliography Series, No. 7). $79.50. LC 85-11798. ISBN 0-8108-1827-2.

Cheyenne

94. Powell, Peter J. **The Cheyennes, Maheoo's People: A Critical Bibliography.** Bloomington: Indiana University Press, 1980. 123p. LC 80-8033. ISBN 0-2533-0416-4.

Chickasaw

95. Hoyt, Anne Kelley. **Bibliography of the Chickasaw**. Metuchen, NJ: Scarecrow Press, 1987. 230p. (Native American Bibliography Series, No. 11). $25.00. LC 87-4871. ISBN 0-8108-1995-3.

Choctaw

95a. Kidwell, Clara Sue, and Charles Roberts. **The Choctaws, a Critical Bibliography**. Bloomington, IN: Indiana University, 1980. 110p. (The Newberry Library Center for the History of the American Indian). LC 80-8037. ISBN 0-253-34412-3.

Chumash

96. Anderson, Eugene Newton. **A Revised Annotated Bibliography of the Chumash and Their Predecessors**. 2d ed. Socorro, NM: Ballena Press, 1978. 82p. (Ballena Press Anthropological Papers, No. 11).

97. Lee, Georgia. **Rock Art of the Chumash Area: An Annotated Bibliography**. Los Angeles: University of California, Los Angeles, Institute of Archaeology, 1979. 48p. (University of California, Los Angeles, Institute of Archaeology Occasional Papers, No. 3).

Creek

98. Green, Michael D. **The Creeks: A Critical Bibliography**. Bloomington: Indiana University Press, 1979. 114p. LC 79-2166. ISBN 0-2533-1776-2.

Crime

99. Horn, Charles, and Curt Taylor Griffiths. **Native North Americans: Crime, Conflict and Criminal Justice: A Research Bibliography**. 4th ed. Burnaby, BC: Northern Justice Society, 1989. 275p. $45.00. ISBN 0864910746.

Delaware

100. Weslager, Clinton Alfred. **The Delawares: A Critical Bibliography**. Bloomington: Indiana University Press, 1978. 84p. ISBN 0-2533-1680-4.

Demography

101. Dobyns, Henry F. **Native American Historical Demography: A Critical Bibliography**. Bloomington: Indiana University Press, 1976. 96p. ISBN 0-2533-3974-0.

Diegueno

102. Almstedt, Ruth R. **Bibliography of the Diegueno Indians**. Ramona, CA: Ballena Press, 1974. 52p. LC 74-162918.

Education

103. **American Indian Education: A Bibliography of ERIC Documents**. Las Cruces: ERIC Clearinghouse on Rural Education and Small Schools, New Mexico State University; Austin, TX: National Educational Laboratory Publishers, 1978. 142p.

104. Brooks, Ian R. **Native Education in Canada and the United States: A Bibliography**. Calgary, AB: University of Calgary, Indian Students University Program Services, Office of Educational Development, 1976. 298p. LC 77-372456.

105. Knox, Douglas R., Roberta Benecke, and Janet Zamora. **Evaluating American Indian Bilingual Education Programs: A Topical Bibliography**. Rosslyn, VA: National Clearinghouse for Bilingual Education, 1982. 60p.

106. Tonemah, Stuart, and Elaine Roanhorse Benally. **Trends in American Indian Education: A Synthesis and Bibliography of Selected ERIC Resources**. Las Cruces, NM: ERIC Clearinghouse on Rural Education and Small Schools, New Mexico State University, 1984. 47p.

106a. Weinberg, Meyer. **The Education of the Minority Child: A Comprehensive Bibliography of 10,000 Selected Entries**. Chicago: Integrated Education Associates, 1970. 530p.

Environment

107. Booth, Annie L., and Harvey M. Jacobs. **Environmental Consciousness—Native American Worldviews and Sustainable Natural Resource Management: An Annotated Bibliography**. Chicago: Council of Planning Librarians, 1988. 40p. $16.00. ISBN 0866022147.

Ethnobotany

108. Lynas, Lothian. **Medicinal and Food Plants of the North American Indians: A Bibliography**. New York: Library of the New York Botanical Garden, 1972. 21p. $1.25. LC 74-157582.

109. Moerman, Daniel E. **American Medical Ethnobotany: A Reference Dictionary**. New York: Garland, 1977. 527p. $51.00. LC 76-24771. ISBN 0824099079.

Family Studies

110. Collinge, William B. **A Bibliography on Native American Child and Family Welfare**. Berkeley: University of California, School of Social Welfare, American Indian/Alaska Native Program, 1982. 50p.

Film

111.   Bataille, Gretchen M., and Charles L. P. Silet. **Images of American Indians on Film: An Annotated Bibliography**. New York: Garland, 1985. 216p. ISBN 0824087372.

112.   Hilger, Michael. **The American Indian in Film**. Metuchen, NJ: Scarecrow Press, 1986. 206p. $22.50. LC 86-10061. ISBN 0-8108-1905-8.

112a.   Weatherford, Elizabeth, and Emelia Seubert, eds. **Native Americans on Film and Video**. New York: Museum of the American Indian, 1981. 151p. LC 81-85266. ISBN 0-934490-38-4.

112b.   Weatherford, Elizabeth, and Emelia Seubert. **Native Americans on Film and Video. Volume II**. New York: Museum of the American Indian, 1988. 112p. $6.00. LC 81-85266. ISBN 0-934490-44-9.

Five Civilized Tribes

113.   Huffman, Mary. **The Five Civilized Tribes: A Bibliography.** Oklahoma City: Oklahoma Historical Society, Library Resources Division, 1991. 51p. LC 92-620620. ISBN 0941498654.

Folklore

114.   Clements, William M., and Frances M. Malpezzi. **Native American Folklore, 1879-1979: An Annotated Bibliography**. Athens, OH: Swallow Press, 1984. 247p. $46.55. LC 83-6672. ISBN 0804008310.
     Over 5,500 items are included in this briefly annotated bibliography of Native American folklore. It is arranged by culture areas and cites books and articles from anthropology, history, religious studies, folklore literature, and other social science and humanities fields of study. The subject index provides access to topics, genres, and concepts within the tribal categories. The emphasis is on the verbal arts, such as legends, myths, songs, and tales.

114a.   Fulton, Jessie Eldred, and Sadie I. Marston. **A First Survey on Indian Folk-Tales and Legends of Ontario, Arranged According to Subject and Locality**. Toronto: Toronto University Library School, 1938. 56p.

115.   Haywood, Charles. **A Bibliography of North American Folklore and Folksong**. New York: Greenberg, 1951. 1,292p. LC 51-1941.

116.   Haywood, Charles. **A Bibliography of North American Folklore and Folksong**. 2d rev.ed. New York: Dover Publications, 1961. 2v. LC 62-3483.
     This revised edition is a comprehensive bibliography covering printed music and recordings as well as books. Volume 2 covers American Indians north of Mexico,

including the Eskimos. The organization of volume 2 is by tribal group, subdivided by genre (e.g., medicine, beliefs).

117. Ullom, Judith C. **Folklore of the North American Indians: An Annotated Bibliography.** Washington, DC: Library of Congress, 1969. 126p. LC 70-601462.

Gabrielino

118. La Lone, Mary. **Gabrielino Indians of Southern California: An Annotated Ethnohistoric Bibliography.** Los Angeles: University of California, Institute of Archaeology, 1980. 72p. (University of California, Los Angeles, Institute of Archaeology Occasional Papers, No. 6). LC 81-180054. ISBN 091795615X.

Ghost Dance

119. Osterreich, Shelley Anne. **The American Indian Ghost Dance, 1870 and 1890: An Annotated Bibliography.** New York: Greenwood, 1991. 96p. (Bibliographies and Indexes in American History Series, No. 19). $37.95. ISBN 0-313-27469-X.

Great Basin

120. Fowler, Catherine S., and Don D. Fowler, eds. **Great Basin Anthropology: A Bibliography.** Reno: University of Nevada System, Western Studies Center, 1970. 418p. $10.00. LC 78-634802. ISBN 0-945920-88-1.

121. Stewart, Omer Call. **Indians of the Great Basin: A Critical Bibliography.** Bloomington: Indiana University Press, 1982. 138p. LC 81-48084. ISBN 0-2533-2979-5.

Great Plains

122. Hoebel, Edward Adamson. **The Plains Indians: A Critical Bibliography.** Bloomington: Indiana University Press, 1977. 75p. ISBN 0-2533-4509-X.

123. McMullen, John. **A Guide to the Christian Indians of the Upper Plains: An Annotated, Selected Bibliography.** Marvin, SD: Blue Cloud Abbey, 1969. 64p.

124. Weist, Katherine M., and Susan R. Sharrock. **An Annotated Bibliography of Northern Plains Ethnohistory.** Missoula: University of Montana, Department of Anthropology, 1985. 299p. LC 85-237614.

Health

125. Barrow, Mark V., Jerry D. Niswander, and Robert Fortuine. **Health and Disease of American Indians North of Mexico: A Bibliography, 1800-1969.** Gainesville: University of Florida Press, 1972. 147p. LC 70-161004. ISBN 08130018.

126. **Nutrition Education Resource Guide for American Indians and Alaska Natives: A Selected Annotated Bibliography for the Food Distribution Program on Indian Reservations.** Alexandria, VA: U.S. Department of Agriculture, Food and Nutrition Service, Nutrition and Technical Services Division, Science and Education Branch, 1988. 75p.

History

127. Calloway, Colin G., ed. **New Directions in American Indian History**. Norman: University of Oklahoma Press, 1988. 288p. (D'Arcy McNickle Center for the History of the American Indian Bibliographical Series, Vol. 1). $32.50. LC 88-5424. ISBN 0-8061-2147-5.

128. Hagan, William Thomas. **The Indian in American History**. 3d ed. Washington, DC: American Historical Association, 1985. 32p. LC 85-47507.

129. Snow, Dean R. **Native American Prehistory: A Critical Bibliography**. Bloomington: Indiana University Press, 1979. 75p. (Newberry Library Center for the History of the American Indian Bibliographical Series). ISBN 0-2533-3498-5.

Hopi

130. Laird, David W. **Hopi Bibliography, Comprehensive and Annotated**. Tucson: University of Arizona Press, 1977. 735p. $35.00pa. LC 77-95563. ISBN 0-8165-0566-7.

Kachinas

131. Muth, Marcia. **Kachinas: A Selected Bibliography**. Santa Fe, NM: Sunstone Press, 1984. 32p. $4.95pa. LC 83-18302. ISBN 0-86534-031-5.

Kansas

132. Unrau, William E. **The Emigrant Indians of Kansas: A Critical Bibliography**. Bloomington: Indiana University Press, 1979. 78p. ISBN 0-2533-6816-2.

Land Tenure

133. Sutton, Imre. **Indian Land Tenure: Bibliographical Essays and a Guide to the Literature.** New York: Clearwater, 1975. 290p. $18.00. LC 74-30668. ISBN 0883541041.
   A series of bibliographical essays are written in seven areas of research: 1) aboriginal occupancy and territoriality, 2) land cessions and the establishment of reservations, 3) land administration and land utilization, 4) aboriginal title and land claims, 5) title clarification and change, 6) tenure and jurisdiction, and 7) land tenure and culture

change. Bibliographies in each chapter refer to the primary bibliography at the end, which is indexed by tribe and geographical area.

Languages and Linguistics

134.   Booker, Karen M. **Languages of the Aboriginal Southeast: An Annotated Bibliography.** Metuchen, NJ: Scarecrow Press, 1991. 265p. (Native American Bibliography Series, No. 15). $32.50. LC 90-28779. ISBN 0-8108-2401-9.

135.   Bright, William. **Bibliography of the Languages of Native California, Including Closely Related Languages of Adjacent Areas.** Metuchen, NJ: Scarecrow Press, 1982. 234p. (Native American Bibliography Series, No. 3). $20.00. LC 82-3331. ISBN 0-8108-1547-8.

136.   Evans, G. Edward, and Karin Abbey. **Bibliography of Language Arts Materials for Native North Americans: Bilingual, English as a Second Language and Native Language Materials 1975-1976, with Supplemental Entries for 1965-1974.** Los Angeles: University of California, Los Angeles, American Indian Studies Center, 1979. 120p. (American Indian Bibliographic Series, No. 2). $5.00. LC 92-217890. ISBN 0-935626-14-X.

137.   Evans, G. Edward, and Jeffrey Clark. **North American Indian Language Materials.** Los Angeles: University of California, Los Angeles, American Indian Studies Center, 1980. 154p. (American Indian Bibliographic Series, No. 3). $5.00pa. ISBN 0-935626-15-8.

138.   Marken, Jack W. **American Indian: Language and Literature**. Arlington Heights, IL: Harlan Davidson, 1978. 204p. LC 76-4624. ISBN 0-8829-5553-5.

139.   Parr, Richard T. **A Bibliography of the Athapaskan Languages**. Ottawa: National Museums of Canada, 1974. 333p. $3.50. LC 75-312128.

Laws and Treaties

140.   De Puy, Henry Farr. **A Bibliography of the English Colonial Treaties with the American Indians, Including a Synopsis of Each Treaty**. Repr. of 1917 ed. New York: AMS Press, 1978. 107p. $11.50. LC 78-164820. ISBN 0-404-07123-6.

140a. Fritz, Linda. **Native Law Bibliography**. 2d ed. Saskatoon, Sask.: Native Law Centre, University of Saskatchewan, 1990. 167p. $30.00. ISBN 0-88880-233-1.

141.   Hargrett, Lester. **A Bibliography of the Constitutions and Laws of the American Indians**. Cambridge, MA: Harvard University Press, 1947. 124p. LC 47-31330.
       The emphasis here is on the constitutions and laws of the Cherokee, Chickasaw, Choctaw, Creek, and Seminole Indians (the Five Civilized Tribes).

141a. Jorgensen, Delores A., and Barbara B. Heisinger, comps. **A Bibliography of Indian Law Periodical Articles, Published 1980-1990**. (with update for 1991). 2d ed. Buffalo, NY: William S. Hein, 1992. 254p. LC 92-070678. ISBN 0-89941-784-4.

141b. Storey, Dorothy S. **A Bibliography of Treaties with the Indians of Canada Included in Government Documents from Earliest Times to 1933**. Montreal: McGill University Library School, 1934. 6p.

Literature

142. Bataille, Gretchen M. **Inside the Cigar Store: A Selected Bibliography**. Ames: Iowa State University, Media Resources Center, 1979. 92p. LC 80-11390.

143. Beidler, Peter G., and Marion F. Egge. **The American Indian in Short Fiction: An Annotated Bibliography**. Metuchen: NJ: Scarecrow Press, 1979. 215p. $20.00. LC 79-20158. ISBN 0-8108-1256-8.

144. Colonnese, Tom, and Louis Owens. **American Indian Novelists: An Annotated Critical Bibliography**. New York: Garland, 1985. 161p. LC 82-49135. ISBN 082409199X.

145. Gilliland, Hap. **Indian Children's Books**. Billings: Montana Council for Indian Education, 1980. 248p. $7.95. ISBN 089925286.

146. Hirschfelder, Arlene B. **American Indian and Eskimo Authors: A Comprehensive Bibliography**. New York: Association on American Indian Affairs; distr., New York: Interbook, 1973. 99p. LC 73-82109.

147. Hirschfelder, Arlene B. **American Indian Authors: A Representative Bibliography**. New York: Association on American Indian Affairs, 1970. 45p. LC 78-121863.
   This bibliography annotates 157 books of 120 American Indian writers, representing 54 tribes.

148. Hirschfelder, Arlene B. **Annotated Bibliography of the Literature on American Indians Published in State Historical Society Publications: New England and Middle Atlantic States**. Millwood, NY: Kraus International Publications, 1982. 356p. $45.00. LC 82-17213. ISBN 0527408891.

149. Jacobson, Angeline. **Contemporary Native American Literature: A Selected and Partially Annotated Bibliography.** Metuchen, NJ: Scarecrow Press, 1977. 247p. $25.00. LC 77-5614. ISBN 0-8108-1031-X.

149a. Lass-Woodfin, Mary Jo, ed. **Books on American Indians and Eskimos: A Selection Guide for Children and Young Adults**. Chicago: American Library Association, 1978. 237p. LC 77-17271. ISBN 08389-0241-3.

150. Littlefield, Daniel F., Jr., and James W. Parins. **A Biobibliography of Native American Writers, 1772-1924.** Metuchen, NJ: Scarecrow Press, 1981. 343p. (Native American Bibliography Series, No. 2). $37.00. LC 81-9138. ISBN 0-8108-1463-3. **Supplement, 1985.** 339p. (Native American Bibliography Series, No. 5). $29.50. LC 85-2045. ISBN 0-8108-1802-7.

These two unique volumes draw together a considerable body of literature not easily found elsewhere: the writings of Indian authors from Colonial times to 1924, when American Indians were granted citizenship in the United States. The two volumes cover over 1,200 Indian writers' contributions to Indian and non-Indian newspapers, newsletters, journals, and magazines and include political essays and addresses, satirical works, myths and legends, poetry, fiction, published letters, historical works, and personal reminiscences. Both volumes are arranged in the same way: Part 1 lists the authors alphabetically, with entries in chronological order; part 2 is a small bibliography of Native American writers known only by pen names; and part 3 provides biographical sketches of each author. An index of tribal affiliation is provided, as well as a detailed subject index.

The only comparable source listing Indian writers of this time period is Arlene Hirschfelder's *American Indian Authors: A Representative Bibliography* (entry 147), which lists writings by Indian authors as well as writings by Indians written down by non-Indians.

150a. Mulroy, Kathleen, comp. **Native Americans: Recommended Books for Children and Young Adults.** Youngstown, OH: NOLA Regional Library System, 1983. 86p.

151. Peck, David R. **American Ethnic Literatures: Native American, African American, Chicano/Latino, and Asian American Writers and Their Backgrounds: An Annotated Bibliography.** Pasadena, CA: Salem Press, 1992. 218p. $40.00. LC 92-12897. ISBN 0-89356-684-5.

152. Rock, Roger O. **The Native American in American Literature: A Selectively Annotated Bibliography.** Westport, CT: Greenwood, 1985. 211p. (Bibliographies and Indexes in American Literature, No. 3). $52.95. LC 84-27972. ISBN 0-313-24550-9.

152a. Ruoff, A. LaVonne Brown. **American Indian Literatures, an Introduction, Bibliographic Review, and Selected Bibliography.** New York: Modern Language Association of America, 1990. 200p. $45.00. LC 90-13438. ISBN 0-87352-188-9.

152b. Schafstall, Marilyn, and Lillian Francois. **Native Americans in Selected Children's Media.** Toledo, OH: Toledo-Lucas County Public Library, 1978. 112p.

153. Slapin, Beverly, and Doris Seale. **Through Indian Eyes: The Native Experience in Books for Children.** 3d ed. Philadelphia: New Society Publishers, 1992. 336p. $49.95; $24.95pa. ISBN 0-86571-212-3; 0-86571-213-1pa.

154. Slapin, Beverly, Doris Seale, and Rosemary Gonzales. **How to Tell the Difference: A Checklist for Evaluating Children's Books for Anti-Indian Bias.** Philadelphia: New Society Publishers, 1992. 32p. $29.95; $7.95pa. ISBN 0-86571-215-8; 0-86571-214-Xpa.

155. Stensland, Anna Lee. **Literature by and About the American Indian: An Annotated Bibliography**. 2d ed. Urbana, IL: National Council of Teachers of English, 1979. 382p. $6.75pa. LC 79-18073. ISBN 0814129846.

155a. Stensland, Anna Lee. **Literature by and About the American Indian: An Annotated Bibliography for Junior and Senior High School Students**. Urbana, IL: National Council of Teachers of English, 1973. 208p. LC 73-83285. ISBN 0-8141-4203-7.

156. Sylvestre, Guy. **Indian-Inuit Authors: An Annotated Bibliography**. Ottawa: Information Canada, 1974. $2.00.

Lumbee

156a. Starr, Glenn Ellen. **The Lumbee Indians: An Annotated Bibliography, with Chronology and Index**. Jefferson, NC: McFarland, 1994. 1,584p. $75.00. ISBN 0-89950-511-2.

Maine

156b. Ray, Roger B. **Indians of Maine and the Atlantic Provinces: A Bibliographic Guide**. Portland, ME: Maine Historical Society, 1977. (Maine History Bibliographical Guide Series). ISBN 0-915592-29-0.

156c. Ray, Roger B. **The Indians of Maine: A Bibliographical Guide**. Portland, ME: Maine Historical Society, 1972.

Menominee

157. **Menominee Indian Tribe of Wisconsin**. Billings, MT: U.S. Bureau of Indian Affairs, Planning Support Group, 1975. 153p. (Bibliography on pp. 63-140). LC 75-602974.

Mental Health

158. Kelso, Dianne R., and Carolyn L. Attneave. **Bibliography of North American Indian Mental Health**. Westport, CT: Greenwood, 1981. 411p. $49.95. LC 81-800. ISBN 0-313-22930-9.

Metis (of Canada)

159. Friesen, John W., and Terry Lusty. **The Metis of Canada: An Annotated Bibliography**. Toronto: OISE Press, 1980. 99p. LC 81-179678. ISBN 0774402156.

Minnesota

160.   Minnesota Historical Society. **Chippewa and Dakota Indians**. St. Paul: Minnesota Historical Society, 1969. 131p. LC 70-102272. ISBN 0873510577.
   Listed are books, periodical articles, pamphlets, and manuscripts on the Chippewa and Dakota Indians.

Missions

161.   Ronda, James P., and James Axtell. **Indian Missions: A Critical Bibliography**. Bloomington: Indiana University Press, 1978. 85p. ISBN 0-2533-2978-7.

Music

162.   Hickerson, Joseph Charles. **Annotated Bibliography of North American Indian Music North of Mexico**. Bloomington: Indiana University Press, 1961. 464p. LC 72-290048.

Navajo

163.   Correll, J. Lee, Editha L. Watson, and David M. Brugge. **Navajo Bibliography: With Subject Index.** Rev. ed. Window Rock, AZ: Navajo Tribe, Museum and Research Department, Research Section, 1969. 2v.

164.   Iverson, Peter. **The Navajos: A Critical Bibliography**. Bloomington: Indiana University Press, 1976. 64p. ISBN 0-2533-3986-3.

164a.   Kari, James M. **A Navajo Reading Bibliography**. Albuquerque: University of New Mexico General Library, 1974. 40p. (Sources, No. 2). LC 74-76955. ISBN 0-913630-02-0.

165.   Kluckhohn, Clyde, and Katherine Spencer. **A Bibliography of the Navaho Indians**. New York: J. J. Augustin, 1940. 93p. $16.00. LC 40-29893. ISBN 0-404-07134-1.

New Mexico

166.   Swadesh, Frances Leon. **20,000 Years of History: A New Mexico Bibliography.** Santa Fe, NM: Sunstone Press, 1973. 129p. $4.95. LC 73-77323. ISBN 0913270148.

Northeast

167.   **Eastern Indians: An Annotated Bibliography with Emphasis on Indigenous Tribes of Connecticut**. Hartford: Connecticut Indian Education Council, Indian Advisory Committee, 1986. 67p. LC 87-621677.

168.   Nelson, Eunice. **The Wabanaki: An Annotated Bibliography of Selected Books, Articles, Documents About Maliseet, Micmac, Passamaquoddy, Penobscot Indians in Maine, Annotated by Native Americans**. Cambridge, MA: American Friends Service Committee, 1982. 108p. $6.50. LC 82-166285.

169.   Porter, Frank W., III. **In Pursuit of the Past: An Anthropological and Bibliographic Guide to Maryland and Delaware**. Metuchen, NJ: Scarecrow Press, 1986. 268p. (Native American Bibliography Series, No. 8). $27.50. LC 85-10889. ISBN 0-8108-1825-6.

170.   Porter, Frank W., III. **Indians in Maryland and Delaware: A Critical Bibliography**. Bloomington: Indiana University Press, 1979. 107p. LC 79-2460. ISBN 0253309549.

171.   Salisbury, Neal. **The Indians of New England: A Critical Bibliography**. Bloomington: Indiana University Press, 1982. 109p. LC 81-48085. ISBN 0253329817.

172.   Tooker, Elisabeth. **The Indians of the Northeast: A Critical Bibliography**. Bloomington: Indiana University Press, 1978. 77p. LC 78-3252. ISBN 0-2533-3003-3.

Northwest

173.   Grumet, Robert Steven. **Native Americans of the Northwest Coast: A Critical Bibliography**. Bloomington: Indiana University Press, 1979. 108p. (Newberry Library Center for the History of the American Indian Bibliographical Series). ISBN 0-2533-0385-0.

174.   Trafzer, Clifford E. **Yakima, Palouse, Cayuse, Umatilla, Walla Walla, and Wanapum Indians**. Metuchen, NJ: Scarecrow Press, 1992. 236p. (Native American Bibliography Series, No. 16). $32.50. LC 91-41052. ISBN 0-8108-2517-1.

Ojibwa

174a. Chippewa and Dakota Indians. **A Subject Catalog of Books, Pamphlets, Periodical Articles, and Manuscripts in the Minnesota Historical Society**. St. Paul, MN: Minnesota Historical Society, 1969. 131p. LC 70-102272. ISBN 87351-057-7.

175.   Tanner, Helen Hornbeck. **The Ojibwas: A Critical Bibliography**. Bloomington: Indiana University Press, 1976. 78p. ISBN 0-2533-4165-5.

Omaha

176.   Tate, Michael L. **The Upstream People: An Annotated Research Bibliography of the Omaha Tribe**. Metuchen, NJ: Scarecrow Press, 1991. 522p. (Native American Bibliography Series, No. 14). $62.50. LC 90-24533. ISBN 0-8108-2372-1.

Osage

177. Wilson, Terry P. **Bibliography of the Osage**. Metuchen, NJ: Scarecrow Press, 1985. 350p. (Native American Bibliography Series, No. 6). $20.00. LC 85-2087. ISBN 0-8108-1805-1.

Pawnees

178. Blaine, Martha Royce. **The Pawnees: A Critical Bibliography**. Bloomington: Indiana University Press, 1980. 109p. ISBN 0-2533-1502-6.

Policy Toward Indians

179. Buchanan, Jim, Fran Burkert, and Mark Jamison. **A Bibliography of Current American Indian Policy. Supplement, 1979-1986**. Monticello, IL: Vance Bibliographies, 1986. 35p. (Public Administration Series Bibliography, P-2053). LC 87-103995. ISBN 1555900933.

180. Prucha, Francis Paul. **A Bibliographical Guide to the History of Indian-White Relations in the United States**. Chicago: University of Chicago Press, 1977. 454p. $30.00. LC 76-16045. ISBN 0-226-68476-8.

180a. Prucha, Francis Paul. **Indian-White Relations in the United States: A Bibliography of Works Published 1975-1980**. Lincoln: University of Nebraska Press, 1982. 179p. $18.95. LC 81-14722. ISBN 0-8032-3665-4.

This reference work and its supplement provide extensive bibliographies and serve as guides for researchers in the history of Indian-nonnative relations from Colonial days to 1980. The initial guide lists over 9,700 citations for books, magazine articles, journal articles, conference proceedings, and U.S. government documents dealing with interactions between Indians and settlers, colonists, traders, and government officials. The 1975-1980 supplement lists 3,400 items. In the first part of *A Bibliographical Guide* (pp. 3-26), researchers are guided to reference materials, government archives, manuscript collections, library catalogs, and other sources for broad-based research. Part two (pp. 27-379) divides the sources by chapters on topics (e.g., military relations, legal relations, Indian health) and subdivides these chapters into specific topics (e.g., Colonial period, water rights, Hampton and Carlisle Institutes). Lots of articles from state historical journals are included. Each work is listed only once in the bibliography, and there is an index to subjects, titles, and authors.

181. Prucha, Francis Paul. **United States Indian Policy: A Critical Bibliography**. Bloomington: Indiana University Press, 1977. 54p. ISBN 0-2533-6165-6.

182. Surtees, Robert J. **Canadian Indian Policy: A Critical Bibliography**. Bloomington: Indiana University Press, 1982. 107p. ISBN 0-2533-1300-7.

Potawatomi

183. Edmunds, Russell David. **Kinsmen Through Time: An Annotated Bibliography of Potawatomi History**. Metuchen, NJ: Scarecrow Press, 1987. 217p. (Native American Bibliography Series, No. 12). $27.50. ISBN 0-8108-2020-X.

Pottery

184. Oppelt, Norman T. **Southwestern Pottery: An Annotated Bibliography and List of Types and Wares**. 2d ed. Metuchen, NJ: Scarecrow Press, 1988. 325p. $42.50. LC 88-6424. ISBN 0-8108-2119-2.

Seminole

184a. Kersey, Harry A., Jr. **The Seminole and Miccosukee Tribes: A Critical Bibliography**. Bloomington, IN: Indiana University Library, 1987. 102p. (D'Arcy McNickle Center for the History of the American Indian Bibliographical Series). LC 85-30545. ISBN 0-253-30662-0.

Seneca

184b. Haas, Marilyn L. **The Seneca and Tuscarora Indians, An Annotated Bibliography**. Metuchen, NJ: Scarecrow Press, 1994. 450p. (Native American Bibliography Series, No. 17). $55.00. LC 94-4415. ISBN 0-8108-2740-9.

Shoalwater Bay

185. Hills, Gordon H. **A List of Sources on the Shoalwater Bay Indian Tribal Heritage**. 2d ed. Tokeland, WA: Heritage Committee, Shoalwater Bay Indian Tribe, 1984. 22p. LC 85-175286.

Sioux (Lakota/Dakota)

186. Hoover, Herbert T. **The Sioux: A Critical Bibliography**. Bloomington: Indiana University Press, 1979. 78p. ISBN 0-2533-4972-9.

186a. Hoover, Herbert T., and Karen P. Zimmerman. **The Sioux and Other Native American Cultures of the Dakotas: An Annotated Bibliography**. Westport, CT: Greenwood, 1993. 265p. (Bibliographies and Indexes in Anthropology, No. 8). $65.00. LC 93-25004. ISBN 0-313-29093-8.

187. Marken, Jack W., and Herbert T. Hoover. **Bibliography of the Sioux**. Metuchen, NJ: Scarecrow Press, 1980. 338p. (Native American Bibliography Series, No. 1). $27.50. LC 80-20106. ISBN 0-8108-1356-4.

Social Sciences

188.   Brennan, Jere L. **The Forgotten American—American Indians Remembered: A Selected Bibliography for Use in Social Work Education**. New York: Council on Social Work Education, 1972. 83p. $3.30. LC 79-176191. ISBN 0-318-35350-4.

189.   Swagerty, W. R., ed. **Scholars and the Indian Experience: Critical Reviews of Recent Writing in the Social Sciences**. Bloomington: Indiana University Press, 1984. 286p. (D'Arcy McNickle Center for the History of the American Indian Bibliographical Series). LC 83-49510. ISBN 0253350956.

190.   Thornton, Russell, and Mary K. Grasmick. **Bibliography of Social Science Research and Writings on American Indians**. Minneapolis: University of Minnesota, Center for Urban and Regional Affairs, 1979. 160p. LC 82-623383.

191.   Thornton, Russell, and Mary K. Grasmick. **Sociology of American Indians: A Critical Bibliography**. Bloomington: Indiana University Press, 1980. 113p. $4.95. LC 80-8035. ISBN 0-2533-5294-0.

Southwest

192.   Dobyns, Henry F., and Robert C. Euler. **Indians of the Southwest: A Critical Bibliography.** Bloomington: Indiana University Press, 1980. 153p. ISBN 0-2533-2658-2.

Stage

193.   Jones, Eugene H. **Native Americans as Shown on the Stage, 1753-1916**. Metuchen, NJ: Scarecrow Press, 1988. 219p. $25.00. LC 87-16121. ISBN 0-8108-2040-4.

Texas

194.   Tate, Michael L. **The Indians of Texas: An Annotated Research Bibliography.** Metuchen, NJ: Scarecrow Press, 1986. 514p. (Native American Bibliography Series, No. 9). $52.50. LC 85-19674. ISBN 0-8108-1852-3.

Urbanization

195.   Bramstedt, Wayne G. **A Bibliography of North American Indians in the Los Angeles Metropolitan Area, the Urban Indian Capital**. Monticello, IL: Vance Bibliographies, 1979. 14p. (Public Administration Series Bibliography, P-233). $1.50. LC 79-110674.

196. Bramstedt, Wayne G. **North American Indians in Towns and Cities: A Bibliography**. Monticello, IL: Vance Bibliographies, 1979. 74p. (Public Administration Series Bibliography, P-234). $7.50. LC 79-110581.

197. Harkins, Arthur M., et al. **A Bibliography of Urban Indians in the United States**. Minneapolis: University of Minnesota Press, 1971. 42p. LC 72-611466.

198. Thornton, Russell, Gary D. Sandefur, and Harold G. Grasmick. **The Urbanization of American Indians: A Critical Bibliography**. Bloomington: Indiana University Press, 1982. 87p. LC 81-48087. ISBN 0253362059.

Ute

198a. Stewart, Omer C. **Ethnohistorical Bibliography of the Ute Indians of Colorado**. Boulder, CO: University of Colorado, 1971. 94p. (University of Colorado, Series in Anthropology No. 18).

199. Tyler, Samuel Lyman. **The Ute People: A Bibliographical Checklist**. Provo, UT: Brigham Young University, Institute of American Indian Studies, 1964. 120p. LC 78-349480.

Virginia

200. Kaufman, Lynn E., James C. O'Neill, and Patricia A. Jehle, eds. **Bibliography of the Virginia Indians: Articles, Books and References to Virginia, with Particular Emphasis on Archaeology.** Richmond, VA: Archaeological Society of Virginia, 1976. 92p. $10.95. ISBN 1-884626-00-9.

Women

201. Green, Rayna. **Native American Women: A Bibliography**. Washington, DC: U.S. Department of Education, 1981. 106p. LC 81-604052.

202. Green, Rayna. **Native American Women: A Contextual Bibliography**. Bloomington: Indiana University Press, 1983. 120p. $25.00. LC 82-48571. ISBN 0253339766.

203. Jamieson, Kathleen. **Native Women in Canada: A Selected Bibliography**. Ottawa: Social Sciences and Humanities Research Council of Canada, 1983. $3.00pa. LC 84-144806. ISBN 0662123964.

Yakimas

204. Schuster, Helen H. **The Yakimas: A Critical Bibliography**. Bloomington: Indiana University Press, 1982. 158p. ISBN 0-2533-6800-6.

Library Book Catalogs

Library book catalogs are special forms of bibliographies listing the materials in libraries and major research centers that are strong in certain fields of study. A book catalog is prepared by photographing the cards in a library's catalog and creating a bound form of the cards. However, book catalogs are not easy to read due to the poor quality of the reproduction process, and researchers must be patient and allow time to use them thoroughly.

Library book catalogs for major collections covering American Indian studies are located in university and large public libraries. Researchers can use these catalogs to discover older materials in libraries other than their own.

Book catalogs are unique in their depth of coverage of the materials. Most book catalogs include some "analytics," which list not only books and periodicals, but also chapters of books and articles within periodicals. Library book catalogs are usually "dictionary catalogs," which means materials are listed alphabetically, by authors, titles, and subjects all together.

Now, most library collections are available as online public access catalogs, which can be searched remotely through the Internet system. But these standard book catalogs in print will continue to serve researchers mainly because many of the older materials listed will not be included in online catalogs, and book catalogs analyzed the contents of many materials included.

The following five library book catalogs are important ones for researchers in American Indian studies who want more than the usual materials found in current periodical indexes and databases and in online public access catalogs of libraries.

205.   Newberry Library. Chicago. Edward E. Ayer Collection. **Dictionary Catalog of the Edward E. Ayer Collection of Americana and American Indians in the Newberry Library.** Boston: G. K. Hall, 1961. 16v. $1,280.00/set. ISBN 0-8161-0586-3. **First Supplement, 1970**. 3v. $365.00/set. ISBN 0-8161-0810-2; **Second Supplement, 1980**. 4v. $500.00. ISBN 0-8161-10326-7.

This valuable collection contains a total of 109,000 books, chapters of books, manuscript holdings, government documents, journal articles, and conference proceedings on American Indians, captivities, Indian wars, early discoveries and explorations of the Americas and the Arctic, missionary activities, and other topics on the history, linguistics, ethnology, and archaeology of North America and South America. The 1980 supplement began a policy of acquiring copies of all identifiable dissertations on American Indians.

206.   Huntington Free Library and Reading Room. New York. **Dictionary Catalog of the American Indian Collection**. Boston: G. K. Hall, 1977. 4v. $435.00/set. ISBN 0-8161-0065-9.

Over 35,000 books, periodicals, periodical articles, and American Indian newspapers are represented in this fine collection on the anthropology, art, history, and contemporary concerns of the native peoples of the western hemisphere.

207.   U.S. Department of the Interior. Washington, DC. **Dictionary Catalog of the Department Library.** Boston: G. K. Hall, 1967. 37v. $4,000.00/set. ISBN 0-8161-0715-7. **First Supplement, 1968.** 4v. $265.00. ISBN 0816113599; **Second Supplement, 1971.** 2v. $200.00. ISBN 0816108455; **Third Supplement, 1973**. 4v. $485.00. ISBN 0816110549; **Fourth Supplement, 1975.** 8v. $910.00/set. ISBN 0-8161-0016-0.

This unique collection combines materials from the Bureau of Biological Survey (begun 1885), the Fish and Wildlife Service (1871), the Bureau of Mines (1910), the Office of the Solicitor (1849), and the Bureau of Indian Affairs (1824), as well as some materials from the Bureau of Land Management and the National Park Service. Included are unpublished government reports, conference proceedings, books, and periodical articles on topics such as government relations with Indians, land policies, law and constitutions affecting Indians, the territories of the United States, biographies, diaries, and letters of individuals.

208. Harvard University. Peabody Museum of Archaeology and Ethnology. Tozzer Library. **Peabody Museum of Archaeology and Ethnology Library Catalogue.** Boston: G. K. Hall, 1963. 54v. (Authors, 26v.; subjects, 28v.) ISBN 0816114005. **First Supplement, 1970,** 12v. ISBN 0816108617; **Second Supplement, 1971,** 6v. ISBN 0816109605; **Third Supplement, 1975,** 7v. ISBN 0816111685; **Fourth Supplement, 1979,** 7v. ISBN 0816102538. Continued by *Author and Subject Catalogues of the Tozzer Library* (formerly the Library of the Peabody Museum of Archaeology and Ethnology). 2d enl. ed. Boston: G. K. Hall, 1988. 12 microfiche in 8 binders. $6,600.00. ISBN 0816117314. Continued by *Anthropological Literature* (entry 229) and the *Bibliographic Guide to Anthropology and Archaeology* (entry 40).

The Tozzer Library of Archaeology and Ethnology at Harvard University is probably the best anthropology library in the world. At the beginning of the twentieth century, it began analyzing the contents of periodicals and other serials and creating catalog cards for the individual articles by authors and subjects, as well as for the complete books in its extensive collection. This created the *Author and Subject Catalogues of the Tozzer Library*, which was first published in book format in 1963 and again in 1988 on microfiche. The new edition cumulates the 1963 edition with all its supplements and combines these with entries through June 1986. This new edition lists about 1.34 million items, including books, serials, periodicals, manuscripts, microforms, and pamphlets specializing in the ethnology and archaeology of the Americas.

The 1963 edition incorporates a difficult-to-use subject headings scheme, which divides materials by topics, geographic areas, and human groups, and requires patience in locating the materials on American Indians. Start by looking under "North America" and checking subdivisions by regions.

In 1981, the *Tozzer Library Index to Anthropological Subject Headings* was published in a second edition. This revised list added many more access points by ethnic group names, subjects, geographical names, and cross-references. Serious researchers cannot overlook this collection of important sources in American Indian studies.

209. New York Public Library. Research Libraries. **Dictionary Catalog of the History of the Americas Collection.** Boston: G. K. Hall, 1961. 28v. $2,520.00/set. ISBN 0-8161-0540-5. **First Supplement, 1974.** 9v. $1,085.00/set. ISBN 0-8161-0771-8.

In the original set of 28 volumes, approximately 600,000 catalog cards were reproduced for author and subject access to this enormous collection of books and periodical articles. The concentration is on the history of North America and South America, with many entries under Indians. The supplement includes cards added to the collection through 1971. After 1971, additions are in the *Dictionary Catalog of the Research Libraries* through 1981 and the *Bibliographic Guide to North American History*, 1978- (annual).

PERIODICAL INDEXES, ABSTRACTS, AND DATABASES

Articles from magazines and journals may be located by using printed periodical indexes, abstracting services, and computerized databases. A myriad of indexes and databases is available for locating topics in American Indian studies. This section deals with the options of using printed tools and computerized tools for research and the advantages and opportunities of each. Chapter 7 of this guide on newspapers covers both printed and computerized sources for newspapers.

Printed Indexes and Abstracts Versus Computerized Databases

Printed indexes and abstracts have long been the tools that make it possible to locate countless pieces of information in magazines and journals. Indexes allow researchers to look up their subjects in hundreds of periodicals over many years, without the limitless task of browsing through all those issues. Periodical indexes (e.g., the *Social Sciences Index*) supply the bibliographic citations to articles in magazines and journals. Abstracting services (e.g., *Sociological Abstracts*) also provide bibliographic citations but include abstracts, or short summaries, of the articles indexed.

Computerized databases are also available for locating articles in magazines and journals. Databases have continued to increase in number dramatically over the last 20 years, as have computer uses in virtually all segments of our society. Our information age continues to expand with databases for periodical references, full-text systems, and directory information, available online and on compact disc.

The tremendous growth of information through the Internet, and other networks such as Bitnet and Usenet, is an indication of our information explosion. Researchers are discovering more and more academic discussion lists, listservs (electronic discussion groups), bulletin boards, interest groups, and full-text files available through these computer networks, which foster information exchange and discussion. One listserv is Nativelit-L, designed for free discussion of Native American literature. For a fairly complete listing of these free and changing online sources of information, check the *Directory of Electronic Journals, Newsletters, and Academic Discussion Lists* (Washington, DC: Association of Research Libraries, Office of Scientific and Academic Publishing, 3d ed., 1993). This third edition lists 240 journals and newsletters online in full text and 1,152 discussion lists. Some of the journals and newsletters are available in print also. The discussion lists are of possible interest to academic researchers. These sources are not substitutes for traditional, scholarly research tools, but they supply additional assistance through sharing of information and resources.

Most research databases are available through computer vendors and producers such as DIALOG, BRS, DATA-STAR, WILSONLINE, and EPIC. These provide the academic and scholarly computer resources corresponding to the printed periodical indexes and abstracts and some full-text files of periodicals. Periodical indexes on CD-ROM (compact disc, read-only memory) are growing rapidly as common tools for researchers in libraries. The ever-popular *InfoTRAC* is sought after by undergraduate college students working on papers and speeches as if it were the only source for references to periodical articles. And hundreds of online databases are available to be searched for a fee through commercial vendors.

The same periodical references and abstracts often may be located by using a printed index, a compact disc database, or an online database. For example, *Psychological Abstracts* is a printed index, *PsycLit* is the CD-ROM version, and *PsycINFO* is the online database version. These various systems are not interchangeable, but offer the researcher a choice in formats for accessing information.

In 1972, DIALOG began offering two online databases, *ERIC* and *NTIS*, and the availability of online bibliographic databases grew rapidly thereafter. In 1994, there were over 500 online databases available through commercial vendors such as DIALOG, DATA-STAR, BRS, ORBIT, WILSONLINE, and EPIC, and many full-text files on systems like *NEXIS*. Most of the online databases through these commercial systems and others around the world similar to them are the equivalents of the printed periodical indexes and abstracts. Increasingly, however, there are many full-text files—journals, magazines, newspapers, directories, statistical sources, and laws and court cases—available online. Some of the online databases, such as *InfoTRAC*, are unique sources, with no exact print equivalents. And conversely, there are printed periodical indexes that do not have computer database equivalents online or on CD-ROM, such as the *Music Index* and *Abstracts in Anthropology*. Full-text databases are also growing rapidly. An evaluation of online database vendors by Carol Tenopir titled "Full-text Searching on Major Supermarket Systems: DIALOG, Data-Star, and NEXIS" (*Database*, Vol. 16, No. 2, October 1993, p. 32) reveals that DIALOG offers over 2,600 full-text sources through 120 databases. DATA-STAR, the European online provider recently acquired by Knight-Ridder, the parent company of DIALOG, has over 50 separate full-text databases. Martha E. Williams, in "The State of

Databases Today: 1993," in *Gale Directory of Databases* (entry 210), notes that in the last seven years, the number of full-text sources has grown nearly 600 percent, now making up 47 percent of the database total.

Information Access, producer of the *InfoTRAC* family of databases, is adding more full-text files to its services. Information Access introduced *Expanded Academic ASAP, Magazine ASAP* in 1993 and *Business ASAP* in 1992, which provide full text for hundreds of their periodicals.

The *LEXIS/NEXIS* system, from Mead Data Central, had been designed from the beginning as a full-text system: *LEXIS* covering the legal texts and *NEXIS* covering magazines, journals, newspapers, and newswires. Other online systems offering full-text sources include *DataTimes* and *Dow Jones News Retrieval.*

This guide will concentrate on the major online and CD-ROM databases of use to researchers in American Indian studies and is not a comprehensive survey of all computerized sources available. Bibliographic databases and indexes are still the core of academic research in American Indian studies, and, therefore, are the focus of this guide.

There is a wide variety of printed and computerized sources available for researching topics in American Indian studies and other fields, and it is understandable that researchers might get confused over which sources are best to use for their particular topics.

Computer databases are popular with many researchers because they are fast, covering several years of periodicals at once. Many times faculty and graduate student researchers say to librarians, "You have just saved me months of looking through indexes and abstracts by this computer search!" There are several reasons they are so delighted by the database searches. Computer databases offer the powerful ability to search more than one word or phrase at a time and to manipulate terms to obtain needed articles (using Boolean logic: AND, OR, NOT). In addition, databases allow searching of words, phrases, names, and dates in all available fields: authors, titles, abstracts, years, and so on. This unique feature allows researchers to be comprehensive when searching for very specific information, such as the name of a questionnaire or theory or program, and in culling records that do not fit the defined parameters. Computer database searching is the way to find the proverbial "needle in a haystack." Therefore, it is normally faster and more comprehensive to use a computer database for locating periodical and newspaper articles rather than traditional printed sources.

The disadvantages of databases are few, but they do impose limits for some researchers. First, most online databases accessible through a computer and a modem are expensive, usually between $20 and $40 per database searched for the typical search. The direct costs vary according to the amount of time one is connected to a database and an online system and the number of citations and abstracts printed or downloaded. There is no accurate way of estimating the costs beforehand. When the search is completed, the online system calculates the exact costs and displays the results. Costs include the telecommunications charges, charges for using the commercial system offering the databases, the online connect costs for each minute of use, and charges for each record that is displayed, printed, or downloaded. The researcher must pay whether any useful information is retrieved.

Researchers can use CD-ROM technology for a lower cost or even for free. CD-ROM databases are commonplace in university and large public libraries. The libraries pay annual fees to lease the CD-ROM versions of the periodical indexes, similar to subscribing to the printed indexes but much more expensive. Sometimes researchers must pay for printing the citations and abstracts retrieved. More and more periodical indexes are available in libraries for free on CD-ROM.

The second limitation to database searching is that usually an intermediary is required to perform the search. Exceptions are with CD-ROM databases and databases loaded onto online public access catalogs, where researchers are usually expected to learn to do their own searches, with assistance from librarians, handouts, and tutorials. The majority of databases available are still online and require a reference librarian to search. Since 1972, when DIALOG Information Services made the education database *ERIC* available, librarians have performed the online database searches for patrons and continue to do them primarily by appointment. Most researchers still do not access online bibliographic databases directly via their own computers and modems at home or work, so time is needed for a librarian or other information professional to conduct the searches for them. Researchers should always call ahead to discuss their search needs. Most university libraries perform online searches only for their own currently registered students and current faculty and staff. Each library has its own policy toward online database searching. And with the growth of personal computers and modems, some researchers are obtaining their own passwords and learning to do their own searches.

A third drawback to computer searching is the limited availability of older materials. Most databases do not cover more than the last 10 to 15 years of literature. The *InfoTRAC* CD-ROM database, for example, which is so popular for locating periodical articles, covers the latest three years only, but the *Readers' Guide to Periodical Literature* covers popular magazines from 1900 to the present. Usually, though, researchers want current materials for most topics.

Databases and Indexes Available

210. Marcaccio, Kathleen Young, ed. **Gale Directory of Databases.** Detroit: Gale Research, 1992-. annual, with semiannual updates. 2v. $280.00pa/set. ISBN 0-8103-5766-1.

This comprehensive directory is the best place to check for databases in any subject area. It lists over 8,500 databases available online, in CD-ROM format, on diskette, on magnetic tape, through batch access, and as handheld database products. This source was created from other directories—*Computer Readable Databases, Directory of Online Databases*, and *Directory of Portable Databases*—to form the largest directory of available databases. Not all of these databases are bibliographic and of interest to researchers for journal literature. Many are numeric, statistical, graphic, directories, and full-text. An index by subjects can be checked for database availability. Addresses, phone numbers, and contact persons are provided for databases and database producers.

211. Katz, Bill, and Linda Sternberg Katz. **Magazines for Libraries**. 7th ed. New Providence, NJ: R. R. Bowker, 1992. 1,214p. $139.95. ISBN 0-917460-37-5. ISSN 0895-4321.

This important reference book is consulted by librarians in universities, public libraries, and school libraries for information on over 6,500 of the most significant English-language research journals and general-interest periodicals in all fields of study. A section called "Abstracts and Indexes" provides a summary of the subject coverage of each periodical index and the availability of the index online or on CD-ROM.

212. **Ulrich's International Periodicals Directory 1993-94, Including Irregular Serials & Annuals**. 32d ed. New Providence, NJ: R. R. Bowker, 1993. 5v. $395.00/set. LC 32-0175. ISBN 0-8352-3368-5/set. ISSN 0000-0175/set.

This superb directory is a classified guide to current periodicals internationally. It lists approximately 140,000 serials and 7,000 newspapers and has separate indexes for online and CD-ROM availability as well as database producers. Also available online through DIALOG.

Major Suppliers of Databases

Because the availability of databases and their access through commercial systems or on CD-ROM can change rapidly, researchers are not expected to keep up with this quickly changing field. Reference librarians who specialize in database searching are the first ones to ask which databases are available for your topic of research and which channels to use for accessing those databases.

The selected guides listed in this section are the major ones offering databases of interest to researchers in American Indian studies in the United States. Other database suppliers have large numbers of databases available (e.g., *Dow Jones News Retrieval, CompuServe*) but overall, these are not applicable to American Indian studies. Also, foreign database vendors are not listed (e.g., DIMDI, a subsidiary of Deutsches Institut Fuer Medizinische Dokumentation und Information, in Cologne, Germany; CISTI, a subsidiary of the National Research Council of Canada, in Ottawa, Ontario). For a complete listing of database vendors and databases available on their systems, see the vendor section in *Ulrich's International Periodicals Directory* (entry 212), pages 5,775-5,798, or check the database catalogs for each vendor. A listing of serials on CD-ROM and producers of CD-ROM products is also available in *Ulrich's.*

Researchers do not usually have to know about database suppliers or producers, unless they want to directly access these databases from their home computers. Most researchers use CD-ROM databases in libraries or have reference librarians search the databases for them.

When a researcher uses a CD-ROM product in a library, it is not so important which database producer created the CD-ROM (e.g., Silverplatter Information, Inc. or DIALOG Information Services, Inc.), but whether the database is available or not. The selected database suppliers are listed below, along with many of the databases they offer, in order to provide researchers an idea of what is available. The major databases are described along with the printed periodical indexes and abstracts in the following section, "Indexes, Abstracts, and Databases Relevant for American Indian Studies" (see page 66).

213. **DIALOG Information Services, Inc.**
(Subsidiary of Knight-Ridder, Inc.)
3460 Hillview Avenue
P.O. Box 10010
Palo Alto, CA 94303-0993
(800) 3-DIALOG

Over 400 databases in a broad range of disciplines are offered on this premier system. Included are bibliographic databases, directories, numeric databases, and full-text sources. Of primary importance to American Indian studies are the databases titled *America: History and Life* and *Historical Abstracts*. The following databases are some of those available through DIALOG (as listed in the 1993 *DIALOG Database Catalogue*) that are applicable for research in American Indian studies:

ABI/Inform

Academic Index

Ageline

America: History and Life

ARTbibliographies Modern

Arts and Humanities Search

Avery Index to Architectural Periodicals

Canadian Index

Ceramics Abstracts

Child Abuse and Neglect and Family Violence

Criminal Justice Periodical Index

Current Contents Search

Enviroline

ERIC (Educational Resources Information Center)

Exceptional Child Education Resources

Family Resources Database

Health Periodicals Database

Health Planning and Administration

Historical Abstracts

Legal Resource Index

Library and Information Science Abstracts (LISA)

Linguistics and Language Behavior Abstracts (LLBA)

Magazine ASAP

Magazine Index

Management Contents

Medline

Mental Health Abstracts

Music Literature International (RILM)

NCJRS (National Criminal Justice Reference Service)

Nursing and Allied Health (CINAHL)

PAIS International

Papers

Philosopher's Index

Pollution Abstracts

PsycINFO

Religion Index

Reuters

Social SciSearch

Sociological Abstracts

U.S. Political Science Documents

Water Resources Abstracts

Waternet

214. **BRS Online Products**
    (Subsidiary of InfoPro Technologies, Inc.)
    8000 Westpark Drive
    McLean, VA 22102
    (800) 289-4277

This database supplier offers over 140 databases specializing in medicine, the biosciences, science, health, and mental health coverage. The database entitled *Social Work Abstracts* is only available through BRS, but many of the major databases are also available here, such as *PsycINFO* and *Social SciSearch*. The indexes and databases produced by the H. W. Wilson Company (e.g., the *Humanities Index*, the *Index to Legal Periodicals*, the *Social Sciences Index*, the *Readers' Guide to Periodical Literature*) are also available through BRS.

The databases listed below are the most appropriate ones for research in American Indian studies (as listed in the 1993 *BRS Database Catalogue*).

ABI/Inform

AgeLine

Alcohol and Alcohol Problems Science Database

Combined Health Information Database

Current Contents Search

DRUGINFO and Alcohol Use and Abuse

ERIC (Educational Resources Information Center)

Exceptional Child Education Resources

Family Resources Database

Health Periodicals Index Database

Health Planning and Administration

Linguistics and Language Behavior Abstracts (LLBA)

Medline

Nursing and Allied Health Database

PsycINFO

Social SciSearch

Social Work Abstracts

Sociological Abstracts

Wilson Applied Science and Technology Index

Wilson Art Index

Wilson Business Periodicals Index

Wilson Education Index

Wilson General Science Index

Wilson Humanities Index

Wilson Index to Legal Periodicals

Wilson Library Literature

Wilson Readers' Guide Abstracts

Wilson Readers' Guide to Periodical Literature

Wilson Social Sciences Index

215. **WILSONLINE**
   H. W. Wilson Company
   950 University Avenue
   Bronx, NY 10452
   (800) 367-6770

H. W. Wilson produces many of the standard periodical indexes that are commonly used in libraries throughout the country, like the *Readers' Guide to Periodical Literature*. These indexes are available as databases that can be accessed online (through WILSONLINE) or on CD-ROM. They are easy to use and cover the most important English-language periodicals in their fields.

The databases listed below are the most useful for topics in American Indian studies:

Applied Science and Technology Index

Art Index

Biography Index

Biological and Agricultural Index

Book Review Digest

Business Periodicals Index

Education Index

Essay and General Literature Index

General Science Index

Humanities Index

Index to Legal Periodicals

Library Literature

Readers' Guide Abstracts

Readers' Guide to Periodical Literature

Social Sciences Index

216. **EPIC SERVICE**
OCLC Online Computer Library Center, Inc.
6565 Frantz Road
Dublin, OH 43017-0702
(800) 848-5800

Many libraries are accessing databases via EPIC, a growing service of OCLC. EPIC offers the *MLA Bibliography* online from 1963-present, compared with the more limited coverage of the *MLA* on WILSONLINE from 1981-present.

The following list includes online databases on EPIC that are useful for American Indian studies:

ABI/Inform

Applied Science and Technology Index

Art Index

Arts and Humanities Search

Business Periodicals Index

ContentsFirst

Education Index

ERIC

General Science Index

Humanities Index

Library Literature

Medline

MLA Bibliography

PAIS

Periodical Abstracts

PsycINFO

Readers' Guide to Periodical Literature

Social Sciences Index

Sociological Abstracts

Indexes, Abstracts, and Databases Relevant for American Indian Studies

Of the many indexes and databases produced, the ones in this section are the most important for researchers studying various aspects of American Indian history, life, and culture. The arrangement is by broad subject categories. Because American Indian studies comprises many fields of study, a variety of subject disciplines is represented.

Printed indexes and abstracts are listed with notations of their availability online or on CD-ROM. Unique databases are listed individually. Printed indexes have annual cumulative volumes, which are not mentioned in the entries. Prices listed for subscriptions to printed indexes are for one year, unless otherwise noted. Costs for searching online databases vary greatly, as do costs for leasing CD-ROM databases. Databases are available from a number of database producers and suppliers, therefore prices are not listed. Check with the database vendors and producers for current prices. Also, online databases and CD-ROM databases usually cover fewer years than do the printed indexes; this span of coverage can vary widely among database producers and vendors.

General Indexes, Abstracts, and Databases

Listed here is a selection of periodical indexes, abstracts, and databases that index general and popular periodicals, such as magazines like *Newsweek, Time,* and *U.S. News & World Report,* instead of the professional journal literature. These indexes and databases are commonly found in college and public libraries. General periodical indexes and databases cover national and international news events. Some of these indexes are regional in their coverage or provide citations to articles in nonmainstream periodicals. General periodical indexes reflect what is going on in society. They take the pulse of social concerns and issues, including some American Indian issues.

The following general periodical indexes, abstracting services, and databases include articles on American Indians.

217. **Readers' Guide to Periodical Literature**. Bronx, NY: H. W. Wilson Co., 1900-. 17/yr., $180.00. ISSN 0034-0464.

The mainstay of periodical indexes, *Readers' Guide* covers more than 200 popular magazines such as *Business Week, Newsweek, Time, Psychology Today,* and *Scientific American.* Easy to use, it is arranged by subjects and authors interfiled in one alphabet. *Readers' Guide* has quarterly and annual cumulations. Articles are on a wide variety of topics, primarily listed under "Indians (American)" and "Indians of North America," with subheadings dealing with art, costume and adornment, government relations, industries, influence on nature, literature, motion pictures, and religion and mythology. The *Readers' Guide* is available online through WILSONLINE and BRS and on CD-ROM.

Other versions are *Readers' Guide Abstracts Print Edition* (1988-present, 10/yr.), which includes over 25,000 abstracts, and *Readers' Guide Abstracts Microfiche Edition* (1986-present, 8/yr.), which features 60,000 abstracts and a much higher subscription cost. These are available online through WILSONLINE and BRS (1983-present) and on CD-ROM.

218. **InfoTRAC**. Foster City, CA: Information Access Co., current year plus 3 years back. monthly, price varies.

There are several versions of this extremely popular CD-ROM periodical index. The *Magazine Index* (entry 219) is part of *InfoTRAC*, with much overlap of coverage. Libraries may subscribe to different editions of *InfoTRAC*; the best one for research is the *Academic Index*. The *Expanded Academic Index* covers around 400 scholarly and general-interest periodicals and is also online through DIALOG. Under the subject "Native Americans," well over 1,000 articles on all aspects of Indian research can be found in magazines, journals, and newspapers from the past three years. Included under "Native Americans" are Indians of all the Americas, with many subdivisions of the topics and regions.

The *General Periodicals Index* is a popular version of *InfoTRAC* found in public and school libraries. It covers over 1,100 periodicals, including all of those from the *Magazine Index* (entry 219) and *IAC's Business Index*. Daily updates are available through *Newsearch* (entry 220).

219. **Magazine Index**. Foster City, CA: Information Access Co., 1977-. weekly, price varies.

Similar to the *Readers' Guide to Periodical Literature* (entry 217), the *Magazine Index* is broader-based, including about 550 periodicals, compared with about 200 for the *Readers' Guide*. It is utilized primarily as a CD-ROM product, as part of *InfoTRAC*, covering the current year plus three years back. It is also available online through DIALOG (1959-March 1970, 1973-present). Some libraries still subscribe to the microfiche version of the *Magazine Index* or have the older years on microfiche. It is the only general periodical database extending as far back as 1959. Daily updates are available in *Newsearch* (entry 220). The *Magazine Index* contains well over 2,000 citations through 1993 on Native Americans. There are articles from a variety of general periodicals, business periodicals, and journals in many fields. Materials on AIDS, art, music, history, gambling, tribal autonomy, government relations, social concerns, and women's roles are indexed. Those beginning research would benefit from checking the *Magazine Index* or *InfoTRAC* (entry 218) first for broad coverage of the periodical field.

220. **Newsearch**. Foster City, CA: Information Access Co., current 2-6 weeks, weekly updates.

Information Access Company has several popular online and CD-ROM products that offer indexing of a wide variety of periodical and newspaper literature. *Newsearch* is a database providing selective coverage of over 5,000 general interest, legal, computer, health, trade, and business publications, as well as coverage of several newspapers and wire services that are indexed in the other periodical indexes offered by Information Access. The database is online on DIALOG and is updated daily with over 3,000 records. This is a good source for current information and topics in the news. Under "Native Americans," articles are discovered in many current periodicals such as *Ms.*, *Natural History*, the *Memphis Business Journal, Maclean's, American History Illustrated*, and *Journal of Commerce and Commercial* on such topics as gambling and casinos on reservations, art, history, health and business issues, women, and Indians in film and television. *Newsearch* has no print equivalent.

221. **Cumulative Magazine Subject Index, 1907-1949**. Boston: G. K. Hall, 1964. 2v.

This is an index to 356 American, Canadian, and English magazines from 1907-1949 originally printed in the *Annual Magazine Subject Index* and not indexed elsewhere. Articles are located under Indian, American; Indians, American; and Indians of North America; and by tribes and subjects. Periodicals include the *Journal of American Folklore, Geographical Journal*, and many state historical journals.

Topics include Indian art, legends, government relations, music, mythology, pottery, and tales and legends. The typeface is difficult to read, but valuable sources from the earlier part of the twentieth century can be discovered.

222. **Poole's Index to Periodical Literature**. Gloucester, MA: Peter Smith, 1963. 6v. $216.00/set. ISBN 0-685-42294-1.

This maiden index covers 105 years of articles from 479 American and English periodicals from 1802-1906. Articles are listed by subjects, but also available is the *Cumulative Author Index for Poole's Index to Periodical Literature, 1802-1906* (Wall, E. Edward, ed. Ann Arbor, MI: Pierian Press, 1971). *Poole's Index* has references under "Indians, American," with subjects such as history, religion, education, languages, arts, myths, and trade, as well as articles on problems of Indians with non-Indians.

223. **Alternative Press Index**. Baltimore, MD: Alternative Press Center, 1969-. quarterly, $125.00. LC 76-24027. ISSN 0002-662X.

Alternative Press Index is the primary index covering nonmainstream periodicals. It indexes around 250 liberal, left-of-center sources that are not usually covered elsewhere. Opinions are expressed that are not found in the mainstream literature. Periodicals included that cover American Indian issues are the *New Left Review, This Magazine, Lies of Our Times, Whole Earth Review*, and NACLA's *Report on the Americas*. Topics are listed under Native American art, culture, history, land disputes, oppression, rights, and women. Much alternative literature is devoted to Indian affairs, probably because most of the periodicals are published in the United States. A similar but more limited source is *The Left Index*, which covers only about 40 periodicals.

224. **Access: The Supplementary Index to Periodicals**. Evanston, IL: John Gordon Burke, 1975-. 3/yr., $157.50. ISSN 0095-5698.

Access indexes about 140 regional and city periodicals such as *New Mexico Magazine, Arizona Highways, San Diego Magazine, The Village Voice, Alaska, Boston Magazine, Oklahoma Observer, Santa Fean Magazine*, and *Southwest Art*, as well as general interest periodicals not indexed in the *Readers' Guide*. Topics include the American Indian Movement, the American Indian Dance Theatre, individual tribes, sports mascots, powwows, art, food, history, government relations, and other topics under "Indians of North America." A similar but more limited source is the *Popular Periodical Index*, which analyzes 37 periodicals.

225. California Periodicals Index. Dekalb, IL: Gabriel Micrographics, 1977-. annual, $95.00 (with microfilm edition, $285.00/yr.). ISSN 0730-1367.

The *California Periodicals Index* covers more than 50 magazines published in or about California, including *News from Native California, California History, Journal of San Diego History, Orange Coast, Pacific Historical Review, Santa Barbara Magazine*, and *West Art*. Many of the magazines indexed are offered on microfilm in full-text from the publisher. Many articles are under "Native Americans," discussing water rights, religions, basketry, art, food preparation, urban life, graves protection, demographic changes, land disputes, dancing, history, and languages.

American Indian Studies (General)

226. Native American Research Information Service (NARIS)
American Indian Institute
Continuing Education and Public Service
University of Oklahoma
555 Constitution Avenue
Norman, OK 73037-0005
(405) 325-4127
(405) 325-7757 (Fax)

This unique database covers over 12,000 published and unpublished items that focus on the human, economic, and community development of Native Americans. Researched since 1969, with periodic updates, *NARIS* originally sought to provide Native American groups with a research database to assist in tribal and community planning, but it grew to be of significant use to government agencies, universities, scholars, businesses, associations, schools, churches, hospitals, research centers, law enforcement agencies, and other groups. *NARIS* offers research covering the entire spectrum of Native American socioeconomic data, community research, and educational studies. Relevant studies are drawn from over 41 other databases to make this singular source. Some of the 41 databases *NARIS* utilizes are *ABI/Inform, American Statistics Index, Agricola, Canadian Business, Child Abuse and Neglect, Dissertation Abstracts, Enviroline, ERIC, Family Resources, Health Planning Administration, Legal Resource Index, Management Contents, Medline, Mental Health Abstracts, NCJRS, PAIS, PsycINFO, Social SciSearch*, and *Sociological Abstracts*.

NARIS provides database searches by direct mail, telephone, and fax requests and charges fees for bibliographic citations and abstracts located. This is the only specialized database specifically for topics in American Indian studies. It is not available through any commercial database vendor, such as DIALOG or BRS.

226a. Index to Literature on the American Indian. San Francisco, CA: Indian Historian, 1970-1973. LC 70-141292.

More than 250 popular and scholarly periodicals from the United States and Canada are indexed by authors and subjects. These volumes were produced by the Indians at the American Indian Historical Society and include articles in 63 broad subject areas (e.g., alcoholism, arts, conservation, education, linguistics, religion).

Periodicals included range from journals such as the *American Anthropologist* to *Time* magazine to some Indian periodicals such as *Indian Life, The Sentinel,* and *Sun Tracks.* Although it was only published for four years, this index is valuable for its coverage during a time of rapid change in public awareness and government policy regarding American Indians. A similar title indexing periodicals, books, and documents from 1953-1968 is the *American Indian Index* (Chicago: J. A. Huebner, 1953-1968), which covered more of the popular periodicals, newspaper articles, newsletters, and government reports.

Aging

227. **Ageline**. Washington, DC: American Association of Retired Persons, 1978-. Bimonthly.

This online database provides bibliographic coverage with abstracts on social gerontology with some materials going back to 1966. *Ageline* focuses on the psychology of aging, health care issues, family and social relationships, economic concerns, business, retirement, policy making, and consumer issues. About two-thirds of the database comprises journal articles, with the rest devoted to citations for books and book chapters, special reports, and government publications, such as those by the Administration on Aging.

Ageline is quite useful for researchers, practitioners, and the general public. Another abstracting service more focused on scholarly materials is *Gerontological Abstracts. Ageline* has many references to "American Indians" and "Alaska Natives" as well as to specific tribes on a wide variety of topics related to aging. Articles are found on menopause, living in harmony with traditional Indian religious beliefs, life stories of Indian elders, government services and funding for older Indians, trends in Indian health, and regional differences in Indian health. *Ageline* is an online database through BRS and DIALOG.

Anthropology

228. **Abstracts in Anthropology**. Amityville, NY: Baywood, 1970-. 8/yr., $249.00. ISSN 0001-3455.

This basic index for anthropology and related fields covers approximately 300 journals in the English language, including Indian periodicals such as *American Indian Culture and Research Journal.* The volumes are divided into broad categories of study, with subject and author indexes available in each issue. Listings are found under "American Indian" and by names of tribes and include topics as diverse as epidemics among American Indians in history, American Indians' service in World War I, language studies of Indians, and archaeological reports. As with all the anthropology indexes, there is a lag of one to two years from the date articles are published until their appearance in the indexes. Most beginning researchers with topics in anthropology should start with this index.

229. **Anthropological Literature: An Index to Periodical Articles and Essays.** Cambridge, MA: Harvard University, Tozzer Library, 1979-. quarterly, $125.00. ISSN 0190-3373.

This distinguished index was established in 1979 as an index to over 1,200 serials in the Tozzer Library collection at Harvard. It provides a continuation of the *Author and Subject Catalogues of the Tozzer Library* (entry 208) for articles and chapters in the journals, proceedings, and edited books that Tozzer receives annually. This collection is very strong in all areas of anthropology internationally and includes materials written in American Indian studies from all over the world.

The overall arrangement of the issues is by broad subfields of anthropology, but the excellent subject indexes provide good access to the entries. The Library of Congress Subject Headings are used, supplemented by additional headings from the Tozzer Library, listing materials under "Indians of North America" and by tribes and subjects. From 1983-1988, this index was only published in microfiche. This is an important source for advanced researchers.

230. **Anthropological Index to Current Periodicals in the Museum of Mankind Library**. London: Royal Anthropological Institute, 1977-. quarterly, $103.00. ISSN 0960-1651. (Continues **Anthropological Index to Current Periodicals Received in the Library of the Royal Anthropological Institute**, Vols. 1-14, 1963-1976).

This major index covers over 700 journals internationally in all areas of anthropology. It is based on the periodical collection of the Royal Anthropological Institute in the Museum of Mankind Library in London. Unlike most periodical indexes, it contains no subject indexes, which makes its use difficult for researchers seeking specific topics. Citations are arranged by continents or geographic regions, such as North America, and subdivided by area studies such as physical anthropology, archaeology, cultural anthropology and ethnology, and linguistics. This requires time to search through the sections on North America for articles on specific topics. However, this is an important collection for the serious researcher.

Another important annual index/bibliography is the *International Bibliography of the Social Sciences—International Bibliography of Social and Cultural Anthropology* (entry 39).

Arts

231. **Art Index**. Bronx, NY: H. W. Wilson Co., 1929-. quarterly, price varies. ISSN 0004-3222.

The *Art Index* is the primary index to art, analyzing over 200 journals. Most are English-language journals published in the United States, but major foreign journals are included. The *Art Index* includes articles on archaeology, architecture, art history, crafts, film, design arts, photography, and other fields related to art. Researchers will find many articles under Indians, Indians of North America (with subheadings such as architecture, art, basketry, costume and adornment, decoration and ornament, exhibitions, painting, photographs, portraits, sculpture, textile industry and fabrics), Indians in art, and tribes (e.g., Haida Indians, Siksisa Indians), as well as under specific subjects (e.g., sand painting, totem poles, pottery pre-Columbian, goldwork pre-Columbian). *Art Index* is easy to use and is also available online through WILSON-LINE and BRS.

Biology and Agriculture

232. **Biological and Agricultural Index**. Bronx, NY: H. W. Wilson Co., 1964-. monthly (except August), price varies. ISSN 0006-3177.

Biological and Agricultural Index is the basic index for English-language periodicals in biology, agriculture, ecology, environmental science, fishery science, food science, forestry, genetics, horticulture, marine biology, microbiology, nutrition, soil science, veterinary medicine, and zoology. There are other more comprehensive indexes, abstracts, and data-bases, such as *Biological Abstracts*, but for American Indian studies, this should suffice. Under "Indians of North America" and under tribal names, there are articles on land disputes, anthropometry, migration studies, DNA, nutrition, Indian health, obesity, ethnobotany, parasitic problems, and other related areas. *Biological and Agricultural Index* is available online through BRS and WILSONLINE and is produced on CD-ROM.

Business

There are many business indexes and databases available in libraries and through commercial vendors and suppliers. The two presented below are good ones for researchers in American Indian studies. The trend for databases, especially in the business field, is toward full text of articles and other materials, and increasing numbers of these are becoming available online and on CD-ROM.

233. **Business Periodicals Index**. Bronx, NY: H. W. Wilson Co., 1958-. monthly, price varies. ISSN 0007-6961.

Another of the standard periodical indexes published by the H. W. Wilson Company, the *Business Periodicals Index* is an excellent source for English-language articles on business topics. Around 300 of the most popular business and industry magazines and journals, chosen by subscriber vote, are indexed by subjects. Researchers will find articles on "Indians of North America—Economic Conditions" (education, industries, land tenure, newspapers, reservations, etc.) as well as entries for Eskimos, American Indian art, tax issues, gambling, mining operations on reservations, Indian businesses, stereotyping, the U.S. Bureau of Indian Affairs, and other organizations and issues confronting Indians in their business and economic development.

Although *Business Periodicals Index* is not as comprehensive as *ABI/Inform* (entry 234), it covers the primary business sources commonly found in libraries. It is available online through BRS and WILSONLINE. A CD-ROM version, called *Wilson Business Abstracts*, is especially useful in that it provides coverage from July 1982-present, with informative abstracts from 1990-present.

234. **ABI/Inform**. Louisville, KY: UMI/Data Courier, 1971-. weekly, price varies.

ABI/Inform is a database offering abstracts and indexing for articles in over 800 business and management periodicals. It is strong in the areas of business trends and business administration and contains references in the fields of accounting, banking, energy, the environment, real estate, and transportation. Topics on Native Americans include a wide variety of issues such as federal Indian policy, management of reservation lands, agriculture, economic development on reservations, and gambling and bingo. *ABI/Inform* is available online through several computer vendors, including BRS and DIALOG, as well as on CD-ROM for the most recent five years.

Criminal Justice

235. **Criminal Justice Abstracts**. Monsey, NY: Willow Tree Press, 1968-. quarterly, $140.00. ISSN 0146-9177.

Formerly called *Abstracts on Crime and Juvenile Delinquency* and *Crime and Delinquency Literature*, this abstracting service has maintained a quality product over the years. It indexes over 50 primary journals in criminal justice and selectively covers around 200 additional journals with criminal justice topics. In addition, *Criminal Justice Abstracts* includes a variety of international publications such as books, dissertations, and reports. Issues are organized by broad subjects (e.g., juvenile justice and delinquency, police, courts and legal processes), but the detailed index by subjects is most useful. Materials are found primarily under "Native Americans" and "Aboriginals" (for Canada).

Articles are found on reservation crime, Indian juvenile delinquency, racial disparity in sentences, substance abuse among Indians, and other issues related to crime and justice. Indexes by authors and geographic areas are also provided. For researchers in the United States, this source provides excellent coverage for the field of criminal justice.

236. **Criminal Justice Periodical Index**. Ann Arbor, MI: University Microfilms International, 1975-. 3/yr., $260.00. ISSN 0145-5818.

This index is more basic than *Criminal Justice Abstracts* (entry 235), covering around 100 journals, newsletters, and law reporters in all areas of criminal justice, primarily in the United States. It is a good starting point for criminal justice research because of ease of use and availability of the journals cited. About 400 citations are listed under "American Indians" through 1993, and these include materials on topics such as drug abuse, homicide, suicide, reservation laws and crimes, adoptions and child custody issues, self-government, laws protecting art and artifacts, tribal courts, land claims, repatriation, uneven sentencing, gambling, civil rights, supreme court cases, and religious use of peyote. *Criminal Justice Periodical Index* is available online through DIALOG.

237. **National Criminal Justice Reference Service Database: NCJRS**. Rockville, MD: National Criminal Justice Reference Service, 1972-. monthly.

This online database, which has no print equivalent, is a major file for all aspects of criminal justice. *NCJRS* is a national and international clearinghouse for criminal justice and law enforcement information and is sponsored by the National Institute of Justice, a division of the U.S. Department of Justice. The database represents the library collection of the National Criminal Justice Reference Service and lists well over 100,000 annotated citations to materials in the collection. This valuable collection contains U.S. government reports, journal articles, and other materials not included in *Criminal Justice Abstracts* (entry 235) and *Criminal Justice Periodical Index* (entry 236). Around 300 citations on American Indians are included through 1993. Materials are cited in corrections, forensics, probation, crime prevention, criminology, juvenile justice, and all related fields of criminal justice. Subject terms include American Indians, Indian affairs, Indian justice, reservation crimes, reservation law enforcement, tribal community relations, tribal court system, tribal history, Canadian Indians, and Eskimos. The *National Criminal Justice Thesaurus* is used to assist researchers in determining the correct subject headings. The *NCJRS* database is available online through DIALOG.

Education

238. ERIC (Educational Resources Information Center). Rockville, MD: U.S. Department of Education, 1966-. monthly.

The main source for topics in education, ERIC comprises two parts: *Current Index to Journals in Education*, or *CIJE* (entry 239), and *Resources in Education,* or *RIE* (entry 240), both available separately in print only. ERIC is commonly used in libraries on CD-ROM and is also available online through several vendors, including BRS and DIALOG. Along with *NTIS*, ERIC was the first online database available on DIALOG and has been one of the most often used databases for scholarly research in university libraries. It is actually highly interdisciplinary but concentrates on education at all levels—schools, universities, students, faculty, administrators—anything that relates to education in the broadest sense, internationally. ERIC covers all the journals in *CIJE* as well as all the educational reports, conference papers, and curriculum materials in *RIE*. ERIC has lots of material on the education of American Indian children and on Indian schools and tribal colleges. As comprehensive as ERIC is, there are still around 60 to 70 journals in the *Education Index* (entry 241) that are not covered in ERIC.

When using ERIC*, CIJE, RIE*, or *Exceptional Child Education Resources* (entry 243), researchers should always start with the latest edition of the *Thesaurus of ERIC Descriptors* to determine the correct subject headings for their topics. Some subject headings in the 12th edition, 1990, of the *Thesaurus of ERIC Descriptors* are "American Indian culture," "American Indian education," "American Indian history," "American Indian languages," "American Indian literature," "American Indian reservations," "American Indian studies," "American Indians," "tribal sovereignty," "tribes," and "trust responsibility (government)."

239. Current Index to Journals in Education (CIJE). Phoenix, AZ: Oryx Press, 1969-. monthly, $235.00. ISSN 0011-3565.

CIJE is the largest printed index for education periodicals, providing complete indexing of over 800 education journals as well as selective indexing of other periodicals for important education-related articles. The *Education Index* (entry 241), in comparison, indexes around 350 education periodicals, and most of these overlap with *CIJE*. *CIJE* features short abstracts of two or three sentences, and the *Education Index* has no abstracts. Loads of articles on American Indian education, history, culture, languages, and literature will be located in *CIJE*. *CIJE* is part of the ERIC database, online through BRS and DIALOG.

240. Resources in Education (RIE). Washington, DC: U.S. Government Printing Office, 1966-. monthly, $42.70. ISSN 0098-0897.

RIE is part of the ERIC database (entry 238) and is also a printed index. *RIE* provides extensive abstracts and indexing of education documents such as program reports and policy papers from education agencies and school systems, research reports done under government contracts, university research reports, dissertations and theses, conference papers, and other miscellaneous education documents that would not be easily located elsewhere. Most of the materials in *RIE* are practical studies, reports, and bibliographies not found in the periodical literature. The materials abstracted are made available on microfiche in libraries or can be ordered for a fee. Over 15,000 documents are indexed annually, providing a unique file of education materials to assist teachers, school administrators, librarians, researchers, and students on all levels. Materials on all aspects of American Indian education and schools can be found here.

241. **Education Index**. Bronx, NY: H. W. Wilson Co., 1929-. 10/yr., price varies. ISSN 0013-1385.

Another of the excellent Wilson indexes, the *Education Index* thoroughly indexes over 350 education journals. Although *CIJE* (entry 239) indexes twice as many journals, the periodicals covered in *Education Index* are the most important ones for research in education. No abstracts are provided, but the arrangement and ease of use facilitate researchers' efforts in locating appropriate articles for their subjects. Many materials are found under "Indians of North America," with subheadings such as antiquities, art, biography, culture, education, games, health and hygiene, history, legends, women, Canada, and Alaska. Entries are also under Indian literature, Indians in literature, and under tribal names and Indian languages. Articles cover all aspects of the education of Indian children and tribal colleges. For articles dealing with college- and university-level education, a better choice is *Higher Education Abstracts* (entry 242). The *Education Index* is available online through WILSONLINE and BRS and on CD-ROM.

242. **Higher Education Abstracts**. Claremont, CA: Claremont Graduate School, 1965-. quarterly, $110.00 ($70.00 individual). ISSN 0748-4364.

Long, informative abstracts make this index an attractive choice for information on all aspects of the college experience for students, faculty, and administrators. *Higher Education Abstracts* does not deal with academic subjects but with the issues of attending college, teaching courses, and administering programs at colleges. Coverage includes around 250 periodicals as well as other materials such as conference proceedings and books. The cumulative indexes for the annual volumes list materials under "Native American students," "Native American faculty," and "Native American studies."

243. **Exceptional Child Education Resources**. Reston, VA: Council for Exceptional Children, 1969-. quarterly, $90.00. ISSN 0160-4309.

The focus of this abstracting service is the education of handicapped students. More than 200 journals are indexed and abstracted, and also books, conference proceedings, special reports from associations, dissertations, and U.S. government publications. Much of this index overlaps with the ERIC system (entry 238), including *CIJE* and *RIE,* but it also offers unique coverage of materials important to researchers. Subjects are found under "American Indians," "American Indian Culture," and "American Indian Education," on issues concerning schoolchildren with congenital impairments, language handicaps, special health problems, emotional disturbances, and behavior problems. *Exceptional Child Education Resources* is available online through DIALOG and BRS.

Environment

244. **Environment Abstracts Annual**. New Providence, NJ: Bowker A & I, 1970-. annual, $1,070.00. ISSN 0000-1198.

Information on the environment related to American Indians may be found in many indexes and databases. This interdisciplinary source includes abstracts and indexing for scientific journals, conference proceedings, institutional reports, newsletters, and popular periodicals. Materials are found on pollution, hazardous waste, conservation of species, and other issues affecting humans and the earth. There are a subject volume and an abstracts volume for each year, along with indexes by author, geographic area, and industry. Under the broad subject of "American Indians," articles are found on water rights issues, the Bureau of Land Management, government and tribal policies affecting the environment, studies of the land and sites in prehistory, landfills on reservations, and the management of Indians' natural resources. *Environment Abstracts Annual* is available on DIALOG as *Enviroline*.

Film

245. **Film Literature Index**. Albany, NY: SUNY Albany, Film and Television Documentation Center, 1973-. quarterly, $300.00. ISSN 0093-6758.

This is the standard source for film periodical literature concerning film topics and movies in the United States. It not only covers articles of interest to the general reader but also indexes journals for the specialist. Over 300 periodicals survey the literature internationally. *Film Literature Index* is the primary source for information on images of American Indians in movies. Check the subject "Indians, American in Film."

Geography

246. **Geographical Abstracts: Human Geography**. Norwich, England: Elsevier/Geo Abstracts, 1966-. monthly, $450.00. ISSN 0953-9611.

This index, formerly part of *Geo Abstracts,* is divided into broad categories of study, such as environment, environmental resources, historical, population, people and regions, urban studies, and agriculture. Cumulative indexes for subject, author, and regional sections are available annually. Under "Native American" and "Indians" are listed articles on ethnic relations, government policies, cultural geography topics, sociocultural studies, and antiquities. *Geographical Abstracts* is available online through DIALOG as *GeoBase.*

Health, Medicine, and Nursing

247. **Index Medicus**. Washington, DC: National Library of Medicine, 1960-. monthly, $310.00 (annual cumulation, $307.00). ISSN 0019-3879.

Index Medicus is the paramount index to the world's medical and biomedical literature, indexing around 3,000 international journals in many languages. It is published monthly, with *Cumulated Index Medicus* printed annually. The subject headings to use are called MESH, for medical subject headings, and should be consulted before beginning a manual or computerized search. The database version is called *MEDLARS* by the National Library of Medicine and *Medline* by commercial database vendors such as DIALOG and BRS. *Medline* is commonly found in larger libraries on CD-ROM. Under "Indians, North American," subjects are found on diet, epidemics, obesity, diseases, mortality, smoking, alcoholism, sudden infant death syndrome, cancer, heart disease, and many other topics related to the health of American Indians and the prevention of diseases.

248. **Cumulative Index to Nursing and Allied Health Literature (CINAHL).** Glendale, CA: Glendale Adventist Medical Center, 1961-. bimonthly, $230.00. ISSN 0146-5554.

CINAHL offers the most comprehensive coverage of English-language nursing journals of any index. It also indexes many journals from allied health fields such as emergency services, occupational therapy, laboratory work, medical records, radiology, respiratory therapy, and social services. Under the subject "Native Americans," articles are found on all aspects of the health and treatment of American Indians. Although there is some overlap with *Index Medicus* (entry 247), unique information will be found here as well. *CINAHL* is available online through BRS and DIALOG and as a CD-ROM database.

249. **Health Index**. Foster City, CA: Information Access Co., 1988-. monthly, price varies.

This CD-ROM product is also available online through BRS. It indexes health-related articles in over 130 magazines, journals, and newsletters, as well as selected articles from over 3,000 other magazines and journals. *Health Index* is better suited for the general public than the comprehensive *Index Medicus* (entry 247), although it compares with the *General Science Index* (entry 250) in its coverage of the major medical journals. Articles can be located on all aspects of health, nutrition, medicine, diseases, and treatment related to Native Americans. It has no print equivalent.

250. **General Science Index**. Bronx, NY: H. W. Wilson Co., 1978-. 10/yr., price varies. ISSN 0162-1963.

Another of the Wilson indexes, the *General Science Index* provides subject access to over 110 of the primary science journals. Most of the articles under "Indians of North America" cover health and medical issues such as alcoholism, prevalent diseases and their treatment and prevention, smoking, and nutrition problems. However, there are articles concerning American Indians from the nonmedical sciences as well (e.g., plants, foods, astronomy). Beginning researchers looking for health or science topics related to Indians may want to begin with the *General Science Index* or the *Health Index* (entry 249).

For more in-depth coverage of the sciences, researchers should check *Applied Science and Technology Index*, *Biological Abstracts*, *Science Citation Index*, *Biological and Agricultural Index* (entry 232), or other more in-depth science indexes and databases covering specific areas of the sciences and technology. The *General Science Index* is an online database through WILSONLINE and BRS and is available on CD-ROM.

History

251. **America: History and Life**. Santa Barbara, CA: ABC-CLIO, 1964-. 5/yr., price varies. ISSN 2626-2627.

America: History and Life is the most important periodical index for most topics in American Indian studies. It indexes and partially abstracts over 2,000 serials from around the world dealing with the history of the United States and Canada from prehistory to the present. All aspects of the history, culture, government relations, trade, and wars of American Indians are recorded in the periodicals indexed here. Most researchers in American Indian studies who need journal literature should start with this significant index. *America: History and Life* is much easier to use, however, as an online database through DIALOG or on CD-ROM.

252. **Bibliography of Native North Americans on Disc**. Santa Barbara, CA: ABC-CLIO, 1993-. annual, $795.00 ($1,200 on network). ISSN 1064-5144.

This CD-ROM database is a significant new tool for research in American Indian studies. ABC-CLIO, publisher of *America: History and Life* (entry 251), has teamed up with the Human Relations Area Files (see pages 26-28) and created a unique, comprehensive source for research on the history and culture of American Indians. The database began in 1993 with over 60,000 citations to journal articles, monographs, dissertations, and essays, more than 10,000 of which were previously unpublished. A cumulative updated disc is published annually with an estimated 2,500 new citations. Libraries that have both *America: History and Life* and the Human Relations Area Files will have access to most of the materials already, although they are not as easy to use as the *Bibliography of Native North Americans on Disc*.

Languages and Linguistics

253. **Linguistics and Language Behavior Abstracts (LLBA)**. San Diego, CA: LLBA, 1967-. quarterly, $225.00. ISSN 0888-8027.

Before April 1985, this index was called *Language and Language Behavior Abstracts*, but it is now known as *LLBA*. Abstracts are provided for articles in over 600 journals in linguistics studies. The arrangement is by 77 broad subject headings (e.g., psycholinguistics, applied linguistics, phonology, syntax, nonverbal communication), with detailed subject indexes provided. Some listings are found under: "American Indian," "Native Language," and "Native Speaker" that are useful to researchers on American Indian languages, reading, and literary instruction. *LLBA* is available as an online database through BRS and DIALOG and on CD-ROM.

Law

254. **Legal Resource Index**. Foster City, CA: Information Access Co., 1980-. monthly, price varies.

Legal Resource Index database contains comprehensive indexing of over 750 law journals, six legal newspapers, and various books and bar association publications, plus selected articles on law topics from over 1,000 additional publications drawn from the *Magazine Index* (entry 219), the *National Newspaper Index* (entry 282), and the *Trade and Industry Index*. Articles are included on Indian legal issues and criminal justice topics. The *Legal Resource Index* is available online through DIALOG, with daily updates available in *Newsearch* (entry 220).

255. **Current Law Index**. Foster City, CA: Information Access Co., 1980-. monthly, $395.00. ISSN 0196-1780.

This printed source indexes over 800 legal periodicals drawn from the *Legal Resource Index* database (entry 254). It does not index the legal newspapers or law-related articles from general periodicals as does the *Legal Resource Index*. However, its coverage of legal periodicals is much more extensive than that of the *Index to Legal Periodicals* (entry 256). The editors state that inclusion is based on the material's "value," not length. Many articles on American Indian law issues are covered in the *Current Law Index*. In the subject index volume for each year, articles are found under tribal names (e.g., Dakota Indians, Tlingit Indians), under proper names (e.g., American Indian Movement), under Supreme Court cases, and especially under the subject heading "Indians of North America." Subheadings under the latter include child welfare, economic aspects, fishing rights, freedom of religion, government relations, hunting, Indian sovereignty and self-determination, land tenure, laws, regulations, reservations, taxation, treaties, tribal courts, and water rights, as well as other issues.

Researchers should consult both *Current Law Index* and *Index to Legal Periodicals* for comprehensive coverage of important legal literature on American Indian topics.

256. **Index to Legal Periodicals**. Bronx, NY: H. W. Wilson Co., 1908-. monthly (except Sept.), $225.00. ISSN 0019-4077.

This standard periodical index covers around 500 important legal periodicals from the United States, Canada, Great Britain, Ireland, Australia, and New Zealand. It is the only legal index covering articles as old as 1908.

The *Current Law Index* (entry 255) began publication in 1980 but offers more extensive coverage of periodicals. The *Index to Legal Periodicals* is not as comprehensive as the *Legal Resource Index* (entry 254) or the *Current Law Index*, focusing instead on what the editors call "high quality legal articles" of at least five pages in length. The *Index to Legal Periodicals* is easy to use and includes an author-subject index together in one alphabet. Articles found under "Indians" deal with legal issues from civil rights to fishing rights.

The *Index to Legal Periodicals* is available online through WILSONLINE and BRS (both 1981-present).

Library Science

257. **Library Literature**. Bronx, NY: H. W. Wilson Co., 1921-. bimonthly, price varies. ISSN 0024-2373.

This is the standard index to library and information science literature, covering primarily the United States. Although some international coverage is presented, most of the journals are in English. Over 200 periodicals, as well as many monographs, theses, books, and audiovisuals are indexed. Subjects include "North American Indians, Library Service for," "North American Indian Literature," "North American Indian Archives," "Public Libraries—Services to North American Indians," and

"Junior and Community College Libraries—Services to North American Indians." For researchers interested in tribal libraries and archives and how to assist in creating them, this is a primary source of information. *Library Literature* is available as an online database through WILSONLINE and BRS and also on CD-ROM.

Literature

258. **MLA International Bibliography of Books and Articles on the Modern Languages and Literatures**. New York: Modern Language Association, 1922-. annual, $850.00. ISSN 0024-8215.

This is the prime index for articles and other materials on literature, indexing over 3,000 journals as well as monographs. It is international in scope and can be a complicated tool for most researchers at first. Two volumes are published each year: part 1, the classified listings and author index, and part 2, the subject index. The classified listings are divided geographically and chronologically into five sub-volumes separating materials as follows: I) British, American, Australian, and other English-language materials; II) European, Asian, African, and South American; III) linguistics; IV) general literature and related topics; and V) folklore. To look under the name of an author for materials written about that author's works, use part 1. However, to look up materials written about American Indian topics, start with part 2, the subject index. In the subject index are found entries for such topics as Native American culture, Native American dramatists, Native American languages, Native American legend, Native American myth, Native American poets, Native American women, Native American writers, and Native Americans. The entry numbers in this section refer to the subvolumes in part 1, the classified lists.

The *MLA* is available online via WILSONLINE from 1981-present and on EPIC from 1965-present, and it is on CD-ROM.

259. **Humanities Index**. Bronx, NY: H. W. Wilson Co., 1974-. quarterly, price varies. ISSN 0095-5981.

The older years of this standard index are called the *Social Sciences and Humanities Index* (1965-1973) and the *International Index* (1915-present). The *Humanities Index* now analyzes around 350 journals in many subject fields of the humanities, including archaeology and classical studies, history, language and literature, folklore, philosophy, religion, and the performing arts. The journals indexed are the major ones in these fields and the ones most commonly found in libraries. It is an excellent source for articles on American Indians. Some of the subject headings found here include the following: "American Literature—Indian Authors"; "Indian Languages"; "Indians in Literature"; "Indians in Art"; "Indians of North America—Antiquities (Art, Baskets, Burial, Culture, Dances, etc.)"; "Indians, Treatment of"; "Indians in Mass Media"; and "Indians in the Press." Listings are also under names of tribes such as Kwakiutl Indians, Lumbee Indians, and so on. The *Humanities Index* is available as an online database on WILSONLINE and BRS.

260. **Essay and General Literature Index**. Bronx, NY: H. W. Wilson Co., 1934-. semiannual. LC 34-14581. ISSN 0014-083X. 1900-1989, 11 vols. $230.00/vol. 5-year cumulation, $80.00, ISBN 0-686-76912-0. annual cumulation, $115.00, ISBN 0-685-57805-4. 1990 vol., 2,031p., $230.00. ISBN 0-685-45836-9.

This is not a periodical index but an author and title index to collections of essays. The essays are primarily in the humanities and social sciences, incorporating a broad spectrum of disciplines including political science, philosophy, religion, law, economics, education, linguistics, literature, the arts, and history. There are many essays under "Indians, Treatment of"; "Indians in Literature"; and "Indians of North America" with all its subdivisions, such as antiquities, art, biography, civil rights, commerce, cultural assimilation, fishing, government relations, history, languages, music, religion, women, and so on. There are essays also under specific subjects and tribes (e.g., ghost dance, sun dance, sand paintings, Navajo Indians). Researchers will locate unique materials not easily found elsewhere.

261. **Arts and Humanities Citation Index**. Philadelphia Institute for Scientific Information, 1977-. 3/yr., $4,375.00 with annual cumulation. ISSN 0162-8445.

There are two other citation indexes, the *Social Sciences Citation Index* (entry 274) and the *Science Citation Index*. These three are unique services with no competitors. The *Arts and Humanities Citation Index* indexes around 6,000 journals, with up to 1,500 of these indexed cover-to-cover and the others selectively indexed. There are three main parts to the index each year: the permuterm subject index, the source index, and the citation index. For subjects, check words or pairs of words likely to appear in the titles of articles in the permuterm subject index (e.g., Lakota and novel, Columbus and Indians, Black Elk, Alaska Native and writing, Indians and myth). The entries here provide the authors' names, which are then located in the source index. The source index provides the citation references for the journal articles. This form of subject searching works best with very specific topics that are difficult to locate in other sources or with new terminology in the literature. The citation indexes allow one to trace who is citing another's works, which is valuable for discovering additional materials related to the article in hand. Unfortunately, researchers are often discouraged by the very fine print of the volumes and the time it takes to flip back and forth from the permuterm subject index to the source index, seeking relevant articles. This expensive index is also an expensive database to use, albeit so much faster and easier than the printed version. It is available online through BRS and DIALOG as *Arts and Humanities Search*, and also on CD-ROM.

Music

262. **Music Index**. Warren, MI: Harmonie Park Press, 1949-. monthly, $1,075. ISSN 0027-4348.

Around 500 periodicals on every facet of music are indexed in this standard source for music information. About half of the periodicals are in English, and entries for subjects, authors, and proper names are in one alphabetical dictionary listing. Music references are found for serious as well as recreational research. Articles about American Indian music, songs, instruments, and cultural aspects of music and dance can be found under subjects such as "Indian, American" and "Indian, North American," as well as specific topics such as "American Indian Dance Theatre." Many of these titles will overlap with the *Arts and Humanities Citation Index* (entry 261) and *RILM Abstracts* (entry 263), which are both more international in coverage.

263. **RILM Abstracts of Music Literature: International Repertory of Music Literature**. New York: City University of New York, 1967-. 2/yr., $360.00 ($90.00 individual). ISSN 0033-6955.

RILM is an international bibliography/periodical index that abstracts the significant literature on music. *RILM* is issued by the Repertoire International de Litterature Musicale under the sponsorship of the International Musicological Society, which does an excellent job of collecting and abstracting the literature in music, including journal articles, books, essays, dissertations, reviews, catalogs, and iconographies. Broad in coverage, *RILM* also includes materials on dance, dramatic arts, film, poetry, visual arts, philosophy, psychology, physiology, sociology, linguistics, acoustics, and other fields as long as the articles relate in some way to music. The volumes are published about three years behind and therefore cannot be used for current issues. Materials are classified by broad sections of art history: medieval art; Renaissance, baroque, and rococo art; neoclassicism and modern art; modern art. The subject indexes list materials on "Indians of North America" (with subheadings such as art, drawing, iconography, painting, photography, sculpture, Southwest, watercolor), and under tribes (e.g., Chippewa Indians, Cree Indians, Kiowa Indians) and other subjects (e.g., iconography, sculpture, American, 19th century). Once a subject is located, the abstract number refers to the bibliography entries. *RILM* is much more international than the *Music Index* (entry 262) and covers a wider variety of materials. *RILM* is available online through DIALOG as *Art Literature International*, while the *Music Index* is not yet available electronically.

Political Science

264. **United States Political Science Documents**. Pittsburgh, PA: University of Pittsburgh, NASA Industrial Applications Center, 1975-. annual, $395.00. ISSN 0148-6063.

USPSD is a major source for political science periodical literature, indexing over 150 major political science journals in the United States. The first volume of each year includes the five indexes: author, subject, geographic, proper name, and journal. The second volume contains the abstracts. Articles from journals in other fields also are covered, such as ethnic studies, anthropology, sociology, and history, when the issues relate in some way to political science. Under the subject "American Indian Studies," articles are found on issues such as criminal and social justice, race relations and inequality of sentencing, and housing and urban issues. *USPSD* is also available online through DIALOG.

265. **ABC Pol Sci; A Bibliography of Contents: Political Science and Government**. Santa Barbara, CA: ABC-CLIO, 1969-. 6/yr. ISSN 0001-0456.

More than 300 essential international political science journals' tables of contents are reproduced in *ABC Pol Sci* and indexed by subjects from key words of the articles. *ABC Pol Sci* provides coverage of political science, government, public policy, international relations, and other related fields. Use the annual cumulative subject indexes for issues concerning Native Americans, such as civil rights, elections, history, and politics. Although more journals are covered than in *United States Political Science Documents* (entry 264), there is not as much material on Native Americans. *ABC Pol Sci* is available on CD-ROM.

Psychology and Mental Health

266. **Psychological Abstracts**. Arlington, VA: American Psychological Association, 1927-. monthly, $1,245.00. ISSN 0033-2887.

Psychological Abstracts is the primary index for information related to American Indian psychological and mental health topics. It indexes and abstracts more than 1,400 journals covering psychology and related fields, mostly in English but from over 50 countries and is highly interdisciplinary in the social sciences. Since 1988, foreign-language materials have not been included in the print version. Dissertations were included until 1980 and still appear in the online database, *PsycINFO*, which is available on BRS and DIALOG among other systems. Cumulative indexes for subjects and authors cover 1927-1983. The online database covers 1967 to the present, and the CD-ROM version (*PsycLit*) covers 1974 to the present. The key to the correct subject headings for all versions of this source is the *Thesaurus of Psychological Index Terms*, which should be consulted before starting a search. Under "American Indians" are references to counseling, rehabilitation, motivation, alcoholism, fetal alcohol syndrome, IQ tests, AIDS, drug abuse, suicide, mental disorders, public health issues, perceptions of Indians in the media, and crime and criminal justice issues.

267. **Mental Health Abstracts**. Alexandria, VA: IFI/Plenum Data Co., 1969-. monthly.

This online database cites mental health literature worldwide, including 1,200 journals, books, technical reports, conference proceedings, and government publications.

It complements *Psychological Abstracts* (entry 266) with the nonjournal literature but does overlap with *Psychological Abstracts* perhaps as much as 50 percent in periodical coverage. *Mental Health Abstracts* was produced by the National Clearinghouse for Mental Health Information of the National Institute of Mental Health from 1969-1982. There is no print equivalent. Long, informative abstracts make the database especially useful to researchers. From 1969-1993, there are over 700 entries under "American Indians," with articles on all aspects of mental health research, including treatment, counseling, and therapy for alcoholism, substance abuse, and suicidal behavior. *Mental Health Abstracts* is available through DIALOG.

Public Administration

268. **PAIS International**. New York: Public Affairs Information Service, 1915-. monthly, $495.00. ISSN 1051-4015.

The combination of the *PAIS Bulletin* and *PAIS Foreign Language Index* created this unique index. *PAIS* indexes over 900 magazines and journals as well over 2,000 books, scores of U.S. government publications, special reports from private organizations, and even pamphlets. There is a cumulated index set for 1915-1974. *PAIS* is much more than a periodical index. The U.S. congressional hearings are especially useful for American Indian studies topics, providing firsthand testimony on issues under debate and important statistics and background information. Under "Indians," researchers can find subheadings for such topics as children, drug problems, economic conditions, education, health, housing, land tenure, legal status, laws, medical care, religion, reservations, and social life and customs. Materials also are found on topics from Indian artifacts, sacred sites, and toxic dumping on reservations to the

Indian Health Service. This is a valuable index to researchers on many topics within American Indian studies. *PAIS* is available online through BRS and DIALOG and also on CD-ROM.

Religion and Philosophy

269. **Religion Index One: Periodicals**. Evanston, IL: American Theological Library Association, 1949-. $400.00. ISSN 0149-8428.

Religion Index One is the most comprehensive English-language index to religious periodicals. *Religion Index Two: Multi-Author Works,* the other part of the set, indexes book chapters and books. *Religion Index One* is comprehensive, covering all areas of religious studies, not just one predominant religious view, as does *Religious and Theological Abstracts*, which is less comprehensive. Under "Indians of North America" in *Religion Index One* are articles on American Indian religions, Indian claims, dances, government relations, legal status and laws, mental health, missions, socio-economic conditions, and Canada. Much material is listed under specific tribal names (e.g., Apache Indians, Pima Indians). Researchers will locate materials on all aspects of American Indian religions and traditional beliefs and ceremonies, such as the ghost dance, manitouism, peyotism, and the Native American Church. *Religion Index One* is available online through DIALOG and on CD-ROM.

270. **Philosopher's Index: An International Index to Philosophical Periodicals and Books**. Bowling Green, OH: Bowling Green State University, Philosophy Documentation Center, 1967-. quarterly, $138.00. ISSN 0031-7993.

The *Philosopher's Index* abstracts and indexes more than 350 serial publications, covering the major philosophy journals in English, French, German, Italian, and Spanish as well as selected journals in other languages and disciplines. Also included are many books and monographic series that pertain directly to topics in philosophy. This is the major index for philosophy, but articles are sparse under "Native Americans." Articles can be found on American Indian beliefs, ethical teachings, and worldviews, but the distinctions among philosophy, religion, and mythology are not so formalized in American Indian traditional life and culture, and other sources will need to be consulted for American Indian philosophy, such as the *Religion Index One* (entry 269). The *Philosopher's Index* is an online database through DIALOG.

Social Sciences (General)

271. **Social Sciences Index**. Bronx, NY: H. W. Wilson Co., 1974-. quarterly, price varies. ISSN 0094-4920.

This multidisciplinary index of over 350 titles includes the major journals from the social and behavioral sciences, including psychology, sociology, social work, and anthropology. It is the best starting point for social science research topics. Under "Indians of North America" and under tribal names, articles are located dealing with government relations, legal status and laws, psychology, political activities, and social conditions of Indians. The *Social Sciences Index* is available online through WILSONLINE and BRS (1983-present) and on CD-ROM.

272. **Sociological Abstracts**. San Diego, CA: Sociological Abstracts, 1952-. 5/yr., $475.00/yr. ISSN 0038-0202.

Covering the world's sociological literature and related disciplines, this abstracting service summarizes and indexes journal articles and conference papers. It is the largest index for sociology-related topics, but the printed index is usually difficult for researchers to use. Many articles and papers are abstracted under the subject headings "American Indians," "American Indian Reservations," "Amerindian Languages," "Potlatches," "Traditional Societies," and "Treaties." Topics vary from ethnic identity and conflict, portrayals of Indians in films and books, stereotyping, sports mascots, and social service support to other sociological issues related to American Indians. It is much easier to use the online database, available through DIALOG or BRS, or the CD-ROM version.

273. **Social Work Research and Abstracts**. Silver Spring, MD: National Association of Social Workers, 1965-. quarterly, $100.00. ISSN 0148-0847.

This is the most important index for social work journals, and it also abstracts articles from many disciplines on social work topics. Original research papers are included with the index on topics of current interest in social work. The winter issue provides a cumulative author and subject index for the preceding year. Under "Native Americans" are materials on delivery of services and therapy related to topics such as AIDS, fetal alcohol syndrome, infant mortality, drug abuse, mental health, child abuse and neglect, and pregnant teenagers. *Social Work Research and Abstracts* is available through BRS as an online database.

274. **Social Sciences Citation Index (SSCI)**. Philadelphia: Institute for Scientific Information, 1969-. 3/yr., $4,300.00. ISSN 0091-3703.

SSCI, an enormous multidisciplinary index, is international in its coverage of the core journals in the social and behavioral sciences disciplines. It is divided into three parts: permuterm subject index, source index, and citation index. The permuterm subject index is the index by topics, as represented by key words in titles of articles. The source index is by authors' names, with bibliographic references for articles published during that time. The citation index is used to determine whether a particular article, book, or thesis has been cited that year. Because about 4,500 journals are indexed here, this is the largest social sciences index available. No abstracts or subject headings are used. Available online as *Social SciSearch* (1972-present) on BRS and DIALOG and also on CD-ROM.

275. **Sage Family Studies Abstracts**. Newbury Park, CA: Sage Publications, 1979-. quarterly, $232.00 ($79.00 individual). ISSN 0164-0283.

This source provides indexing and abstracts for family and marriage topics. It includes references to journals, books, government publications, dissertations, and other "fugitive" materials. Arrangement is by broad categories (e.g., trends in marriage, family, and society; sexual attitudes; gender roles; reproduction; singlehood; family economics; child care; divorce; minority issues), with cumulative subject and author indexes in the final quarterly issue each year.

Women's Studies

276. **Women's Studies Index**. Boston: G. K. Hall, 1989-. annual, $150.00/yr. ISSN 1058-6369.

Over 100 women's studies journals and magazines are indexed annually by subjects, authors, and titles in one alphabet. This surpasses similar indexes in the number of periodicals analyzed, although no abstracts are provided. Among periodicals included are popular ones (e.g., *Ms.*, *Redbook*, *Glamour*, and *Good Housekeeping*) and scholarly ones (e.g., *Journal of Feminist Studies in Religion*, *Feminist Review*, *Journal of Marriage and the Family*, and *Canadian Woman Studies*). The subject index at the end of each volume lists "Indians of North America," with subdivisions by specific areas of research, such as literature and arts, religion, status of women, domestic violence, housing, politics, and personal narratives. Researchers will find articles on such topics as the representation of American Indian women in the media and Canadian aboriginal family violence.

277. **Women Studies Abstracts**. Rush, NY: Rush Publications Co., 1972-. quarterly, $112.00/yr. ($56.00/yr. individual). ISBN 0049-7835.

This source abstracts around 34 scholarly journals such as *Gender and Society*, *Journal of Women and Aging*, *Signs*, *Sex Roles*, and *Journal of Women's History*. The arrangement is by broad subject areas (e.g., employment, history, media, family) with subject and author indexes at the end of each issue and annual volume. Under "Indians (North American)" and "Indians (Canadian)," researchers will discover articles on topics dealing with Indian women and their roles in the history and culture of tribes, contemporary issues of Indian women, and interviews with Indian women. *Studies on Women Abstracts* is a similar title, based in England, that offers a more international perspective than entries 276 and 277.

NEWSPAPER INDEXES, ABSTRACTS, AND DATABASES

Newspaper articles are useful to researchers for current and historical information, local stories, interviews, case studies, and primary source perspectives. Researchers in American Indian studies can find newspaper articles on reservation activities, tribal issues, summaries of government studies, Indian health statistics, and a variety of other topics concerning American Indians.

The following indexes, databases, and computer systems are important ones for American Indian topics, and they are the ones most likely to be available in research libraries.

278. **NEXIS**
Mead Data Central
9443 Springboro Pike
P.O. Box 933
Dayton, OH 45401
(800) 346-9759

NEXIS is the largest online, full-text news database. (Mead Data Central also produces *LEXIS*, which has full texts of laws and court cases, as does its competitor, *WESTLAW*). *NEXIS* is an amazing system, providing the full text of newspapers, newswires, magazines, and journals, plus some reference books. Over 350 newspapers are available through *NEXIS*, to be searched in a group or individually. The years of coverage vary with each title, with most titles available for the past three to ten years. *NEXIS* began in 1979 and has daily updates. Currency and comprehensiveness make *NEXIS* an extremely valuable source for news around the country and the world, including many issues on American Indians.

279. **DataTimes**
  14000 Quail Springs Parkway
  Suite 450
  Oklahoma City, OK 73134
  (800) 642-2525

DataTimes is an international, full-text, online information network similar to *NEXIS* (entry 278). *DataTimes* offers over 2,000 local, regional, national, and international newspapers, newswire services, and trade and industry sources. Even transcripts of certain television news programs are available. Most newspapers do not have their own indexes, and most libraries cannot afford to subscribe to hundreds of newspapers. Remarkable systems like *DataTimes* and *NEXIS* make it possible to search hundreds of newspapers that otherwise would be practically inaccessible to researchers. Newspapers in *DataTimes* can be searched separately or in groups such as All New Mexico News, All North Carolina Newspapers, or all sources. The coverage is usually from around 1988-present. Both *DataTimes* and *NEXIS* are expanding the number of newspapers and time spans covered.

280. **Newsbank**
  Newsbank, Inc.
  58 Pine Street
  New Canaan, CT 06840-5426
  (203) 875-2910

Newsbank is a valuable source of information for newspaper articles on American Indians. It provides access to selected articles in newspapers of over 450 cities in the United States. The full texts are reproduced on microfiche. Libraries may subscribe to *Newsbank* in print (1970-present, ISSN 0737-3813) and on CD-ROM (1986-present, with a back file available). *Newsbank* is divided into broad categories that reflect the range of coverage of the articles: arts and literature, business and economic development, consumer affairs, education, employment, environment, government structure, health, housing and land development, international affairs and defense, law and legal systems, people, political development, science and technology, social relations, transportation, and welfare and social problems.

From 1986-August 1993, there were 6,597 entries under "Indians, North American," and 776 entries under "Alaskan Natives." Articles cover a wide variety of contemporary topics such as Indian health issues, gambling on reservations, powwows, land claims, race relations, and images in the media. This is an important source for current information on American Indians, althouh it is time-consuming to look through the many subheadings to find specific topics needed.

281. **Ethnic Newswatch Database**
  17103 Preston Road
  LB 107 Suite 250
  Dallas, TX 75248-1373
  (214) 713-8170

This CD-ROM database became available in 1993, offering access to thousands of articles from ethnic newspapers and magazines in the United States. *Ethnic Newswatch* is a multicultural database with articles in both English and Spanish and is dedicated to the collection of information from the ethnic and minority press.

Articles on American Indians are included and provide a unique perspective on issues of importance to the Indian community.

282. **National Newspaper Index and Newsearch**
Information Access Company
362 Lakeside Drive
Foster City, CA 94404
(800) 321-6388
These two newspaper files are available online through DIALOG, and the *National Newspaper Index* is also on CD-ROM. *Newsearch* is designed for access to current news, covering the most recent two to six weeks of articles and stories indexed and abstracted by the databases produced by Information Access. Daily updates can be found in *Newsearch*, although only *The New York Times* and *The Wall Street Journal* are available within 24 hours. References come from more than 5,000 general interest, legal, trade, and business publications, newspapers, and wire services. The *National Newspaper Index* covers 1979-present for the online database and the most recent year plus three years back on the CD-ROM version. However, only five of the major U.S. newspapers are indexed: *The New York Times,* the *Los Angeles Times, The Wall Street Journal, The Washington Post*, and *The Christian Science Monitor*. The *National Newspaper Index* is updated monthly with over 15,000 records. From 1990-October 1993, there were 595 articles under "Native Americans."

283. **Newspaper and Periodical Abstracts**
UMI Data Courier
620 South Third Street
Louisville, KY 40202
(502) 583-4111
Over 25 national and regional newspapers are indexed and abstracted daily in this online database. The newspaper coverage is from 1989-present, and the coverage of more than 300 periodicals is from 1988-present. Also, citations to weekly transcripts of more than 30 television programs are provided. *Newspaper and Periodical Abstracts* overlaps considerably with other news sources but is available online through DIALOG and EPIC.

284. **Papers**
Dialog Information Services, Inc.
3460 Hillview Avenue
P.O. Box 10010
Palo Alto, CA 94303-0993
(800) 3-DIALOG
Around 50 major national and regional U.S. newspapers are included in *Papers*, an electronic file. The time coverage varies for each newspaper, but most span from around 1988-present. The complete text, with daily updates, began in January 1993. *Papers* provides access to some newspapers not covered in other newspaper sources. It is available online through DIALOG and on CD-ROM.

285. **The New York Times Index**
     The New York Times Company
     229 West 43d Street
     New York, NY 10036
     (800) 521-0600

Distributed by University Microfilms International. 1913-; 1851-1912 prior series. $850.00/yr. ISSN 0147-538X.

The New York Times is the finest newspaper in the country and the only American newspaper with an index spanning such a long period of time. *The New York Times Index* is an excellent subject index, providing brief synopses of the articles, with references to the dates, pages, and columns of the newspaper. Many cross-references are provided for names and related subjects. *The New York Times Index* and *The New York Times* newspaper are available online.

AMERICAN INDIAN PERIODICALS, NEWSPAPERS, AND NEWSLETTERS

8

American Indian periodicals (magazines and journals), newspapers, and newsletters are important vehicles of information for researchers as well as for Indian people. They focus on current news, concerns, and research affecting Indians. However, researchers must often browse through issues of American Indian periodicals, newspapers, and newsletters because most are not indexed in the standard periodical indexes or databases. Examples of Indian periodicals that are indexed are *American Indian Culture and Research Journal* and *American Indian Quarterly.* These two are indexed in *America: History and Life,* a printed index and computerized database. The *Journal of American Indian Education* is indexed in *Current Index to Journals in Education* and in the ERIC database. *Akwesasne Notes*, the significant Indian newspaper out of Mohawk country, is indexed in the *Alternative Press Index.* This is the only Indian newspaper indexed anywhere.

Some special microfilm sets have compiled American Indian periodicals into a single location. See chapter 12 for microform collections listing periodicals and newspapers in microform.

There are many newspapers and newsletters published by tribes and associations concerning Indian affairs. The largest newspapers are *Indian Country Today* (formerly the *Lakota Times*), the *Navajo Times*, and *Akwesasne Notes.* Many tribal centers and Indian libraries subscribe to Indian periodicals, newspapers, and newsletters that are seldom found in most university and public libraries.

The directories listed earlier in this book are excellent sources for American Indian periodicals, newspapers, and newsletters. *Native Americans Information Directory* (entry 5) lists some of the most important American Indian journals and magazines, newsletters, and newspapers, with descriptions, subscription costs, addresses and telephone numbers.

A more extensive listing is found in the *Reference Encyclopedia of the America Indian* (entry 6). A section on periodicals lists important magazines, journals, newsletters, and newspapers for American Indians of the United States and lists Canadian periodicals.

Directories of Periodicals, Newspapers, and Newsletters

The sources that follow list American Indian periodicals, newspapers, and newsletters that existed or still exist today.

286.   Littlefield, Daniel F., Jr., and James W. Parins, eds. **American Indian and Alaska Native Newspapers and Periodicals**, 1826-1924, Vol. 1; 1925-1970, Vol. 2; 1971-1985, Vol. 3. Westport, CT: Greenwood, 1984-1986. (Historical Guides to the World's Periodicals & Newspapers Series). 3v. $95.00/vol. LC 83-1483. Vol. 1 ISBN 0-313-23426-4; Vol. 2 ISBN 0-313-23427-2; Vol. 3 ISBN 0-313-24834-6.

This is the best directory and guide to newspapers and periodicals edited or published by American Indians or Alaska Natives and to newspapers and periodicals whose central purpose was to publish contemporary information about Indians or Alaska Natives. Publications concerning Indians of Mexico and Canada are not included. The three volumes alphabetically list sources published from 1826-1985, beginning with the *Cherokee Phoenix,* a tribal newspaper established in 1828. Long essays provide publication histories and summaries of the contents of the titles. Included are tribal newspapers, nontribal newspapers, intertribal newspapers and periodicals, literary periodicals, reform periodicals, independent newspapers and periodicals, native-language periodicals, English-language periodicals, the Indian school press, and Indian agency periodicals. Bibliographic references and notes conclude each entry.

Good indexes allow access by name of the sources, individuals involved with the publications, associations, and subject fields covered. Appendixes list titles chronologically. This source is the most important contribution to the history of Indian periodicals, newspapers, and newsletters.

287.   Danky, James P., ed. **Native American Periodicals and Newspapers, 1828-1982**. Westport, CT: Greenwood, 1984. 532p. $59.95. LC 83-22579. ISBN 0-313-23773-5.

Arranged alphabetically by title, this guide lists 1,164 periodicals and newspapers published by or about American Indians from 1828-1982. Brief information is given on the publication histories, editors, dates, and subjects on which the publications focus. Holdings information is given for 147 university and research libraries in the United States and Canada, with strong coverage of Wisconsin libraries. Microform availability is provided for each title. Good indexes provide access by subjects covered, editors, publishers, states and geographic regions, and time periods of publication. This guide does not cover the histories of the periodicals and newspapers as does Littlefield (entry 286), and the typeface is terrible, but it does offer a lasting contribution for researchers seeking information on Indian periodicals and newspapers and which libraries contain them.

288. Katz, Bill, and Linda Sternberg Katz, eds. **Magazines for Libraries**. 7th ed. New Providence, NJ: R. R. Bowker, 1992. 1,214 p. $139.95. ISBN 0-8352-3166-6.

The 7th edition of this useful guide for periodicals lists 6,600 periodicals, from over 70,000 possibilities. These represent some of the best and most useful magazines and journals for libraries in elementary and secondary schools, public libraries, special libraries, and college and university libraries. This standard source is relied upon by librarians for collection development, and by researchers for descriptions of periodicals. It lists 40 major periodicals in American Indian studies (under "Indians of North America") and analyzes their subject content.

289. **Newsletters in Print**. 6th ed. Detroit: Gale Research, 1992-. irreg. $175.00. ISSN 0899-0425. (Formerly: **Newsletter Directory** and **National Directory of Newsletters and Reporting Services**).

The 6th edition lists over 8,000 newsletters issued in the United States in print or online. Forty-one of these are Native American newsletters. Directory information is given, such as addresses, phone numbers, and subscription information, along with short descriptions of the contents.

290. **Oxbridge Directory of Newsletters**. New York: Oxbridge Communications, 1992. annual, $325.00. ISSN 0163-7010.

Oxbridge lists more than 20,000 newsletters published in the United States and Canada, primarily overlapping with *Newsletters in Print* (entry 289). It is arranged by major subject categories, listing directory information with only short editorial descriptions.

Core American Indian Periodicals and Newspapers

The following selective list of American Indian magazines, journals, and newspapers represents a small fraction of those currently published. However, these are some of the major ones useful for researchers. There are also many newsletters that provide timely information that are not included here. Newsletters such as the *Sentinel,* published by the National Congress of American Indians, and the *NARF Legal Review,* published by the Native American Rights Fund, are important sources of legal and political news affecting all Native Americans. Comprehensive listings of current periodicals, newspapers, and newsletters may be found in the directories (entries 5 and 6) of this guide.

291. **Akwe Kon Journal** (until 1992, **Northeast Indian Quarterly**). Ithaca, NY: Cornell University, American Indian Program, 1984-. quarterly, $15.00/yr. ISSN 0897-7354.

This interdisciplinary journal with emphasis on politics, economic concerns, and community issues of the Iroquois and other northeastern Indian groups also publishes articles of interest to the national Indian community.

292.   **Akwesasne Notes: A Journal for Native and Natural People.** Rooseveltown, NY: Mohawk Nation at Akwesasne, 1968-. bimonthly, $20.00/yr. ISSN 0002-3949.

One of the most widely read Indian newspapers, this is the official paper of the Mohawk Nation in upstate New York. It gives broad coverage to important issues of native peoples everywhere as well as local Mohawk Nation news. Articles are often politically charged, and many are drawn from other Indian publications in the United States and Canada.

It is indexed by the *Alternative Press Index, Chicano Index, Human Rights Internet Reporter*, and *Anthropological Index*.

293.   **American Indian and Alaska Native Mental Health Research: The Journal of the National Center** (formerly: **White Cloud Journal**). Denver, CO: Center for American Indian and Alaska Native Mental Health Research, University of Colorado Health Sciences Center, 1978-. 3/yr., $35.00/yr. ISSN 0893-5394.

This scholarly journal publishes empirical research studies, program evaluations, and case studies in the area of mental health of American Indians and Alaska Natives.

It is indexed by *Psychological Abstracts, Social Work Research and Abstracts, Current Index to Journals in Education, Sociological Abstracts*, and *Anthropological Literature*.

294.   **American Indian Art Magazine**. Scottsdale, AZ: American Indian Art, 1975-. quarterly, $20.00/yr. ISSN 0192-9968.

This beautiful periodical has excellent pictures of Indian art, articles by experts in the field, coverage of gallery shows, auctions, and museum exhibitions, and much advertising. It is useful to collectors and museums primarily.

American Indian Art Magazine is indexed by *Artbibliographies Modern, Anthropological Literature, America: History and Life*, and *Historical Abstracts*.

295.   **American Indian Culture and Research Journal.** Los Angeles: American Indian Studies Center, University of California, Los Angeles, 1971-. quarterly, $30.00/yr. ($20.00/individual). ISSN 0161-6463.

This is one of the more scholarly journals on American Indian culture, history, and anthropology, as well as an excellent source for book reviews. It is indexed by *America: History and Life, Abstracts in Anthropology, Anthropological Literature, Historical Abstracts, Current Index to Journals in Education, Sociological Abstracts,* and *Special Needs Abstracts*.

296.   **American Indian Law Review**. Norman: University of Oklahoma, College of Law, 1973-. semiannual, $15.00/yr. ISSN 0094-002X.

This scholarly publication is concerned with important legal issues affecting American Indians. Articles are presented on U.S. judicial and congressional decisions affecting Indians and on topics such as child welfare, repatriation of Indian remains, water rights, and gambling on reservations.

American Indian Law Review is indexed by *Current Law Index, Index to Legal Periodicals, LegalTrac,* and *Selected Water Resources Abstracts*.

297. **American Indian Quarterly**. Berkeley: University of California, Berkeley, Native American Studies Program, 1974-. quarterly, $45.00/yr. ($25.00/individual). ISSN 0095-182X.

American Indian Quarterly is an important scholarly journal covering interdisciplinary topics on American Indians in the areas of folklore, law, education, anthropology, history, women's studies, culture, and literature. It compares with the *American Indian Culture and Research Journal* (entry 295) in its scholarly content and excellent book reviews.

It is indexed by *Abstracts in Anthropology, Anthropological Literature, America: History and Life, Historical Abstracts, Current Index to Journals in Education,* and *Humanities Index.*

298. **Canadian Journal of Native Education**. Edmonton: University of Alberta, Department of Educational Foundations, 1973-. semiannual, $24.00/yr. Canada, ($30.00/yr. foreign). ISSN 0710-1481.

This academic journal focuses on the education of Canada's Inuit, Metis, and Indian populations but also discusses education of the Alaska Native population. A wide variety of educational and social issues facing educators and schoolchildren are presented. It is indexed by the *Canadian Education Index.*

299. **European Review of Native American Studies**. Vienna: Christian Feest, 1987-. semiannual, $25.00/yr. ISSN 0238-1486.

This scholarly journal is the first outlet for Native American studies research in Europe. Articles are written either by Europeans, or written about the history and contact of Europeans and Indians.

One feature of the journal is a current European bibliography of Native American studies. This journal is useful for researchers who are interested in the European perspective.

300. **Indian Business and Management**. Mesa, AZ: National Center for American Indian Enterprise Development, 1990-. bimonthly, free.

The concern of this magazine is the development of successful Indian-run businesses on reservations. Articles address tribal entrepreneurs and economic opportunities on reservations and report on cooperative endeavors between businesses and tribes.

301. **Indian Country Today** (until Oct. 8, 1992, **Lakota Times**). Rapid City, SD: Native American Publishing, 1981-. weekly, $40.00/yr.

The largest Native-American-owned weekly newspaper in the United States, this award-winning paper provides detailed coverage of local Indian news as well as state, national, and international news affecting Indians. It primarily serves the Lakota Sioux Nation, with sections on regional news and news at the Pine Ridge and Rosebud reservations. Because this newspaper is not tribally owned, it expresses independence in its editorial stances.

302. **Inuit Art Quarterly**. Nepean, Ont: Inuit Art Foundation, 1986-. quarterly, $25.00/yr. ISSN 0831-6708.

This glossy magazine is well illustrated to present the sculpture and graphic arts of Canada's Inuit peoples. It reviews art exhibitions and informs of forthcoming conferences and exhibitions.

303. **Journal of American Indian Education**. Tempe, AZ: Arizona State University, College of Education, Center for Indian Education, 1961-. 3/yr., $16.00/yr. ISSN 0021-8731.

A small, scholarly journal publishing articles on the education of American Indians, including Alaska Natives, this publication emphasizes basic and applied research, historical research, and field study reports. The *Journal of American Indian Education* is indexed by *Current Index to Journals in Education,* the *Education Index,* and *Linguistics and Language Behavior Abstracts.*

304. **Native Nations: News and Analysis from Indian Country**. New York: Solidarity Foundation, 1985-. monthly, $50.00/yr. ($20.00/individual).

Contributors to this journal are usually Indian leaders who present a wide spectrum of news and opinion on political issues and other affairs affecting American Indians today.

305. **Native Peoples: The Arts and Lifeways**. Phoenix, AZ: Media Concepts Group, 1987-. quarterly, $18.00/yr. ISSN 0895-7606.

A colorful magazine dedicated to sensitively portraying the arts and cultures of native peoples of the Americas, *Native Peoples* features a wide variety of topics in art, education, culture, events, and exhibits.

306. **Native Studies Review**. Saskatoon: University of Saskatchewan, Native Studies Department, 1985-. semiannual, $30.00/yr. ($20.00/individual).

This scholarly journal is devoted to studies of Native Canadian history, culture, law, politics, government relations, and contemporary concerns.

307. **Navajo Times**. Window Rock, AZ: Navajo Nation, 1959-. weekly, $25.00/yr.

This official tribal newspaper serves the Navajo Nation with news articles on Navajo tribal affairs, politics, laws, social conditions, economy, sports, and education. The *Navajo Times* also contains articles on national issues of concern to Indians.

308. **News from Indian Country**. Hayward, WI: Indian Country Communications, 1988-. semimonthly. $40.00/yr. ($24.00/individual). (Formerly: **Lac Courte Oreilles Journal**).

This large, independently owned Indian tabloid publishes articles of interest to Indians in Wisconsin and the Great Lakes region. It also covers issues important to the national Native American community. It is known for its balanced coverage of controversial issues.

309. **News from Native California**. Berkeley, CA: Heyday Books, 1987-. quarterly, $16.00/yr. ISSN 1040-5437.

This important journal represents contemporary and historical issues of California's Indians. Articles are written primarily by Native Californian authors and cover the music, food, arts, crafts, education, legends, languages, and other cultural aspects of life of California Indians. A calendar of powwows and other Indian happenings around the state is provided in each issue.

310. **Studies in American Indian Literatures**. San Bernardino: California State University, San Bernardino, 1977-. quarterly, $16.00/yr. ISSN 0730-3228.

This scholarly journal focuses on traditional and contemporary Native American literatures, including translated oral texts, versions of myths, poetry, and interviews with native writers.

311. **Tribal College: Journal of American Indian Higher Education**. Sacramento, CA: American Indian Higher Education Consortium, 1989-. quarterly, $14.00/yr.

Tribal College is the only periodical devoted to tribal college issues. It is a glossy magazine publishing articles about individual tribal colleges and programs and issues affecting them.

312. **Tundra Times**. Anchorage, AK: Eskimo, Indian, Aleut Press, 1962-. weekly, $20.00/yr. ISSN 0049-4801.

This is Alaska's oldest statewide newspaper, publishing articles and commentary about contemporary issues of interest to Native Americans, Eskimos, and Aleuts across the state.

313. **Wicazo Sa Review/Red Pencil Review: A Journal of Native American Studies**. Davis: University of California, Davis, Native American Studies Department, 1985-. semiannual, $20.00/yr. ISSN 0749-6427.

This scholarly journal aims to serve Native American studies as an academic discipline and functions as a forum for students and scholars in the discipline.

314. **Winds of Change: American Indian Education and Opportunity**. Boulder, CO: American Indian Science and Engineering Society, 1986-. quarterly, $24.00/yr. ISSN 0888-8612.

This attractive magazine specializes in career development in the fields of science and engineering for American Indians and also has articles on tribal culture and identity.

315. **Windspeaker**. Edmonton, Alta: Aboriginal Multi-media Society of Alberta, 1983-. biweekly, $40.00/yr.

This Canadian tabloid covers native issues and activities in Alberta and Saskatchewan, Canadian government policies toward Indians, and social issues of Native Canadians.

BIOGRAPHICAL SOURCES

9

Information about people may be found in directories, books, periodicals, newspapers, and databases. The scope of biographical sources varies, covering historical or contemporary figures, persons in particular occupations or fields, men or women, or other limiting factors. And the amount of information varies from basic brief summaries to long articles.

This chapter lists major sources of biographical information available in research libraries and does not attempt a comprehensive listing of all sources providing biographical information on American Indians.

There are whole books written about famous Indians from the past and present, such as Chief Joseph, Black Elk, and Ben Nighthorse Campbell. And there are many collective biographies of prominent American Indians. Some of the collective biographies that have remained popular over the years are *Great North American Indians: Profiles in Life and Leadership,* by Frederick J. Dockstader (New York: Van Nostrand Reinhold, 1977), *American Indian Leaders: Studies in Diversity,* by R. David Edmunds (Lincoln: University of Nebraska, 1980), and *The Patriot Chiefs: A Chronicle of American Leadership,* by Alvin M. Josephy, Jr. (New York: Viking, 1961).

Some historical accounts of biographical information provide primary-source views of Indian leaders. One example is a collective biography titled *Indian Tribes of North America: With Biographical Sketches & Anecdotes of the Principal Chiefs*, by Thomas Loraine McKenney and James Hall (reprint, St. Clair Shores, MI: Scholarly Press, 1974). McKenney (1785-1859) began his research and writings around 1821 in an attempt to create a record of prominent American Indians from various tribes in the United States. He held government positions dealing with Indians, such as superintendent of Indian trade in 1816 and another post in the Bureau of

Indian Affairs beginning in 1824. Through his official and personal relations with Indians and his travels in Indian country, he produced letters and reports on tribes and individuals. This set provides insights on more than 100 important Indian chiefs (all men), their lives, personalities, and attributes. Such leaders as Red Jacket, a Seneca war chief, and Tenskwautawaw, the Prophet, are included. Accompanying the text are 123 full-page color plates of portrait-sketches by J. O. Lewis. Volume 3 also contains the 262-page "Essay on the History of the North American Indians" by James Hall. Each volume contains a separate index in the back for individual and tribal names.

Books about American Indian writers and their literature usually include some biographical information. Examples are *American Indian Authors,* by Natachee Scott Momaday (Boston: Houghton Mifflin, 1972), which has short biographical essays preceding each author's short story in the volume, and *American Indian Novelists: An Annotated Critical Bibliography,* by Tom Colonese and Louis Owens (New York: Garland, 1985), which includes biographical information on some of the major Indian writers.

Photographic, portrait, and picture collections are held in libraries and government archives such as the Smithsonian Institution, the National Archives, and the Library of Congress. The Library of Congress, Prints and Photographs Division, contains an amazingly rich collection of around 10 million photographs of American Indians, of which 8,000 have been processed and cataloged. Of these, 3,200 photographs taken from 1863-1940 by many individuals, including Edward S. Curtis, Frank Bennett Fiske, and A. Zeno Shindler, are available to researchers. These pictures have been reproduced in William H. Geotzmann's book *The First Americans: Photographs from the Library of Congress* (Washington, D.C.: Starwood, 1991). The index lists negative numbers, which researchers can use to order copies of the photographs. The outstanding photographs of Edward S. Curtis are also published in books, such as his collection titled *The North American Indian* (New York: Johnson Reprint Corp., 1970). In 1992, the Library of Congress also published *Portrait Index of North American Indians in Published Collections*, edited by Patrick Frazier (Washington, D.C.: Library of Congress, 1992), which indexes the portraits of American Indians in 75 different books in the Library of Congress. Indian names and alternate names are listed (e.g., Ah-yaw-ne-tah-car-ron, Black Hawk) under tribal names and also in an alphabetical index. Many books are published containing portraits and drawings of American Indians, such as those by George Catlin.

This section concentrates on major biographical sources, bibliographies, and reference works that focus on American Indians from the past and present and that provide textual information on Indians who gained prominence in various ways.

General Biographical Indexes

316. **Biography Index**. New York: H. W. Wilson, 1946-. quarterly, price varies. ISSN 0006-3053.

The *Biography Index* covers articles in periodicals, books, and book chapters about individuals in all fields. Materials are drawn from the other Wilson indexes, selected additional periodicals, and books of individual and collected biographies. Articles on individuals in over 2,600 periodicals are analyzed in this convenient source. Mostly Americans are included, and the main section is alphabetically arranged by the people's names. An index by profession or occupation is provided at the end of each issue. This is a valuable source for information on contemporary American Indians, such as Wilma Mankiller or Dennis Banks, who are written about in magazines and books. The *Biography Index* is available online through WILSONLINE, BRS, and EPIC and is also a CD-ROM database.

317. **Biography and Genealogy Master Index**. Detroit: Gale Research, 1975-. annual, $275.00 (1980 cumulative, $950.00/8v.). ISSN 0730-1316. (microfiche edition: Bio-Base).

This unique, monumental source is a master index to more than 8 million references to biographical entries in over 350 biography sources. The basic set, plus the cumulations and the annual volumes, provides a quick way to check for individuals in hundreds of directories and who's who sources. *Biography and Genealogy Master Index* is also available online through DIALOG and on CD-ROM.

Bibliographies and Reference Works

318. Bataille, Gretchen M., and Kathleen M. Sands. **American Indian Women: A Guide to Research**. New York: Garland, 1991. 444p. (Women's History and Culture, Vol. 4). $57.00. LC 91-2961. ISBN 0-8240-4799-0.

This research guide has a chapter listing 340 citations to autobiographies, biographies, and interviews (pp. 281-365) on American Indian women. The citations and short abstracts refer to periodical articles, books, and book chapters on Indian women from the nineteenth century to the present.

319. Bataille, Gretchen M., ed. **Native American Women: A Biographical Dictionary**. New York: Garland, 1993. 333p. (Biographical Dictionaries of Minority Women, Vol. 1). $55.00. LC 92-19990. ISBN 0-8240-5267-6.

The lives of contemporary and historical American Indian women are told in one- to two-page summaries. These include Indian women representing diverse roles within their cultures, including legendary and historical figures. The arrangement is alphabetical with bibliographic references listed with each entry for articles and books about the women. An index lists names and subjects, and four appendixes are provided. The first appendix lists individuals by primary area of specialization, which reveals the variety of entries in this volume: activism, anthropology, architecture, arts, business, captive, Christian leadership, cosmetology, cultural interpretation, education, fur trade, historian, law, library, linguistics, literature/criticism, medicine (Western), medicine (traditional), missionary work, music, performance, photography, social work, storytelling, tribal leadership, and warrior. The other three appendixes list entries by decades of birth, by state or province of birth, and by tribal affiliation.

319a. Champagne, Duane. **Native America, Portrait of the Peoples**. Detroit, MI: Visible Ink, 1994. 786p. $18.95. ISBN 0-8103-9452-9.

This very attractive book profiles significant Native Americans from the past and present who have contributed to their culture. Biographical essays highlight Indian activists, musicians, educators, tribal leaders, religious leaders, artists, poets, writers, actors, politicians and others, such as Tecumseh, Jay Silverheels, Leslie Marmon Silko, Kicking Bear, and Maria Martinez. Much additional information is presented in chapters on historical and cultural events in Indian history.

320. **Biographical Dictionary of Indians of the Americas**. Newport Beach, CA: American Indian Publishers, 1992. 2v. $285.00. ISBN 0937862290.

These two volumes provide brief summaries of nearly 2,000 noteworthy Indians, both contemporary and historical. Alphabetically arranged by individuals and illustrated with drawings, the biographical entries often include references to books, encyclopedias, periodicals, and government reports containing information on the individuals. Indexes are provided for variant names of the subjects included and for tribal names. Like *Who Was Who in Native American History* (entry 329), this is a starting point for beginning researchers. A similar title with most of the same information is *Dictionary of Indians of North America* (St. Clair Shores, MI: Scholarly Press, 1978. 3v. LC 78-65222. ISBN 0-403-01799-8).

321. Brumble, H. David, III. **An Annotated Bibliography of American Indian and Eskimo Autobiographies**. Lincoln: University of Nebraska, 1981. 177p. $25.00. LC 80-23449. ISBN 0-8032-1175-9.

American Indian autobiographies reveal firsthand what it was like to live in the past, and what really happened between Indians and non-Indians. Autobiographies were written by Indians or recorded by non-Indians from the earliest encounters. Brumble attempts a comprehensive list of printed versions of first-person narratives of American Indians and has compiled over 500 autobiographical narratives in books and periodicals. More than 100 of these are book-length. Included are athletes, authors, artists, hunters, religious leaders, warriors, musicians—the gamut of occupations and backgrounds, from the eighteenth century forward.

322. Brumble, H. David, III. **American Indian Autobiography**. Berkeley: University of California Press, 1988. 336p. $42.50; $13.00pa. ISBN 0-520-06245-0; 0-520-07182-4pa.

This analysis of American Indian autobiography contains a list of autobiographies on pages 211-258 that updates Brumble's *Annotated Bibliography of American Indian and Eskimo Autobiographies* (entry 321). Books, sections of books, periodical articles, and special anthropological papers from associations and schools are included.

323. **Encyclopedia of Indians of the Americas**. St. Clair Shores, MI: Scholarly Press, 1981. $59.00/v. LC 75-170347. ISBN 0-403-03586-4.

This eight-volume set is rich in biographical information on Indians of all the Americas. The lives of Indians from the past and present in all fields are summarized, and many have photographs or drawings accompanying the text. No bibliographic references are provided, however.

324. Hirschfelder, Arlene B. **American Indian and Eskimo Authors: A Comprehensive Bibliography**. New York: Association on American Indian Affairs, 1973. 99p. LC 73-82109.

Hirschfelder identifies material written by or narrated by American Indians and Eskimos. Authors are listed by tribes, with an alphabetical listing of the authors and their works following the main section. Brief annotations are provided for each entry.

325. Klein, Barry T. **Reference Encyclopedia of the American Indian**. 6th ed. West Nyack, NY: Todd, 1993. 679p. $125.00. ISBN 0-915344-30-0.

Klein's directory includes an impressive section (pp. 451-666) of short biographies on contemporary Native Americans and non-Indians. These are prominent American Indians involved in Indian affairs, the business world, the arts, and various other professions, as well as non-Indians active in Indian affairs, anthropology, art, history, archaeology, and other fields with connections to American Indians. Included are tribal chairpersons, chiefs, curators of museums, educators, doctors, artists, and businesspeople. Information is provided on their professional achievements and positions but not personal information on spouses, children, dates of marriage, and social interests.

326. Littlefield, Daniel F., Jr., and James W. Parins. **A Biobibliography of Native American Writers, 1772-1924**. Metuchen, NJ: Scarecrow Press, 1981. 343p. (Native American Bibliography Series, No. 2). LC 81-9138. ISBN 0-8108-1463-3. **Supplement, 1985**. 339p. (Native American Bibliography Series, No. 5). $29.50. LC 85-2045. ISBN 0-8108-1802-7.

These two volumes draw together a considerable body of writing not easily found elsewhere: the writings of Indian authors from Colonial times to 1924. More than 1,200 American Indian authors are represented here, and biographical sketches are given in section 3 of each volume.

The length of the biographical notes varies from a single sentence identifying an author's tribal affiliation and place of birth to a paragraph summarizing the author's life, education, marriage, family, work, offices held, writings, and other activities. Indexes are provided in each volume for tribal affiliations. These volumes are unique in their coverage of early American Indian writers.

327. Snodgrass, Jeanne O., ed. **American Indian Painters: A Biographical Directory with 1,187 Indian Painters**. New York: Museum of the American Indian, Heye Foundation, 1968. 269p. $7.50pa. LC 67-27949. ISBN 0-934490-30-9.

American Indian painters of all artistic styles are listed alphabetically. Biographical summaries are short, with basic information on birth date and place, spouses and children, education, publications, exhibitions, collections held by individuals, tribal affiliations, and careers. A tribal index is included. This directory is of value only for information on obscure Indian painters.

327a. Monthan, Guy, and Doris Monthan. **Art and Indian Individualists: The Art of Seventeen Contemporary Southwestern Artists and Craftsmen**. Flagstaff, AZ: Northland, 1975. 197p. LC 74-31544. ISBN 0-87358-137-7.

Seventeen prominent contemporary American Indian artists who have received national recognition for their work are highlighted. The articles are two to three pages long with color illustrations of the works, which include jewelry, painting, sculpture, pottery, basketry, and weaving.

328. U.S. Department of the Interior Library. **Biographical and Historical Index of American Indians and Persons Involved in Indian Affairs**. Boston: G. K. Hall, 1966. 8v. $940.00. ISBN 0-8161-0716-5.

This subject index is a reproduction of the card file developed by the library in the Bureau of Indian Affairs, which is now incorporated into the Department of the

Interior Library. There are over 200,000 cards reproduced. Biographical information can be located on Indians and non-Indians involved with Indian affairs during the late nineteenth and early twentieth centuries. Featured are Indian chiefs, prominent Indians from history, Bureau of Indian Affairs personnel, Indian agents, and anthropologists.

Although it contains irregularities in forms of persons' names, descriptions are added to assist in identifying individuals. For example, under "Walking Rain (Iowa Chief)," the entry states "Signer of Treaty with Osage, September 12, 1815." The dictionary catalog also lists entries by tribes and descriptions (e.g., "New Mexico Supt'y"). The entries provide citations to the biographical sources, which include monographs, journal articles, government publications, and archival and manuscript materials from the Bureau of American Ethnology. This set is for the serious researcher.

329.   Waldman, Carl. **Who Was Who in Native American History: Indians and Non-Indians from Early Contacts Through 1900**. New York: Facts on File, 1990. 416p. $45.00. ISBN 0-8160-1797-2.

Summaries are provided of the lives of American Indians and non-Indians from early contacts through 1900. Articles range from short paragraphs to over a page in length, highlighting major events of the subjects' lives and the roles they played in history. Indian chiefs, leaders, and educators are included, such as Seattle, Sequoyah, and Cochise. Also, non-Indians important in American Indian history and affairs are found here, such as George Catlin, Edward S. Curtis, and Frederick Webb Hodge. The non-Indians are scholars, writers, anthropologists, photographers, and others who have contributed in positive ways to the preservation of the cultures, histories, arts, and autonomy of Indian tribes. This excellent biographical encyclopedia is a starting point for research but would be more useful if it contained bibliographic references for each entry for additional information.

DISSERTATIONS AND THESES

Dissertations and theses written in partial fulfillment of requirements for doctoral and master's degrees are important sources for researchers because they often concentrate on very specialized areas of research. Most dissertations and theses provide a review of the literature in the second chapter, which is valuable for the researcher working on a closely related topic. Researchers will discover some dissertations and theses in bibliographies. And the Edward E. Ayer Collection of Americana and American Indians in the Newberry Library (entry 205) established a policy around 1970 of acquiring copies of every dissertation on the American Indian. Dissertations and theses are not often cited in periodical indexes or databases. Generally, they must be sought in the special sources listed below.

330. **Dissertation Abstracts International**. Ann Arbor, MI: University Microfilms International, 1969-. monthly. (Continues **Dissertation Abstracts, 1939-1968**). **Part A: The Humanities and Social Sciences**, $525.00. ISSN 0419-4209. **Part B: The Sciences and Engineering**, $525.00. ISSN 0419-4217.

This is the primary source for identification of doctoral dissertations in all fields of study, covering dissertations written as far back as 1861, when academic doctoral degrees were first granted in the United States. Over 550 universities in the United States and Canada and throughout the world send their dissertations to University Microfilms International (UMI) for publication in paper copy and on microform. UMI publishes about 45,000 dissertations each year, and most of these are abstracted in *Dissertation Abstracts International*.

Authors supply abstracts up to 350 words in length, describing in detail the original research projects.

Researchers will need to use the key word-title indexes or author indexes, because the abstracts are organized in such broad categories. Part A: The Humanities and Social Sciences is divided into five sections: "Communication and the Arts," "Education," "Language, Literature, and Linguistics," "Philosophy, Religion, and Theology," and "Social Sciences." Part B: The Sciences and Engineering is also divided into five major sections: "Biological Sciences," "Earth Sciences," "Health and Environmental Sciences," "Physical Sciences," and "Psychology." These broad categories are subdivided further (e.g., "Social Sciences" has "History" as a subdivision, which is further divided to the United States and other regions).

Part C: Worldwide covers all disciplines, listing dissertations internationally. This part was titled "European Abstracts" through spring 1989. Most of the dissertations indexed here are not available from UMI, and those that are available are listed in parts A and B as well. The database version of *Dissertation Abstracts International* includes British and European dissertations from 1988 forward.

Cumulative indexes make the set much easier to use. The *Comprehensive Dissertation Index 1861-1972* lists more than 417,000 dissertations, the *Comprehensive Dissertation Index 1973-1982* cites 351,000 dissertations, and the *Comprehensive Dissertation Index 1983-1987* contains 162,000 cites. However, even these cumulations take time to use because they are divided into broad subject categories.

Many master's theses are also included in *Dissertation Abstracts International,* although the coverage is much more selective than that of dissertations. More than 40,000 master's theses are listed through 1993, and approximately 3,000 master's thesis citations are added each year. *Masters Abstracts International* is also published by UMI as a separate source. However, *Masters Abstracts International* has no specific subject indexes but is divided into broad subject categories. This severely limits its usefulness to researchers seeking specific topics. There is no comprehensive index to master's theses, so this is limited in coverage anyway.

The most efficient and thorough way to use *Dissertation Abstracts International* is through a computerized version, especially because dissertations on topics in American Indian studies may be found in many subject disciplines. Several computer vendors offer *Dissertation Abstracts International* online, including DIALOG and BRS. It is also produced on CD-ROM.

331.   Dockstader, Frederick J., and Alice W. Dockstader. **The American Indian in Graduate Studies: A Bibliography of Theses and Dissertations**. New York: Museum of the American Indian, Heye Foundation, 1973-74. 2v. $18.00pa./set. ISBN 0-934490-06-6.

Totalling 7,446 reports from 274 universities, this bibliography claims to cover 90 percent of the dissertations and theses written on American Indians from 1890-1970. Dissertations known to be available from University Microfilms are indicated with an M after the citation. Part 1 covers theses and dissertations from 1890-1955, and Part 2 covers 1955-1970. The subject index at the end refers back to the author entries, which are arranged alphabetically. This bibliography is very useful for its comprehensiveness and scope of coverage through 1970.

332.   **North American Indians: A Dissertation Index**. Ann Arbor, MI: University Microfilms International, 1977. 169p. $28.00. ISBN 0-8357-0134-4.

Key word and author indexes lead to over 1,700 doctoral dissertations completed between 1904 and 1976 and summarized in *Dissertation Abstracts International*. A supplement, published in 1979, provides access to 455 dissertations completed in 1977-1978 and 102 master's theses published by University Microfilms from 1962-1978.

333.   Manson, Spero M., et al. **Psychosocial Research on American Indian and Alaska Native Youth: An Indexed Guide to Recent Dissertations**. Westport, CT: Greenwood, 1984. 228p. (Bibliographies and Indexes in Psychology, No. 1). $45.00. LC 84-6583. ISBN 0-313-23991-6.

A total of 345 dissertations completed between 1960-1982 are included in this bibliography, which reports on psychosocial research on American Indian and Alaska Native youth. The arrangement is by 13 topical areas of research, such as mental health and adjustment, self-imagery, and intelligence, with author entries in alphabetical order. Summaries of the dissertations include the subject of study, sample size, sampling techniques, research questions, data collection procedures, results, and conclusions. Researchers will need to utilize the glossary of terms with subject entries in the back of the volume to locate specific topics.

334.   Reynolds, Michael. **A Guide to Theses and Dissertations: An International Bibliography of Bibliographies**. rev. ed. Phoenix, AZ: Oryx Press, 1985. 263p. $31.50. LC 85-43094. ISBN 0-89774-149-8.

This bibliography draws together citations to bibliographies of theses and dissertations from around the world. The theses and dissertations are from a broad range of sources and are arranged by a classified system from the general to the more specific. The subject index lists 16 entries for Native North Americans. Besides the standard sources listed in this guide, there are additional ones dealing with Canadian Indians and Indian education published as bibliographies in journals or as ERIC documents.

GOVERNMENT PUBLICATIONS AND ARCHIVAL MATERIAL

The U.S. government is the largest publisher in the world. However, many researchers overlook this vast source of information out of lack of knowledge of what is available and how to access the materials. Many current and archival materials on American Indians are produced by government departments and agencies such as the Bureau of Indian Affairs and the Indian Health Service. Researchers will discover congressional reports and hearings, census materials, and publications from government agencies on all aspects of American Indian life, culture, and history.

The sources in this chapter are a selective list of some of the major tools for locating U.S. government publications, or government documents, as they are often called. State governments also publish many materials on American Indians, and these must be searched through separate sources. Researchers should check with university and state libraries for depositories of state documents.

U.S. government publications designated for general distribution are sent to libraries throughout the country to provide access for the general public. There are more than 1,400 libraries designated as depository libraries, and these libraries receive government publications free of charge. Depository libraries are usually state libraries, large public libraries, and university libraries. Government publications are normally segregated from book and periodical sections because government publications have their own classification system and indexes. Few libraries have integrated their government publications into their online and card catalogs. Therefore, researchers must know how to access the valuable materials available within the government publications collections.

Superintendent of Documents Classification

Government publications have a unique classification system. Whereas, library classification schemes like the Library of Congress Classification and the Dewey Decimal Classification allow the arrangement of books and periodicals on the same subject to be shelved together, the Superintendent of Documents (SuDocs) classification system groups materials together by the issuing departments, bureaus, and agencies of the government. The SuDocs classification is alphanumeric, beginning with a letter, or letters, representing the departments and agencies issuing the documents:

A	Agriculture Department
C	Commerce Department
D	Defense Department
E	Energy Department
ED	Education Department
EP	Environmental Protection Agency
HE	Health and Human Services Department
I	Interior Department
J	Justice Department
L	Labor Department
NAS	National Aeronautics and Space Administration
PREX	Executive Office of the President
S	State Department
SBA	Small Business Administration
SI	Smithsonian Institution
T	Treasury Department
TD	Transportation Department
VA	Veterans Affairs Department

These letters in combination with series numbers create class stems, which subdivide publications within the government departments and agencies. Within the Department of the Interior, for example, is the Bureau of Indian Affairs (BIA). BIA publications begin with the letter "I" for Interior Department. The publication *List of Classes of United States Government Publications Available for Selection by Depository Libraries* lists the following class divisions in use today.

INDIAN AFFAIRS BUREAU

I 20.2:	General Publications
I 20.9/2:	Laws
I 20.12/2:	Handbooks, Manuals, Guides
I 20.27:	Addresses
I 20.46:	Statistics Concerning Indian Education, Fiscal Year
I 20.47:	Maps and Atlases
I 20.48:	Bibliographies and Lists of Publications
I 20.51:	Indians of (various states)
I 20.51/2:	Indians (various subjects)
I 20.58:	Tribal and Bureau of Law Enforcement Services Automated Data Report
I 20.61:	Annual Report of Indian Lands
I 20.61/2:	Annual Report of Indian Land and Income from Surface and Subsurface Leases
I 20.61/3:	Indian Forest Management (biannual)
I 20.62:	Posters
I 20.65:	BIA Administration Reports
I 20.66:	Southwestern Indian Polytechnic Institute, Catalog
I 20.67:	Horizons, Indian Mineral Resource (semiannual)

Each publication has additional numbers assigned to create a unique SuDocs number for that title. Some examples are the following:

HE 23.3002:AM 3	*American Indian Elderly: A National Profile*
I 29.2:C 16	*Canyon de Chelly: The Story of Its Ruins and People*
ED 1.319	*Indian Reading Series*
Y4.IN 2/11:S.hrg.99-207	*Gambling on Indian Reservations and Lands*
SI 1.43:2	*Ojibwa Dance Drum: Its History and Construction*

Reports on American Indians may be found with many different SuDocs numbers because they are issued by different departments and agencies such as the Interior Department, the Education Department, the Agriculture Department, and Health and Human Services. In addition, there are hundreds of congressional hearings and reports on American Indians.

Guides to U.S. Government Publications

335.   Morehead, Joe, and Mary Fetzer. **Introduction to United States Government Information Sources**. 4th ed. Englewood, CO: Libraries Unlimited, 1992. 474p. (Library Science Text Series). $38.50; $32.50pa. LC 92-13251. ISBN 0-87287-909-7; 1-56308-066-4pa.

This is a thorough and comprehensive guide to U.S. government publications. Thirteen chapters divide the guide and include sections on catalogs and indexes, branches of government, departments and agencies, the judiciary, statistical sources, technical report literature, and government periodicals. This excellent textbook is filled with illustrations and explanations and includes indexes by subject, title/series, and personal name.

336.   Robinson, Judith Schiek. **Tapping the Government Grapevine: The User-Friendly Guide to U.S. Government Information Sources**. 2d ed. Phoenix, AZ: Oryx Press, 1993. 227p. $34.50pa. LC 92-40201. ISBN 0-89774-712-7.

Another useful guide to government documents, this one attempts to simplify the search process and sources available. Robinson has produced a teaching aid for librarians and students that answers questions of what, who, why, when, how, and where for each chapter on bibliographies and indexes; scientific information; patents, trademarks, and copyrights; legislative information; regulations; executive branch and judicial branch information; statistics; and other fields of coverage in government publications. She enhances the text with search tips, illustrations, and explanations on using government sources. References for further reading are included at the end of each chapter, along with exercises for practicing use of the sources covered. Robinson compares favorably with Morehead (entry 335) and provides excellent guidance in navigating the world of government publications.

337.   Sears, Jean L., and Marilyn K. Moody. **Using Government Publications. Vol. 1: Searching by Subjects and Agencies. Vol. 2: Finding Statistics and Using Special Techniques**. Phoenix, AZ: Oryx Press, 1985. Vol. 1, 216p. $41.50, LC 83-43249, ISBN 0-89774-094-7. Vol. 2, 231p. $41.50, LC 83-43249, ISBN 0-89774-124-2.

A somewhat older set describing government publications, Sears's volumes are organized differently from Morehead (entry 335) and Robinson (entry 336). Arranged by subjects in volume 1, this guide focuses on specific areas of research, such as foreign policy, occupations, business aids, directories, tax information, travel information, climate, elections, maps, genealogy, agriculture, education, geology, health, and environmental and natural resources. Researchers may more easily focus on areas of research and tools used in those areas than in the two preceding guides. Volume 2 is concerned with statistical sources and is divided into chapters on such topics as population statistics, vital statistics, economic indicators, business and industry statistics, income, earnings, employment, prices, consumer expenditures, foreign trade statistics, crime and criminal justice statistics, defense and military statistics, energy statistics, and projects. Each section explains what is available to be searched: general sources, current sources, online databases, and other categories and sources of reports. The second half of volume 2 covers special techniques or strategies for locating information in historical, legislative, budgetary, technical, and specialized report areas. Some researchers will appreciate the more focused approach of Sears's guide.

Archival and Historical Material

This section deals with the official government archives of the United States. However, researchers will also discover specialized archives within museums, libraries, and universities. The section on directories of this guide will guide researchers to collections such as the Indiana University Archives of Traditional Music, which has one of the largest collections of North American Indian music, and the Thomas Gilcrease Institute of American History and Art Library, University of Oklahoma, with extensive materials on the Five Civilized Tribes. The University of Oklahoma

Western History Collections is one of the finest for Native American archival materials, and includes manuscripts, photographs, and sound recordings, as well as books. There are also archival collections of American Indian materials in countries outside the United States and Canada. A guide to some of these is *Time's Flotsam: Overseas Collections of California Indian Material Culture* by Thomas C. Blackburn and Travis Hudson (Santa Barbara, CA: Santa Barbara Museum of Natural History by Menlo Park, CA: Ballena, 1990. 224p. Ballena Press Anthropological Papers, no. 35. $34.95. LC 90-308. ISBN 0-87919-117-1). The advanced researcher will need to visit specialized archival collections for the extensive and rare materials available at museums and universities.

338.   Johnson, Steven L. **Guide to American Indian Documents in the Congressional Serial Set: 1817-1899**. New York: Clearwater, 1977. 503p. LC 75-45321. ISBN 0-88354-107-6.

The main source of historical government publications is the *U.S. Congressional Serial Set*, from 1789-present. The *Serial Set* is an ongoing series of volumes containing the reports and documents of the House and Senate and other reports by government agencies and commissions that were submitted to Congress. Although various indexes and finding aids are available for this monumental collection of materials, the best is the *CIS U.S. Serial Set Index, 1789-1969* (entry 347). The Johnson guide contains a chronological list of documents dealing primarily with U.S. government relations with Indians before 1900; this is a great assist for researchers in American Indian studies. The *Serial Set* contains more than 14,000 volumes, so this guide is a time-saver for the serious researcher seeking noncurrent documents such as the *Annual Reports of the Commissioner of Indian Affairs and the Secretary of War*.

Appendix I of *Guide to American Indian Documents in the Congressional Serial Set: 1817-1899* lists documents relevant to Indian affairs from 1817-1881 that were not published in the *Serial Set*. These are mainly publications from the Bureau of Indian Affairs and the Interior Department. The subject index is valuable for locating information on specific tribes and topics, and references are made to the chronological entries.

339.   Hill, Edward E., comp. **Guide to Records in the National Archives of the United States Relating to American Indians**. Washington, DC: National Archives and Records Service, General Services Administration, 1981. 467p. $25.00. LC 81-22357. ISBN 0-911333-13-4.

Hill's guide is a valuable, specialized supplement to the general *Guide to the National Archives of the United States* (entry 340). Hill makes the records in the National Archives better discovered and easier to use. The great mass of papers, photographs, recordings, maps, and films that deal with American Indians are described, including the Indians who lived along the international boundaries in Canada and Mexico. The record groups containing Indian materials are described for dozens of government departments and agencies, such as the Bureau of Indian Affairs, the Secretary of the Interior, the Bureau of Land Management, the Secretary of War, the U.S. Army Continental Commands, 1821-1920, and many other governmental divisions.

A detailed subject index is provided. The serious researcher must utilize this invaluable guide to determine what materials are available.

340. **Guide to the National Archives of the United States**. Washington, DC: National Archives and Records Administration, 1987. 896p. $25.00. LC 87-28205. ISBN 0-911333-23-1.

This reprint of the 1974 edition explains the whole mass of documents in the National Archives and how the materials are organized. Records are described from the legislative, judicial, and executive branches, the independent agencies, and other government bodies. This guide is a monumental achievement that describes the contents and scope of the multitude of noncurrent papers and reports preserved by the U.S. government.

341. Smithsonian Institution. National Museum of Natural History. Department of Anthropology. National Anthropological Archives. **A Catalog to Manuscripts at the National Anthropological Archives**. Boston: G. K. Hall, 1975. 4v. ISBN 0-8161-1194-4.

The Bureau of American Ethnology collected materials written on American Indians between 1879 and 1965, and these materials now comprise much of the material in the National Anthropological Archives. The catalog lists over 6,000 manuscript collections, including correspondence, maps, vocabularies, grammar notes, linguistic texts, field notes, journals, and Bureau of American Ethnology administrative records.

The first section of the catalog lists manuscripts on Indians north of Mexico by tribe, linguistic group, name of individual, and sometimes by descriptive heading. These manuscripts are only for the most serious researchers interested in breaking new ground.

342. Szucs, Loretto Dennis, and Sandra Hargreaves Luebking. **The Archives: A Guide to the National Archives Field Branches**. Salt Lake City, UT: Ancestry, 1988. 340p. $35.95. LC 87-70108. ISBN 0-916489-23-X.

The Archives is divided into three broad sections. Section I explains the holdings of the National Archives Field Branches in Atlanta, Boston, Chicago, Denver, Fort Worth, Kansas City, Los Angeles, New York, Philadelphia, San Francisco, and Seattle. For example, the Los Angeles branch maintains the permanently valuable federal records of the Pacific Southwest region, including the records from 11 southern counties of California, Arizona, and Nevada. Explanations are supplied for the amount and types of information kept in that branch. Records of the Bureau of Indian Affairs constitute the second-largest collection of records there, covering southern California, Arizona, and some from New Mexico.

Section II covers textual and microfilm holding in common to all or several branches of the National Archives. Section III is a listing of the 149 record groups available at the various field branches. These include everything from the National Aeronautics and Space Administration to the Centers for Disease Control to the Supreme Court to the Bureau of Indian Affairs. This section summarizes, for example, that the Los Angeles branch has 38 collections of records from various Indian agencies such as the La Jolla Superintendency, 1909-1911, and the Pala Subagency, 1922-1947.

343. Viola, Herman J. **The National Archives of the United States**. New York: Harry N. Abrams, 1984. 287p. $49.50. LC 84-2889. ISBN 0-8109-1367-4.

This beautifully illustrated volume on the National Archives and its contents shows the types of materials preserved and the purposes for the archives. The beginning researcher will get inspired looking at the photographs of materials to be explored, such as the family tree and marriage license submitted to the Bureau of Indian Affairs in 1907 by members of the Brown family as proof of their Chickasaw ancestry (p. 177).

343a. Ross, Norman A., ed. **Index to the Decisions of the Indian Claims Commission**. New York: Clearwater, 1973. 158p. LC 72-13850. ISBN 0-88354-001-0.

The Indian Claims Commission was formed in 1946 to hear and determine claims by Indian tribes against the United States arising prior to August 13, 1946. This volume indexes the 370 petitions and 611 claims filed with the Commission from August 1946 through August 1973. The indexes include a Tribal Index, Docket Index, and Table of Cases. The result was the determination of the areas of land claimed by the Indians, and the value of the land for monetary disposition. A microfiche collection of the cases accompanies the index in most libraries. Another important tool for researching Indian claims is the *Index to the Expert Testimony Before the Indian Claims Commission: The Written Reports* (Ross, Norman A., ed. New York: Clearwater, 1973. 102p. LC 72-13851. ISBN 0-88354-002-9), with a microfiche collection with it.

343b. Hill, Edward E. **The Office of Indian Affairs, 1824-1880: Historical Sketches**. New York: Clearwater, 1974. 246p. LC 73-16321. ISBN 0-88354-105-X.

There is a microfilm collection for the BIA correspondence received between 1824-1880 which provides valuable insight on the state of Indian affairs during that time. Researchers may use this guide to the collection produced by the National Archives and Records Service to locate needed microfilm reels. The majority of this guide is devoted to brief histories of superintendencies and agencies. There is a tribal index and a jurisdictional index, which allow the serious researcher to locate the units under study.

Indexes, Abstracts, and Databases

There are many access tools for locating government publications. These include printed and computerized sources for congressional, executive, and judicial information. The major sources are listed below.

General

344. **Monthly Catalog of United States Government Publications**. Washington, DC: U.S. Government Printing Office, 1895-. monthly, $201.00/yr. ISSN 0362-6830.

The *Monthly Catalog* is the standard index for government reports. Most of the publications included are depository and available for use at depository libraries, although some are only for sale through the Government Printing Office, NTIS (National Technical Information Service), or directly from the issuing agency.

The monthly and annual indexes list subjects (Library of Congress Subject Headings): authors; titles; key words; and series, report, and contract numbers. The indexes also provide the SuDocs numbers needed to locate the government reports on the shelves. Use the cumulative subject index to the *Monthly Catalog 1900-1971* for the older years. Several computerized equivalents of the *Monthly Catalog* are available on compact disc from July 1976-present. These are the fastest routes to locating publicly available documents. The *Monthly Catalog* is also online through commercial vendors such as DIALOG.

345. **Government Reports Announcements & Index**. Springfield, VA: U.S. Department of Commerce, National Technical Information Service (NTIS), 1975-. semi-monthly, $535.00. (Continues **Government Reports Announcements, 1946-1975**). ISSN 0097-9007.

NTIS, an agency of the U.S. Department of Commerce, is the central source for processing and selling technical reports from other government agencies and from foreign governments. The reports are abstracted and indexed in *Government Reports Announcements & Index*, and prices and order information are provided. These materials are primarily U.S. government-sponsored research, development, and engineering reports but also include social, business, and economic reports. Approximately 2 million reports are contained in the set, with some 6,000 reports added each month. The quarterly issues cumulate into *Government Reports Annual Index*. Thirty-eight broad subject categories (e.g., behavior and society, business and economics, health care, medicine and biology, transportation) are further separated into over 350 subcategories. The key word index is the specific subject approach, with additional indexes for personal authors, corporate authors, contract/grant numbers, and NTIS order/report numbers. Key word indexes list reports on such topics as the Indian Health Service, Indian lands, Indian reservations, Navajo Indians and other tribes, and native peoples. Most of the reports deal with topics such as the management and protection of Indians lands, the reservation environment, fisheries, logging, and community wastewater. Some reports are produced on social, linguistic, and education issues of American Indians. The *NTIS Bibliographic Database* is the computerized equivalent of *Government Reports Announcements & Index* and includes all documents received and processed by NTIS since 1964. *NTIS* is online through BRS, DIALOG, and other vendors and is on CD-ROM. The electronic *NTIS* allows for title searching whereas the printed index does not.

Congressional Information

Congressional Information Service, Inc., publishes many important indexes and guides for U.S. government information. These include the *CIS Index to Unpublished U.S. House of Representatives Committee Hearings, CIS Index to Unpublished U.S. Senate Committee Hearings, CIS Congressional Committee Prints Index, CIS Congressional Committee Hearings Index, CIS U.S. Senate Executive Documents & Reports, CIS Index to U.S. Executive Branch Documents, 1789-1909*, and *CIS Index to Presidential Executive Orders & Proclamations, 1789-1983*. Only the two most important CIS indexes are listed here. Most research libraries with government documents divisions offer specialized research assistance with these tools. Consult a reference librarian for your detailed research needs.

346. **CIS Index to Publications of the United States Congress**. Bethesda, MD: Congressional Information Service, 1970-. price varies. ISSN 0007-8514.

The *CIS Index* covers an array of publications from the U.S. Congress. These include congressional hearings, House and Senate reports and documents, committee prints, Senate executive reports, Senate treaty documents, legislative histories, and special publications of the House and Senate. An index volume and an abstract volume for each year cover 1970 to date. Researchers in American Indian studies will be especially interested in congressional hearings on Indian concerns. These hearings may be exploratory or investigative and often provide testimony and information on issues of public concern. For older materials, use the *CIS U.S. Serial Set Index* (entry 347). The *CIS Index* is online via DIALOG and is available on CD-ROM from Congressional Information Service, Inc. as *Congressional Masterfile 2*.

347. **CIS U.S. Serial Set Index 1789-1969**. Bethesda, MD: Congressional Information Service, 1975. 36v. LC 75-27448.

The *U.S. Congressional Serial Set*, known as the *Serial Set*, is a serially numbered collection of congressional publications dating back to 1789. It includes House and Senate reports and documents, the *American State Papers*, and other non-congressional materials. The *Serial Set* is a rich source of historical materials for serious researchers. The Johnson guide (entry 338) and other guides to government publications listed earlier in this chapter discuss the many indexes and guides available for searching these historical sources. The most important is the *CIS U.S. Serial Set Index 1789-1969*, which effectively permits researchers to bypass these other tools.

The indexes provide coverage by subjects and key words as well as a number of other access points. The 36 volumes of the *CIS U.S. Serial Set Index 1789-1969* are divided into groups of congresses and years (e.g., 1789-1857, 1857-1879). The subject arrangement is under topics such as "Indians," "Appropriation, Indian Affairs," "Hostile," "Hostilities," "Depredations," "Wild," "Boundary," "Difficulties," "Disturbances," "Half Breed," "Indian Territory," and "Indian Wars," and under names of tribes and reservations. Researchers can quickly figure out that most of the reports and documents during these early years deal with money paid by the government to Indians for treaties and settlements and with problems the government had with Indians.

The *American State Papers*, indexed in the *CIS U.S. Serial Set Index 1789-1969*, is a large collection of executive and legislative documents of the first 14 congresses, 1789-1823, grouped by subject categories such as "Indian Affairs," "Foreign Affairs," and "Public Lands." The *New American State Papers 1789-1860* (Wilmington, DE: Scholarly Resources, 1972) comprises 13 volumes on Indian affairs covering the formative years of our country. These volumes were drawn from three major sources: the original *American State Papers*, the serial volumes of the official documents of the U.S. Congress printed continuously after 1817, and the Legislative Records Section of the National Archives in Washington, D.C. These primary source reprints are important materials reflecting the relations between the federal government and Indians at that time. There are government reports concerning treaties, agreements, settlements, expenditures, letters, correspondence, and congressional reports and documents. For example, pages 115-436 of volume 10, *Indian Affairs*, of the *New American State Papers* deal with removal of the Cherokees around 1836. This is fascinating reading for the researcher looking for primary source material.

The Congressional Information Service has even further simplified and streamlined historical searching with its CD-ROM database called *Congressional Masterfile 1*. This merges the CIS indexes to the *Serial Set*, published and unpublished committee hearings, committee prints, and Senate Executive Documents and Reports from 1789-1969. Many *Serial Set* publications after 1969 are indexed in the *CIS Index* (entry 346).

Laws

348. **United States Code. Title 25. Indians**. Washington, DC: U.S. Congress. House, 1926-. Every 6 years, with annual supplements. $57.00. (revised April 1, 1993).

The *United States Code* is a consolidation and codification of the general and permanent laws of the country. It is arranged under titles, with *Title 25* covering laws related to American Indians. The *Code* is updated every six years, with annual cumulative supplements, and is available on CD-ROM.

New laws are issued initially as slip laws, then in chronological order in the *United States Statutes at Large*. Later, they are arranged in subject order in the *U.S. Code*. Other commercial publications of the laws include the *U.S. Code Congressional and Administrative News*, the *United States Code Annotated*, and the *United States Code Service*. The computerized systems *WESTLAW* and *LEXIS* offer the full text of the laws.

For summaries of current key congressional bills and laws, researchers may want to start with *CQ Weekly Report* or the *CQ Almanac*.

348a. Getches, David H., Charles F. Wilkinson, and Robert A. Williams, Jr. **Federal Indian Law, Cases and Materials**. 3d ed. St. Paul, MN: West, 1993. 1,055p. (American Casebook Series). $46.00. ISBN 0-3140-2268-6.

This excellent handbook to Indian law reveals the complexity of the topic, with an overview of Indian law, the history of federal Indian law, and policy stemming from the era of discovery and Spanish and English colonial law to the formative years of the European founding of the country to the shifting policies of the contemporary era. Important cases are summarized, criminal and civil jurisdiction analyzed, and topics concerning taxation and regulation, Indian religion and culture, water rights, fishing and hunting rights, and the rights of Alaska Natives and Native Hawaiians are discussed through legislation and court cases. Researchers should consult a law library for additional materials or contact the Native American Rights Fund (NARF) (1506 Broadway, Boulder, CO 80302, 303-447-8760).

A listing of legal materials on American Indians held by 28 law libraries in the United States is *American Indian Legal Materials: A Union List* compiled by Laura N. Gasaway, James L. Hoover, and Dorothy M. Warden (New York: Earl M. Coleman Enterprises, 1980. 152p. [American Indians at Law Series]. LC 79-22718. ISBN 0-930576-31-4). Handbooks are also available as brief guides for understanding the complexity of the laws affecting Indians. Three good examples are *The Rights of Indians and Tribes, the Basic ACLU Guide to Indian and Tribal Rights*, by Stephen L. Pevar (Carbondale, IL: Southern Illinois University, 1992. 338p. [An American Civil Liberties Union Handbook]. $7.50. LC 91-11872. ISBN 0-9093-1768-0), the reprint of the U.S. government one from 1942: *Handbook of Federal Indian Law, with Reference Tables and Index* by Felix S. Cohen (Buffalo, NY: W. S. Hein. 662p. $78.00. ISBN 0-89941-671-3) and *American Indian Law in a Nutshell*, 2d ed., by William C. Canby, Jr. (St. Paul, MN: West, 1993. 336p. [Nutshell Series]. $15.95pa. ISBN 0-314-41160-7).

Treaties

Volume 7 of the *United States Statutes at Large* contains the texts of Indian treaties from 1778-1842. After that, treaties and agreements between the U.S. government and tribes are printed in the *United States Statutes at Large* in chronological order. The guides below provide identification and compilations of treaties.

349. **A Chronological List of Treaties and Agreements Made by Indian Tribes with the United States**. Oklahoma City, OK: Institute for the Development of Indian Law. (American Indian Treaty Series, No. 9). $5.00. ISBN 0-944253-19-9.

This is a listing of all Indian treaties and agreements, ratified or unratified, covering 1778-1909, in chronological order.

350. Kappler, Charles J., comp. and ed. **Indian Affairs: Laws and Treaties**. Washington, DC: U.S. Government Printing Office, 1904-1941. 5v. Repr., New York: AMS, 1978. 5v. $895.00. LC 78-128994. ISBN 0-404-06710-7. Vol. 2: **Indian Treaties, 1778-1883**. Repr., New York: Interland, 1972. 1,099p. ISBN 0879890258. **Kappler's Indian Affairs: Laws and Treaties**. Vols. 6, 7. Washington, DC: U.S. Government Printing Office, 1979. $22.00/set (vols. 6 and 7).

The first five volumes provide a record of the relationship between Indians and the federal government from 1778-1938. Included are treaties from 1778-1871, when the last treaty was made, records of sales of Indian lands, statistics on tribes and agencies, presidential proclamations, reservation establishment records, U.S. Supreme Court decisions, and laws. Volume 1 contains laws, executive orders, and proclamations related to Indians from 1871-1902; volume 2 contains the texts of all treaties and agreements between the federal government and Indians. This volume was reprinted in 1972 under the title *Indian Treaties, 1778-1883*. Volume 3 is a compilation of laws through 1912 that were subject to adjudication; volume 4 contains laws, unratified treaties, the text of *Title 25* of the *U.S. Code*, and discussions of legal matters related to Indians; volume 5 is an update of the laws in the compilation through 1938. An index is provided in the back of each volume.

The original five-volume set contains treaties and laws enacted through the 75th Congress. Volumes 6 and 7, published in 1979, supplement the original set by extending the work to include all treaties, laws, executive orders, and regulations relating to Indian affairs in force on September 1, 1967.

351. Prucha, Frances Paul, ed. **Documents of United States Indian Policy**. 2d ed. Lincoln: University of Nebraska, 1990. 338p. $37.50. LC 89-16408. ISBN 0-8032-3688-3.

In this one volume, Prucha lists almost 200 documents relevant to government policies toward American Indians. These include statutes, U.S. Supreme Court decisions, and treaties and agreements from the past and present. Another source of treaties by the Confederate states is *Jefferson Davis and the Confederacy and Treaties Concluded by the Confederate States with Indian Tribes*, edited by Ronald Gibson (Dobbs Ferry, NY: Oceana, 1977. 205p. $18.00. LC 77-10189. ISBN 0-379-12095-X).

351a. Washburn, Wilcomb E. **The American Indian and the United States: A Documentary History**. New York: Random House, 1973. 4v. LC 72-10259. ISBN 0-394-47283-7.

This impressive guide to relations between the U.S. government and American Indians reproduces important government documents, reports, congressional debates, laws, treaties, and legal decisions as evidence of the treatment of Indians by the government. It covers Reports of the Commissioners of Indian Affairs in volumes 1 and 2, congressional debates on Indian affairs in volumes 2 and 3, acts, ordinances, and proclamations in volume 3, Indian treaties in volumes 3 and 4, and legal decisions in volume 4. Prucha (entry 351) and this guide are concerned with government-produced documents and treaties. For speeches and congressional testimony given by Indians to express their points of view about the government policies, check books on Indian oratory, such as *Great Documents in American Indian History* by Wayne Moquin and Charles Van Doren (New York: Praeger, 1973. 416p. LC 72-80583).

Regulations

352. Office of the Federal Register. National Archives and Records Administration. **Code of Federal Regulations, Title 25 Indians**. Washington, DC: U.S. Government Printing Office, 1939-. annual, $31.00.

Rules and regulations of the federal government are printed in 50 titles of the *Code of Federal Regulations (CFR),* creating around 175 volumes. These are not congressional laws or judicial opinions but administrative regulations written by executive agencies.

Title 25 of the *CFR* covers regulations of the Bureau of Indian Affairs, the Indian Claims Commission, the Indian Arts and Crafts Board, and the Navajo and Hopi Indian Relocation Commission. The *Federal Register* provides daily updates of the *CFR* to document changes and additions in federal agency regulations and new presidential proclamations and executive orders. The *Federal Register* is available on CD-ROM, covering the most current six months, and is online through DIALOG.

Statistics

353. **American Statistics Index (ASI).** Bethesda, MD: Congressional Information Service, 1973-. monthly, price varies. ISSN 0091-1658.

ASI is the best source for determining whether the federal government has compiled statistics on a subject and where those statistics are found. *ASI* is a master index to U.S. government statistics in government periodicals, congressional hearings, and other reports as well as statistical sources published separately. *ASI* indexes and abstracts statistical publications of the executive branch, Congress, the judiciary, and other federal government entities. The abstracts enable researchers to determine the scope of the statistics available. Although begun in 1973, *ASI*'s first issue, *ASI Annual & Retrospective Edition*, provides selective indexing and abstracting for publications issued from the 1960s to January 1974. *ASI* is available as an online database through DIALOG and also on CD-ROM through the *CIS Statistical Masterfile*.

Congressional Information Service, Inc. also produces the *Statistical Reference Index (SRI)* for statistics produced by non-federal government sources, such as associations, business organizations, commercial publishers, independent research organizations, state governments, and universities. *SRI* is also part of the CD-ROM product from CIS called *Statistical Masterfile*.

354. **Statistical Abstract of the United States**. Washington, DC: U.S. Government Printing Office, 1878-. annual, $29.00pa. ISSN 0-16-038080.

This is the first stop for most researchers in locating statistics on any topic. The *Statistical Abstract* is a convenient and quick way to determine whether the U.S. government compiles statistics on a particular topic and what the original source is for the statistics. Also, statistics from private sources are listed and cited. Researchers will praise a new title edited by Marlita A. Reddy, *Statistical Record of Native North Americans* (Detroit: Gale Research, 1993) which compiles U.S. government and privately published statistics on native populations of the United States and Canada.

354a. Reddy, Marlita A., ed. **Statistical Record of Native North America**. Detroit, MI: Gale Research, 1993. 1,659p. $89.50. ISBN 0-8103-8963-0.

This extraordinary volume compiles statistics from the U.S. government, state governments, tribal governments, associations and other organizations on Indians of the United States and Canada. Many of the statistics would be difficult to locate separately, and much of the information is not even available in published format. The range of statistics is historical to current, from population estimates of pre-Columbian contact population to projections for 2040. United States and Canadian Census data are reformatted and easier to use for locating specific statistics. The arrangement is by 12 chapters on broad topics: history, demographics, the family, education, culture and tradition, health and health care, social and economic conditions, business and industry, land and water management, government relations, law and law enforcement, and Canada. Some of the census tables only cover through 1980, while some are current through 1990. The thorough coverage of Canadian statistics is something most libraries will not have in any other source. The sources used in this important work are listed and indexed in the detailed keyword index, which includes 3,000 subjects, names, people, tribes, organizations, and places. Students on all levels will turn to this handy source for a wide variety of statistics concerning Native Americans.

For more maps detailing historical statistics on tribal populations, reservation lands and other government statistics, use the *Atlas of American Indian Affairs* by Francis Paul Prucha (Lincoln, NE: University of Nebraska, 1990. 191p. $50.00. LC 90-675000. ISBN 0-8032-3689-1). For a shorter handbook of useful facts and figures on American Indians drawn from U.S. government sources, there is *Nations Within a Nation, Historical Statistics of American Indians* by Paul Stuart (Westport, CT: Greenwood, 1987. 251p. $55.00. LC 86-33618. ISBN 0-313-23813-8).

Census

The U.S. Census Bureau conducts the decennial census to collect data on families, heads of households, housing, and other social, demographic, and economic factors such as age, race, marital status, income, and so forth. The 1990 Decennial Census marked the 200th anniversary of the general census. Census Bureau statistics are available in print and online databases and on CD-ROM, floppy disc, microfiche, and magnetic tape. The bulk of the census data is only available in computerized format. *CENDATA* is the online system from the Census Bureau that provides current statistics, news releases, and ordering information. *CENDATA* is available through DIALOG and CompuServe.

355. **1990 Census of Population and Housing.** Washington, DC: U.S. Bureau of the Census, 1992. CD-ROM.

The most efficient way to obtain census statistics is through the CD-ROM database version, available in most large libraries. The CD-ROM database of the census for population and housing is very easy and quick to use. Information is available from the Summary Tape Files (STF) for the United States as a whole and by each state.

Under the U.S. Summary, *1990 Census of Population and Housing (STF 3C),* choices are given for searching "American Indian Reservation," "Tribal Jurisdiction Statistical Area," "Tribal Designated Statistical Area," and "Alaska Native Village." Under "American Indian Reservation" is an alphabetical list of the reservations. Under each reservation are choices of data for such topics as persons, families, sex, age, race, household type, language spoken at home, ancestry, marital status, place of birth, place of work, travel time to work, school enrollment, educational attainment, period of military service, sex by employment status, occupation, household income, earnings, poverty status, housing units, rooms, source of water, sewage disposal, year structure built, bedrooms, kitchen facilities, plumbing facilities, and value of housing. It is easy to check under Acoma Pueblo and locate per capita income in 1989 ($4,130) and median family income in 1989 ($14,049).

For those with access to print materials only, the following publications are available:

356. U.S. Commerce Department. Census Bureau. Economics and Statistics Administration. Population Division. **Census of Population, 1990. General Population Characteristics: American Indian and Alaska Native Areas**. Washington, DC: U.S. Government Printing Office, 1993. 638p. $36.00. ($45.00/foreign).

357. U.S. Commerce Department. Census Bureau. Economics and Statistics Administration. **Census of Housing, 1990. General Housing Characteristics: American Indian and Alaska Native Areas**. Washington, DC: U.S. Government Printing Office, 1992. 638p. $35.00 ($43.75/foreign).

MICROFORM COLLECTIONS

Thousands of research items on American Indians have been reproduced in microform. Most of these are on either microfilm or microfiche and are detailed primary-source materials for serious researchers needing in-depth information on specialized topics. The publishing companies and the National Archives, which produce these microforms, provide catalogs of their products. These catalogs should be consulted for the latest information on titles and prices. The sources presented below are guides to the available microforms.

358. Dodson, Suzanne Cates. **Microform Research Collections: A Guide.** 2d ed. Westport, CT: Meckler, 1984. 670p. $125.00. ISBN 0930466667.

Dodson's guide lists many special microform sets on American Indians. These include such items as books and collections of books from the eighteenth century forward, Indian newspapers and periodicals, government reports and congressional hearings, association papers, oral histories, collected personal papers of individuals working with Indians, tribal meetings, Indian activist group meetings, early pioneer accounts, religious organization reports, and other esoteric materials.

359. **American Indians: A Select Catalog of National Archives Microfilm Publications**. 1984. Repr., Washington, DC: National Archives and Records Administration, 1991. 96p. LC 83-13412. ISBN 0-911333-09-6.

Since 1941, the National Archives has microfilmed groups of selected federal records that have high research value. This catalog is designed to increase public awareness of the availability of the National Archives records on American Indians. Thousands of files are available, such as the Records of the Bureau of Indian Affairs, the Records of the Indian Division of the Office of the

Secretary of the Interior, the Records Relating to Indian Treaties, the Records Relating to Territories, and the Records of Miscellaneous Civilian Agencies. Individual reels of microfilm can be ordered for $23.00/reel from the National Archives or from Scholarly Resources, Inc. (104 Greenhill Avenue, Wilmington, DE 19805-1897; (800) 772-8937).

359a. Grimshaw, Polly Swift. **Images of the Other: A Guide to Microform Manuscripts on Indian-White Relations**. Champaign, IL: University of Illinois, 1991. 174p. $27.50. LC 90-45132. ISBN 0-252-01759-5.

This guide provides lengthy descriptions of 65 manuscript collections that have been reproduced on microform. The documents are grouped into seven categories: reports of government agencies, missionary letters, treaties, reservations, Indian reform organizations, Indian constitutions, laws and tribal code, and other manuscript sources. The time period covers 1631 to 1978, and examples include the annual reports of the commissioners of the Bureau of Indian Affairs, the ratified Indian treaties, 1722-1869, the Indian removals, and the Indian Rights Association papers. Information is given on the companies and organizations that originally produced the sets. These materials are for the serious researcher seeking primary sources.

360. **Guide to Microforms in Print, Incorporating International Microforms in Print**. Munich, Germany: K. G. Saur, 1990-. 1993 annual supplement, $145.00. ISBN 3-598-10930-X.

Guide to Microforms in Print is a comprehensive, international source for currently available books, journals, newspapers, government publications, archival materials, and other special collections and projects on microform. The subject volume is arranged by the Dewey Decimal classification, making it difficult for researchers to locate sets for which they are unfamiliar. There is no specific subject index. Entries for American Indians are under classes such as 970 (North American History), 971 (Canadian History), 301 (Anthropology, General), and 306 (Anthropology, Social). A related annual title is *Serials in Microform*, published by University Microfilms International.

361. **Microform Review**. Munich, Germany: K. G. Saur, 1972-. quarterly. $140.00. ISSN 0002-6530.

Microform Review is the primary source for reviews of microform collections. An article by Timothy Troy titled "American Indian Materials in Microform: An Overview" (*Microform Review* Vol. 16, No. 2, Spring 1987, pp. 112-17) provides an excellent survey of American Indian materials available up to 1987 in microform. Troy makes recommendations on what size and type of library should purchase these collections. Because of the high prices of most collections and the esoteric subject matter, most libraries will have only a few. Troy discusses the various types of collections published, such as Indian periodicals and newspapers, monographs, personal papers, oral histories, and government documents. He also lists reviews of material on American Indians appearing in *Microform Review*.

362. **Bibliographic Guide to Microform Publications**. Boston: G. K. Hall, 1987-. annual, $260.00. ISSN 0891-3749.

The *Bibliographic Guide to Microform Publications* lists microforms cataloged during the previous year by the New York Public Library and the Library of Congress. Each year there are entries under "Indians of North America" for items such as nineteenth-century books, congressional reports, monographs on captivities, and other nonserial microforms either filmed by these two libraries or purchased for their collections from commercial publishers.

The following list of microform collections are some of the most important ones for scholarly research on topics in American Indian studies. Graduate students and faculty may utilize these for analysis of Indian issues where primary-source materials are important. Only large research libraries will hold many of these titles, but serious scholars should be aware of their existence as unique materials, preserved for those patient enough to investigate their contents.

363. **The Alaska Mission Collection of the Oregon Province Archives of the Society of Jesus**. Wilmington, DE: Scholarly Resources, 1980. $3,150.00. (42 rolls of 35mm microfilm with guide).

364. **The Alaska Indian Language Collection of the Oregon Province Archives of the Society of Jesus**. Wilmington, DE: Scholarly Resources, 1976. $2,100.00. (28 rolls of 35mm microfilm with guide).

365. **American Indian Periodicals from the Princeton University Library, 1839-1982**. Bethesda, MD: University Publications of America. Part I, $6,535.00; Part II, $1,310. (Part I: 95 titles on 401 microfiche and 2 reels of microfilm with printed guide; Part II: 34 titles on 401 microfiche and 2 reels of microfilm with printed guide).

366. **American Indian Periodicals from the State Historical Society of Wisconsin, 1884-1981**. Bethesda, MD: University Publications of America. $770.00. (40 titles on 13 reels of 35mm microfilm with printed guide).

367. **Constitutions and Laws of the American Indian**. Millwood, NY: Kraus. $360.00. (7 reels of 35mm microfilm with hardbound copy of **A Bibliography of the Constitutions and Laws of the American Indians,** by Lester Hargrett, Cambridge, MA: Harvard University Press, 1947, and a listing of the titles filmed).

368. **Duke Indian Oral History Collection**. Millwood, NY: Kraus, 1972. $1,450.00. (310 microfiche with index on 8 reels of 35mm microfilm).

369. **FBI File on Osage Indian Murders**. Wilmington, DE: Scholarly Resources, 1986. $225.00. (3 rolls of 35mm microfilm with guide).

370. **The FBI Files on the American Indian Movement and Wounded Knee**. Bethesda, MD: University Publications of America, 1986. $1,985. (26 reels of 35mm microfilm with printed guide). ISBN 0-89093-989-6.

371.   Harrington, John Peabody. **The Papers of John Peabody Harrington in the Smithsonian Institution, 1907-1957**. Millwood, NY: Kraus. Prepared in the National Anthropological Archives, Department of Anthropology, National Museum of Natural History, Washington, DC. Edited by Elaine L. Mills and Ann J. Brickfield, 1982-1991. Part 1: **Alaska/Northwest Coast**, $1,500.00. 30 reels of 35mm microfilm and paper guide/index, 1982; Part 2: **Northern and Central California**, $5,050.00. 101 reels of 35mm microfilm and paper guide/index, 1985; Part 3: **Southern California/Basin**, $9,100.00. 182 reels of 35mm microfilm and paper guide/index, 1986; Part 4: **Southwest**, $2,900.00. 58 reels of 35mm microfilm and paper guide/index, 1986; Part 5: **Plains**, $850.00. 17 reels of 35mm microfilm and paper guide/index, 1987; Part 6: **Northeast/Southeast**, $900.00. 18 reels of 35mm microfilm and paper guide/index, 1987; Part 7: **Mexico/Central America/South America**, $ 1,800.00. 36 reels of 35mm microfilm and paper guide/index, 1988; Part 8: **Notes and Writings on Special Linguistics Studies**, $1,750.00. 35 reels of 35mm microfilm and paper guide/index, 1989; Part 9: **Correspondence and Financial Records**, $850.00. 17 reels of 35mm microfilm and paper guide/index, 1991. A printed guide to the Harrington collection field notes is *John Peabody Harrington: The Man and His California Fieldnotes* by Jane MacLaren Walsh of the Smithsonian Institution (Ramona, CA: Ballena, 1976. 58p. ISBN 0-87919-061-2).

372.   **Indian Pioneer Papers: 1860-1935**. Millwood, NY: Kraus, 1981. $3,057.00. (1,019 microfiche).

373.   **The Indian Rights Association, 1885-1901**. Wilmington, DE: Scholarly Resources, 1972. $1,950.00. (26 rolls of 35mm microfilm).

374.   **The Lake Mohonk Conference of Friends of the Indian: Annual Reports**. Bethesda, MD: University Publications of America, 1975. $260.00. (80 microfiche).

375.   **Major Council Meetings of American Indian Tribes**. Bethesda, MD: University Publications of America, 1982. $4,310.00/set. Part One, Section I: **1914-1956: Navaho, Five Civilized Tribes, Ute, Pueblo, Cheyenne, and Arapaho**, $1,135.00. ISBN 0-89093-406-1; Part One, Section II: **1911-1956: Sioux (Standing Rock, Rosebud, Pine Ridge, and Cheyenne River), Chippewa, and Klamath**, $1,135.00. ISBN 0-89093-407-X; Part Two, Section I: **1957-1971: Navaho, Five Civilized Tribes, Ute, Pueblo, Cheyenne, and Arapaho**, $1,225.00. ISBN 0-89093-408-8; Part Two, Section II: **1957-1971: Sioux (Standing Rock, Rosebud, Pine Ridge, and Cheyenne River), Chippewa, and Klamath**, $1,045.00. ISBN 0-89093-409-6.

376.   **Native Americans and the New Deal: The Office Files of John Collier, 1933-1945**. Bethesda, MD: University Publications of America, 1993. $2,040.00. (18 reels of 35mm microfilm with printed guide). ISBN 1-55655-491-5.

377.   **The Native Americans Reference Collection: Documents Collected by the Office of Indian Affairs**. Bethesda, MD: University Publications of America, 1991. Part I, 1840-1900, $2,895.00. ISBN 1-55655-408-7 (29 reels of 35mm film); Part II, 1901-1948, $4,590. ISBN 1-55655-409-5 (46 reels of 35mm film), 1992.

378. **The Pacific Northwest Tribes Indian Language Collection of the Oregon Province Archives of the Society of Jesus**. Wilmington, DE: Scholarly Resources, 1976. $1,575.00. (21 rolls of 35mm microfilm with guide).

379. **The Pacific Northwest Tribes Missions Collection of the Oregon Province Archives of the Society of Jesus, 1853-1960**. Wilmington, DE: Scholarly Resources, 1986. $2,720.00. (34 rolls of 35mm microfilm with guide).

380. **The Papers of Carlos Montezuma, M.D.** Wilmington, DE: Scholarly Resources, 1984. $675.00. (9 rolls of 35mm microfilm, with guide).

381. **The Papers of the Society of American Indians, 1906-1946**. Wilmington, DE: Scholarly Resources, 1986. $750.00. (10 rolls of 35mm microfilm with guide). LC 86-24843.

382. **Records of the U.S. Indian Claims Commission**. Bethesda, MD: University Publications of America. $16,465.00. (6,128 microfiche with 2-volume printed guide).

383. **Reports of the Commissioner to the Five Civilized Tribes**. Bethesda, MD: University Publications of America, 1975. $250.00. (3 reels of 35mm microfilm with printed guide). ISBN 0-89093-005-8.

384. **Survey of Conditions of the Indians in the United States**. Bethesda, MD: University Publications of America, 1975. $665.00. (8 reels of 35mm microfilm with printed guide). ISBN 0-89093-004-X.

385. **Survey of Indian Reservations**. Bethesda, MD: University Publications of America, 1975. $265.00. (3 reels of 35mm microfilm with printed guide). ISBN 0-89093-011-2.

APPENDIX: LIBRARY OF CONGRESS SUBJECT HEADINGS

The *Library of Congress Subject Headings* provide the correct terms to use when looking for books by subjects in the computerized catalogs or card catalogs of libraries. There are four large volumes to the *Subject Headings*, which is published annually. This appendix was taken from the 15th edition (1991) and provides all the subject terms and cross-references from the set under:

Indians of North America

The researcher will find additional subject headings for some specific topics (e.g., Navajo Literature), specific people (e.g., Sitting Bull 1834-1890), and other American Indian topics, and should check under the most specific subjects needed.

Library of Congress classification numbers (combinations of letters and numerals) are listed in brackets ([]). They group specific subjects together (e.g., E98.A27 for Indians of North America — Aged). These class numbers allow the researcher to browse the bookstacks. When books are cataloged, author numbers are added to the last line of the classification numbers to create unique call numbers for each book.

Subjects are arranged from the general to the specific, with alphabetical subdivisions designated by dashes (—). Subjects are listed first, then Indian tribes by regions or states. All terms listed after BT, NT, RT, SA, and USE are correct subject terms as well as those listed alphabetically in bold print. Terms listed after UF are not used.

KEY: UF = used for
        BT = broader term
        NT = narrower term
        RT = related term
        SA = see also
        USE means to look under the following word or phrase instead of the one designated above it.
        (May Subd Geog) = May Subdivide Geographically

Indians of North America
 (May Subd Geog) [E77-E99]
 UF   American aborigines
      American Indians
      Indians of North America—
        Culture
      Indians of North America—
        Ethnology
      Indians of North America—
        United States
      Indians of the United States
      Native Americans
      North American Indians
 NT   Algonquian Indians
      Athapascan Indians
      Caddoan Indians
      Eskimos
      Mound-builders
      Ojibwa Indians
      Piegan Indians
      Sewee Indians
      Shoshoni Indians
      Tinne Indians
      United States—Civiliza-
        tion—Indian influences
—**Adoption**
 BT   Adoption
—**Aesthetics** *[E98]*
 BT   Aesthetics
—**African influences**
 BT   Africa—Civilization
—**Aged** *[E98.A27]*
 BT   Aged
— — **Mental health**
—**Agriculture** *[E98.A3]*
 NT   Indians of North
        America—Domestic
        animals
      Indians of North
        America—Irrigation
— — **Health aspects**
—**Alcohol use** *[E98.L7]*
 UF   Indians of North
        America—Liquor
        problem
 BT   Indians of North
        America—Beverages
—**Amusements**
 USE Indians of North
        America—Recreation
—**Anecdotes**
 UF   Indians of North
        America—Anecdotes,
        facetiae, satire, etc.
—**Anecdotes, facetiae, satire, etc.**
 USE Indians of North
        America—Anecdotes
      Indians of North
        America—Humor
—**Animals, Domestic**

 USE Indians of North
        America—Domestic
        animals
—**Anthropometry** *[E98.A55]*
 RT   Indians of North
        America—Craniology
—**Antiquities** *[E98.A6]*
 BT   United States—
        Antiquities
 NT   Adena culture
      Blackduck culture
      Folsom culture
      Hopewell culture
      Indians of North
        America—Implements
      Indians of North
        America—Pottery
      Kitchen-middens
      Mississippian culture
      Mound-builders
      Mounds
      Woodland culture
— — **Collection and preservation**
— — **Collectors and collecting**
      (May Subd Geog)
— — **Law and legislation**
      (Not Subd Geog)
— — **Private collections**
      (May Subd Geog)
— — **Religious aspects**
—**Appellate courts**
 BT   Appellate courts
      Indians of North
        America—Courts
—**Appropriations** *[E91-E93]*
 UF   Appropriations, Indian
      Indian Appropriations
 BT   Indians of North
        America—Govern-
        ment relations
—**Arbitration and award**
 BT   Arbitration and award
      Indians of North
        America—Legal
        status, laws, etc.
—**Architecture** *[E98.A63]*
 NT   Kivas
— — **Conservation and
      restoration**
—**Archives** *[E97.9]*
 BT   Archives
—**Armor** *[E98.A65]*
 UF   Indians of North
        America—Arms
        and armor
      Indians of North
        America—Weapons
—**Art** *[E98.A7]*
 BT   Art, Primitive
      Ethnic art—United
        States

 NT   Indians of North
        America—Embroidery
      Indians of North
        America—
        Feather-work
      Indians of North
        America—Metal-work
      Indians of North
        America—Painting
      Indians of North
        America—Sculpture
      Indians of North
        America—Shell
        engraving
      Indians of North
        America—
        Wood-carving
      Mound-builders—Art
      Quillwork
      Sandpaintings
— — **Endowments** *[E98.A7]*
— — **Exhibitions**
—**Arts** *[E98.A73]*
 UF   Arts, Indian
      Indian arts
— — **Management**
 BT   Arts—Management
—**Astrology**
 BT   Astrology
—**Astronomy**
—**Attitudes**
 BT   Attitude (Psychology)
—**Basket making** *[E98.B3]*
 BT   Indians of North
        America—Industries
—**Beading**
 USE Indians of North
        America—Beadwork
—**Beadwork**
 UF   Indians of North
        America—Beading
 BT   Indians of North
        America—Costume
        and adornment
 NT   Beadwork
      Wampum belts
—**Beverages**
 BT   Beverages
 NT   Indians of North
        America—Alcohol use
—**Bibliography** *[Z1209-Z1210]*
—**Biography** *[E89-E90]*
— — **History and criticism—
      Boats** *[E98.C2]*
 UF   Birch-bark canoes
 BT   Canoes and canoeing
 NT   Eskimos—Boats
—**Boxing**
 BT   Boxing
      Indians of North
        America—Sports

—Burial
USE Indians of North
America—Mortuary
customs
—**Business enterprises**
BT Indians of North
America—Commerce
Indians of North
America—Economic
conditions
Minority business
enterprises
—**Calendar** *[E98.C14]*
—**Captivities** *[E85-E87]*
BT Frontier and pioneer life
SA *subdivision* Captivity,
[dates] *under names*
of individual persons
—**Census** *[E98.C3]*
NT Indians of North
America—Population
—**Census, [date]**
—**Child welfare** *[E98.C5]*
BT Child welfare
Indians of North
America—Children
Indians of North
America—Public
welfare
NT Indians of North
America—Children—
Day care
Indians of North
America—Orphanages
—**Children** *[E98.C5]*
BT Children—United States
NT Indians of North
America—Child
welfare
Indians of North
America—Handi-
capped children
Indians of North
America—Orphanages
Indians of North
America—Youth
— — **Day care**
BT Day care centers
Indians of North
America—Child
welfare
— — **Legal status, laws, etc.**
BT Indians of North
America—
Domestic relations
Indians of North
America—Legal
status, laws, etc.
—**Chinese influences**
—**Chronology**
BT Chronology

—**Citizenship** *[E91-E93]*
Here are entered works on
United States citizenship of
American Indians. Works on tribal
citizenship of American Indians
are entered under Indians of North
America—Tribal citizenship.
BT Citizenship
—**City planning**
—**Civil rights**
BT Civil rights
NT Indians of North
America—Freedom
of religion
—**Claims** *[E98.C6]*
BT Indians of North
America—Legal
status, laws, etc.
—**Claims against** *[E98.C62]*
UF Indians of North
America—Claims
(against the Indians)
United States—Claims
against Indians of
North America
BT Indians of North
America—Legal
status, laws, etc.
—**Claims (against the Indians)**
USE Indians of North
America—Claims
against
—**Colonization**
(May Subd Geog)
—**Commerce** *[E98.C7]*
BT Commerce
NT Indians of North
America—Business
enterprises
Indians of North
America—Trading
posts
—**Constitutional law**
BT Constitutional law
Indians of North
America—Legal
status, laws, etc.
—**Costume and adornment**
[E98.C8]
BT Costume
RT Wampum
NT Indians of North
America—Beadwork
Indians of North
America—Footwear
Indians of North
America—Jewelry
Wampum belts
—**Councils** *[E98.C]*
—**Courts** *[E93]*
BT Courts

Indians of North
America—Legal
status, laws, etc.
NT Indians of North
America—
Appellate courts
—**Cradleboards**
USE Indians of North
America—Cradles
—**Cradles**
UF Indians of North
America—
Cradleboards
BT Cradles
—**Craniology** *[E98.C85]*
BT Indians of North
America—Physical
characteristics
RT Indians of North
America—
Anthropometry
—**Crime** *[E98.C87]*
UF Indian criminals
BT Crime
Criminals
NT Indians of North
America—Juvenile
delinquency
Indians of North
America—Wife abuse
—**Crimes against**
—**Criminal justice system**
[E98.C87]
BT Criminal justice,
Administration of—
Canada
Criminal justice,
Administration of—
United States
Indians of North
America—Govern-
ment relations
—**Cultural assimilation**
BT Indians, Treatment of—
North America
Indians of North
America—Govern-
ment relations
—**Culture**
USE *subdivision* Chinese,
[Egyptian, Transpa-
cific, etc.] *influences*
under Indians of
North America for
specific foreign
influences on the
culture of Indians
of North America
Indians of North
America

Indians of North America
—Culture *(Continued)*
    Indians of North
      America—Foreign
      influences
    Indians of North
      America—Hindu
      influences
—Customs
  USE Indians of North
      America—Social
      life and customs
—**Dances** *[E98.D2]*
  BT Indians of North
      America—Religion
      and mythology
      Indians of North
      America—Social
      life and customs
  NT Butterfly dance
      Calumet dance
      Corn maidens' dance
      Eagle dance
      Ghost dance
      O-kee-pa (Religious
      ceremony)
      Snake-dance
      Urine dance
      Wolf ritual
—**Dental care**
—**Dentistry**
  BT Indians of North
      America—Medicine
—Dentition
  USE Indians of North
      America—Teeth
—**Dictionaries**
  UF Indians of North
      America—
      Dictionaries and
      encyclopedias
—Dictionaries and encyclopedias
  USE Indians of North
      America—Dictionaries
      Indians of North
      America—
      Encyclopedias
—**Diseases** *(May Subd Geog)*
  [E98.D6]
  NT Indians of North
      America—Hospitals
—**Dogs**
  BT Indians of North
      America—Domestic
      animals
—**Dolls** *[E98.D65]*
  UF Dolls, Indian
  BT Indians of North
      America—Games
—**Domestic animals**

  UF Indians of North
      America—Animals,
      Domestic
  BT Indians of North
      America—Agriculture
  NT Indians of North
      America—Dogs
      Indians of North
      America—Horses
—**Domestic relations**
  BT Domestic relations
      Indians of North
      America—Legal
      status, laws, etc.
  NT Indians of North
      America—Children
      —Legal status, laws,
      etc.
—**Drama**
—**Drinking vessels**
—**Drug use** *[E98.N5]*
  UF Indians of North
      America—Narcotics
—**Dwellings** *[E98.D9]*
  Here are entered works on the
architecture, construction, ethnol-
ogy, etc. of dwellings. Works on
the social or economic aspects of
housing are entered under Indians
of North America—Housing.
  UF Teepee rings
      Teepees
      Tepee rings
      Tepees
      Tipi rings
      Tipis
      Wigwams
  NT Pueblos
—**Economic conditions**
  [E98.E2]
  NT Indians of North
      America—Business
      enterprises
      Indians of North
      America—Public
      welfare
—**Education** *[E97 (United States)]*
  [LC2629 (Canada)]
  Here are entered works on the
education of Indians of North
America. Works on courses of
study, research, etc. about Indians
of North America are entered under
Indians of North America—Study
and teaching.
  UF Indians of North
      America—Schools
  NT Indians of North
      America—Scholar-
      ships, fellowships, etc.
— — **Law and legislation**
—**Education (Higher)**

—**Egyptian influences**
  [E99.C9]
  BT Egypt—Civilization
—**Embroidery** *[E98.E5]*
  UF Embroidery, Indian
  BT Indians of North
      America—Art
      Indians of North
      America—Textile
      industry and fabrics
—**Employment** *[E98.E6]*
— — **Law and legislation**
    BT Labor laws and
      legislation
—**Encyclopedias**
  UF Indians of North
      America—Dictionar-
      ies and encyclopedias
—**Ethics**
  UF Ethics, Indian
      Indian ethics
—**Ethnic identity**
  UF Indians of North
      America—Race
      identity
—**Ethnobotany**
  BT Ethnobotany
—Ethnology
  USE Ethnology—North
      America
      Indians of North America
—**Ethnozoology**
  BT Ethnozoology
—**Exhibitions**
—**Extraterrestrial influences**
  UF Extraterrestrial influences
      on Indians of North
      America
  BT Interplanetary voyages
—Factory system
  USE Indians of North
      America—Trading
      posts
—**Feather-work**
  BT Feather-work
      Indians of North
      America—Art
      Indians of North
      America—Industries
—**Fiction**
—**Financial affairs** *[E98.F3]*
  BT Indians of North
      America—Property
— — **Law and legislation**
—**Fire use**
  UF Fire use by Indians of
      North America
      Use of fire by Indians
      of North America
  BT Fire
—**First contact with Europeans**

UF Contact, First, of the
Indians of North
America with
Europeans
Indians of North
America—First
contact with Occidental
civilization
BT Europeans
First contact of
aboriginal peoples
with Westerners
—First contact with Occidental
civilization
USE Indians of North
America—First
contact with
Europeans
—**Fishing** *[E98.F4]*
— — **Law and legislation**
BT Fishery law and
legislation
—Five Civilized Tribes
USE Five Civilized Tribes
—**Folklore**
UF Folk-lore, Indian
Indians of North
America—Mythology
NT Indians of North
America—Legends
—**Food** *[E98.F7]*
NT Indians of North
America—Salt
—**Footwear**
BT Indians of North
America—Costume
and adornment
NT Moccasins
—Forced removal
USE Indians of North
America—Removal
—**Foreign influences**
UF Indians of North
America—Culture
—**Freedom of religion**
UF Indians of North
America—Religious
liberty
BT Freedom of religion
Indians of North
America—Civil rights
—**Gambling**
—**Games** *[E98.G2]*
BT Indians of North
America—Recreation
Indians of North
America—Social
life and customs
NT Indians of North
America—Dolls

Indians of North
America—Sports
—**Genealogy**
BT Genealogy
—**Gifts**
BT Gifts
Indians of North
America—Govern-
ment relations
Indians of North
America—Social
life and customs
NT Potlatch
—**Goldwork**
BT Goldwork
—Government policy
USE Indians of North
America—Govern-
ment relations
—**Government relations** *[E91]*
[E93 (United States)]
Here are entered works on the
Indian policy of the United States
government and on relations be-
tween the government and the In-
dians, or on North American
government relations with the Indi-
ans in general. For works on govern-
ment relations with Indians of a
particular state an additional subject
entry is made under Indians of North
America—[local subdivision].
UF Indians of North
America—Govern-
ment policy
SA *subdivision Government*
relations under
individual tribes,
e.g. Dakota Indians—
Government relations;
and names of agencies,
e.g. Red Cloud Agency
NT Indian agents
Indians of North
America—
Appropriations
Indians of North
America—Canada
Indians of North
America—Criminal
justice system
Indians of North
America—Cultural
assimilation
Indians of North
America—Gifts
Indians of North
America—Removal
—Government relations
— — **To 1789**
— — **1789-1869**
— — **1869-1934**
— — **1934-**

NT Trail of Broken
Treaties, 1972
Wounded Knee
(S.D.)—History
—Indian occupation,
1973
—**Handicapped**
—**Handicapped children**
BT Handicapped children
Indians of North
America—Children
—Handicraft
USE Indians of North
America—Industries
—**Health and hygiene**
BT Medical anthropology
NT Indians of North
America—Hospitals
Indians of North
America—Mental
health services
— — **Law and legislation**
—**Hindu influences**
UF Indians of North
America—Culture
—**Historiography**
—**History** *[E77]*
NT Indians of North
America—Wars
— — **16th century**
— — **17th century**
— — **Colonial period, ca.**
1600-1775 *[E77]*
— — **18th century**
— — **Revolution, 1775-1783**
— — **19th century**
— — **Civil War, 1861-1865**
[E540.I3]
— — **20th century**
— — **Chronology**
Here are entered works con-
taining listings of events and
dates in order of occurence in
the history of the Indians of
North America. Works on the
system of arranging time used
by the Indians of North America
are entered under Indians of
North America—Chronology.
— — **Study and teaching** *(May*
Subd Geog)
— — Text-books
USE Indians of North
America—History
—Text-books
— — **Textbooks**
UF Indians of North
America—
History—Textbooks
—**Horses** *[E98.H55 (Indians of*
North America)]
UF Indian ponies

Indians of North America

—Horses *(Continued)*

    Indians of North America—Ponies

    BT Horses

        Indians of North America—Domestic animals

—Hospital care

    BT Hospital care

        Indians of North America—Medical care

—Hospitals *[RA981.A35]*

    UF Hospitals, Indian

        Indian hospitals

    BT Indians of North America—Diseases

        Indians of North America—Health and hygiene

—Housing

    Here are entered works on the social or economic aspects of housing. Works on the architecture, construction, ethnology, etc. of dwellings are entered under Indians of North America—Dwellings

— — Finance

— — — Law and legislation

— — Law and legislation

    (May Subd Geog)

—Humor

    UF Indians of North America—Anecdotes, facetiae, satire, etc.

—Hunting *[E98.H8]*

    BT Indians of North America—Industries

        Indians of North America—Social life and customs

    NT Buffalo jump

— — Law and legislation

    BT Game-laws

—Implements *[E98.I4]*

    BT Indians of North America—Antiquities

        Indians of North America—Quarries

    NT Folsom points

        Harpoons

        Indians of North America—Knives

        Scottsbluff points

        Tomahawks

—Incantations *[E98.M2]*

    UF Incantations, Indian

        Indian incantations

    BT Indians of North America—Magic

—Industries *[E98.I5]*

    UF Indians of North America—Handicraft

        Indians of North America—Manufactures

    BT Handicraft

        Indians of North America—Material culture

        Industries, Primitive

    NT Indians of North America—Basket making

        Indians of North America—Featherwork

        Indians of North America—Hunting

        Indians of North America—Metal-work

        Indians of North America—Pottery

        Indians of North America—Quarries

        Indians of North America—Salt

        Indians of North America—Textile industry and fabrics

        Indians of North America—Trading posts

        Indians of North America—Trapping

        Quillwork

—Inheritance and succession

    BT Indians of North America—Property

    RT Indians of North America—Probate law and practice

    NT Indians of North America—Wills

—Interviews

—Irrigation

    BT Indians of North America—Agriculture

        Irrigation

—Jewelry

    BT Indians of North America—Costume and adornment

—Joking

    BT Joking

—Juvenile delinquency

    [E98.C87]

    BT Indians of North America—Crime

        Juvenile delinquency

—Kings and rulers

—Kinship

    BT Indians of North America—Social life and customs

—Knives *[E98.K54]*

    BT Indians of North America—Implements

        Knives

—Land tenure *[E98.L3]*

    UF Indians of North America—Land titles

        Indians of North America—Real property

    BT Indians of North America—Legal status, laws, etc.

        Indians of North America—Property

—Land titles

    USE Indians of North America—Land tenure

—Land transfers *[E91-E93]*

    BT Indians of North America—Legal status, laws, etc.

    RT Indians of North America—Treaties

    NT Indians of North America—Property

        Indians of North America—Removal

—Languages *[PM1-PM7356]*

    SA *names of languages, e.g.* Algonquian languages, Chippewa language, Hupa language

    NT Iroquoian languages

        Kutenai language

        Michif language

        Muskogean languages

        Na-Dene languages

        Proto-Athapascan language

        Salishan languages

        Tanoan languages

        Wakashan languages

— — Imprints *[Z7118]*

— — Texts

—Leather work

    BT Leather work

    NT Parfleches

—Legal status, laws, etc.

    NT Indians of North America—Arbitration and award

        Indians of North America—Children—Legal status, laws, etc.

        Indians of North America—Claims

Indians of North
America—Claims
against
Indians of North
America—Constitu-
tional law
Indians of North
America—Courts
Indians of North
America—Domestic
relations
Indians of North
America—Land
tenure
Indians of North
America—Land
transfers
Indians of North
America—Mediation
Indians of North
America—Pensions
Indians of North
America—Probate
law and practice
Indians of North
America—Property
Indians of North
America—Suffrage
Indians of North
America—Treaties
Indians of North
America—Water
rights
Indians of North
America—Wills
—Legends [E98.F6]
   BT   Indians of North
America—Folklore
   NT   Coyote (Legendary
character)
—Library resources
—Liquor problem
   USE Indians of North
America—Alcohol use
—Magic [E98.M2]
   UF   Magic, Indian
   BT   Indians of North
America—Religion
and mythology
   NT   Indians of North
America—Incantations
—Manufactures
   USE Indians of North
America—Industries
—Maps
—Marriage customs and rites
   BT   Indians of North
America—Social
life and customs
—Masks [E98.M3]
—Mass media

   BT   Mass media
—Material culture
   BT   Material culture
   NT   Indians of North
America—Industries
—Mathematics
   BT   Mathematics
—Medals
—Mediation
   BT   Indians of North
America—Legal
status, laws, etc.
Mediation
—Medical care
   NT   Indians of North
America—Hospital
care
 — — Law and legislation
—Medicine [E98.M4]
   NT   Indians of North
America—Dentistry
 — — Formulae, receipts, pre-
scriptions [E98.M4]
—Mental health
—Mental health services
   BT   Indians of North
America—Health
and hygiene
—Metal-work [E98.M45]
   BT   Indians of North
America—Art
Indians of North
America—Industries
—Military capacity and organi-
zation
   USE Indian warfare—North
America
—Mineral resources
   USE Indians of North
America—Mines
and mining
—Mines and mining
   UF   Indians of North
America—Mineral
resources
 — — Law and legislation
   BT   Mining law
—Missions [E98.M6]
   UF   Missions to Indians of
North America
—Mixed bloods
   USE Indians of North
America—Mixed
descent
—Mixed descent [E99.M693]
   UF   Guineas (Mixed bloods,
United States)
Indians of North
America—Mixed
bloods

   BT   Racially mixed people—
North America
   NT   Melungeons
Ramapo Mountain people
Wesorts
—Money [E98.M7]
   BT   Shell money
   RT   Wampum
—Mortality
—Mortuary customs [E98.M8]
   UF   Indians of North
America—Burial
—Museums [E56]
   BT   Archaeological museums
and collections
Ethnological museums
and collections
 — — Law and legislation
     (Not Subd Geog)
—Music [E98.M9] [ML3557]
—Mythology
   USE Indians of North
America—Folklore
Indians of North
America—Religion
and mythology
—Names [E98.N2]
   UF   Names, Geographical—
Indians of North
America
Names, North American
Indian
—Narcotics
   USE Indians of North
America—Drug use
—Newspapers
—Nutrition
—Oratory [E98.O7]
     Here are entered collections of
orations in Indian languages as
well as works about Indian ora-
tions. Collections of orations by
American Indians belonging to a
specific tribe and in an individual
Indian language receive additional
subject entries under the name of
the tribe subdivided by Oratory
and the heading for orations in that
language, e.g. Pima Indians—Oratory
and Speeches, addresses, etc.,
Pima. Collections of orations by
American Indians in an individual
non-Indian language are entered
under the appropriate heading for
orations in that language with the
subdivision Indian authors, e.g.
Speeches, addresses, etc., American—
Indian authors.
   NT   Speeches, addresses,
etc., American—Indian
authors
Speeches, addresses,
etc., Dakota

Indians of North America
—**Oratory** (Continued)
  Speeches, addresses,
   etc., Iroquois
  Speeches, addresses,
   etc., Pima
  Speeches, addresses,
   etc., Tohono O'Odham
—**Origin**
—Orphan-asylums
 USE Indians of North
   America—Orphanages
—**Orphanages**
 UF Indians of North
   America—Orphan-
   asylums
 BT Indians of North
   America—Child
   welfare
  Indians of North
   America—Children
—Ownership of slaves
 USE Indians of North
   America—Slaves,
   Ownership of
—**Painting**
 BT Indians of North
   America—Art
—Paper making
 USE Indians of North
   America—Paper-
   making
—**Papermaking**
 UF Indians of North
   America—Paper-
   making
 BT Papermaking
—**Pensions** [E98.P3]
 BT Indians of North
   America—Legal
   status, laws, etc.
  Indians of North
   America—Public
   welfare
—**Philosophy**
 BT Ethnophilosophy
—**Physical characteristics**
 [E98.P53]
 UF Indians of North
   America—Somatology
 NT Indians of North
   America—Anthro-
   pometry
  Indians of North
   America—Craniology
—**Pictorial works** [E77.5]
 UF Indians of North
   America in art
— — **Exhibitions**
—**Poetry**
 BT Indians in literature

—**Politics and government**
 UF Indians of North
   America—Tribal
   government
—Ponies
 USE Indians of North
   America—Horses
—**Population**
 BT Indians of North
   America—Census
  North America—
   Population
 NT Indians of North
   America—Statistics,
   Vital
—**Portraits** [E89]
 This heading covers general
collections of portraits of Indians
and also works containing portraits
of Indians of a particular tribe or of
the tribes of a specific locality. The
latter are entered also under the
name of the tribe or under the local
subdivision, e.g. a work which
deals with portraits of Indians of
Oregon will appear under: 1. Indians
of North America—Portraits. 2. In-
dians of North America—Oregon.
—**Pottery** [E98.P8]
 BT Indians of North
   America—Antiquities
  Indians of North
   America—Industries
—**Probate law and practice**
 BT Indians of North
   America—Legal
   status, laws, etc.
 RT Indians of North
   America—Inheritance
   and succession
—**Property** [E98.P9]
 BT Indians of North
   America—Land
   transfers
  Indians of North
   America—Legal
   status, laws, etc.
 NT Indians of North
   America—Financial
   affairs
  Indians of North
   America—Inheritance
   and succession
  Indians of North
   America—Land
   tenure
—**Psychology** [E98.P95]
—**Public contracts**
—**Public opinion**
—**Public welfare**
 BT Indians of North
   America—Economic
   conditions

  Public welfare
 NT Indians of North
   America—Child
   welfare
  Indians of North
   America—Pensions
—**Quarries** [E98.15]
 BT Indians of North
   America—Industries
  Quarries and quarrying
  Quarries and quarrying,
   Prehistoric
 NT Indians of North
   America—Implements
—Race identity
 USE Indians of North
   America—Ethnic
   identity
—Real property
 USE Indians of North
   America—Land
   tenure
—**Recreation** [E99.G2]
 UF Indians of North
   America—Amusements
 BT Indians of North
   America—Social
   life and customs
 NT Indians of North
   America—Games
—Relations with Afro-Americans
 USE Afro-Americans—
   Relations with Indians
—**Religion and mythology**
 [E98.R3]
 UF Indians of North
   America—Mythology
 NT Corn maidens' dance
  Indians of North
   America—Dances
  Indians of North
   America—Magic
  Indians of North
   America—Rites
   and ceremonies
  Medicine wheels
  Peyotism
  Totems
  Vision quests
—Religious liberty
 USE Indians of North
   America—Freedom
   of religion
—**Removal** [E93 (United States)]
 UF Forced removal of Indians
  Indian removal
  Indians of North
   America—Forced
   removal
  Removal of Indians

BT   Indians, Treatment of—
       United States
       Indians of North
       America—Govern-
       ment relations
       Indians of North
       America—Land
       transfers
NT   Cherokee Removal,
       1838

—Research *(May Subd Geog)*

—Reservations *[E78] [E91-E93]*
[E99]
UF   Indian reservations
       Reservations, Indian
SA   *names of reservations*
NT   Indian agents
       Navajo Indian
       Reservation

—Rites and ceremonies
BT   Indians of North
       America—Religion
       and mythology
SA   *names of special*
       ceremonies, e.g.
       O-kee-pa (Religious
       ceremony)
NT   Ajilee (Navajo rite)
       Butterfly dance
       Indians of North
       America—Sweatbaths
       Peyotism

—Roads
BT   Indian trails
       Roads

—Rugs
USE   Indians of North
       America—Textile
       industry and fabrics

—Salt *[E98.S26]*
BT   Indians of North
       America—Food
       Indians of North
       America—Industries
       Salt

—Sanatoriums

—Scholarships, fellowships, etc.
(May Subd Geog)
UF   Indian scholarships
BT   Indians of North
       America—Education

—Schools
USE   *names of individual*
       schools
       Indians of North
       America—Education

—Sculpture
UF   Indians of North
       America—Stone-
       sculpture

BT   Indians of North
       America—Art
       Sculpture, Primitive

—Secret societies *[E98.S75]*
BT   Secret societies

—Semitic influences
BT   Civilization, Semitic

—Sexual behavior
BT   Sex customs

—Shell engraving
BT   Indians of North
       America—Art
       Shell engraving

—Sign language *[E98.S5]*
UF   Gesture language
BT   Sign language

—Silversmithing
USE   Indians of North
       America—Silverwork

—Silverwork
UF   Indians of North
       America—Silver-
       smithing
BT   Silverwork

—Slaves, Ownership of
UF   Indians of North
       America—Ownership
       of slaves
       Ownership of slaves by
       Indians
BT   Slavery—United States

—Smoking
USE   Indians of North
       America—Tobacco use

—Social conditions
NT   Indians of North
       America—Urban
       residence

—Social life and customs
[E98.S7]
UF   Indians of North
       America—Customs
NT   Indians of North
       America—Dances
       Indians of North
       America—Games
       Indians of North
       America—Gifts
       Indians of North
       America—Hunting
       Indians of North
       America—Kinship
       Indians of North
       America—Marriage
       customs and rites
       Indians of North
       America—Recreation
       Potlatch

—Societies, etc.

—Somatology

USE   Indians of North
       America—Physical
       characteristics

—Sports
BT   Indians of North
       America—Games
NT   Indians of North
       America—Boxing

—Statistics

—Statistics, Vital
BT   Indians of North
       America—Population
       Vital statistics

—Stone-sculpture
USE   Indians of North
       America—Sculpture

—Study and teaching
(May Subd Geog)
       Here are entered works on
courses of study, research, etc.
about Indians of North America.
Works on the education of Indians
of North America are entered under Indians of North America—
Education.
UF   Indian studies, North
       American

—Suffrage
BT   Indians of North
       America—Legal
       status, laws, etc.

—Suicidal behavior

—Sweatbaths
       Here are entered works which
deal with the sweatbath as an important Indian social and religious
institution and the structure where
the sweatbath takes place.
UF   Indians of North
       America—
       Sweathouses
       Indians of North
       America—
       Sweatlodges
BT   Baths, Vapor
       Indians of North
       America—Rites
       and ceremonies

—Sweathouses
USE   Indians of North
       America—Sweatbaths

—Sweatlodges
USE   Indians of North
       America—Sweatbaths

—Taxation
— — Law and legislation

—Teeth
UF   Indians of North
       America—Dentition
BT   Dental anthropology
       Teeth

Indians of North America
(Continued)
—Textile industry and fabrics
[E98.T35]
 UF Indians of North
 America—Rugs
 BT Blankets
 Indians of North
 America—Industries
 Textile fabrics
 Textile industry
 NT Indians of North
 America—Embroidery
—Tobacco-pipes *[E98.T6]*
 UF Calumets
 Pipes, Indian
 BT Indians of North
 America—Tobacco-
 pipes
—Tobacco use
 UF Indians of North
 America—Smoking
 BT Smoking
 Tobacco
 NT Indians of North
 America—Tobacco-
 pipes
—Trading posts *[E98.C7]*
 UF Indian trade factories
 Indians of North
 America—Factory
 system
 Trading posts (North
 American Indian)
 BT Indians of North
 America—Commerce
 Indians of North
 America—Industries
—Trails
 USE Indian trails
—Transatlantic influences
 UF Transatlantic influences
 on Indians
—Transpacific influences
 UF Transpacific influences
 on Indians
 BT America—Discovery
 and exploration—
 Pre-Columbian
 Indians—Origin
 Man—Migrations
—Transportation
—Trapping *[E98.T75]*
 BT Indians of North
 America—Industries
 Trapping
—Treaties *[E95]*
 BT Indians of North
 America—Legal
 status, laws, etc.

 RT Indians of North
 America—Land
 transfers
 SA *names of specific
 treaties*
—Treaties, [date]
—Treatment
 USE Indians, Treatment of—
 North America
—Tribal citizenship
 Here are entered works on
 tribal citizenship of American Indi-
 ans. Works on United States citi-
 zenship of American Indians are
 entered under Indians of North
 America—Citizenship.
—Tribal government
 USE Indians of North
 America—Politics
 and government
—Urban residence
 BT City and town life
 Indians of North
 America—Social
 conditions
 Urbanization
—Wars *[E81-E83]*
 BT Indians of North
 America—History
 RT Indian warfare—North
 America
 NT Indians of North
 America as seamen
— — **1600-1750** *[E82]*
 NT Ackia, Battle of, 1736
 Chickasaw Indians—
 Wars, 1739-1740
 Eastern Indians, Wars
 with, 1722-1726
 Esopus Indians—
 Wars, 1655-1660
 Esopus Indians—
 Wars, 1663-1664
 King Philip's War,
 1675-1676
 Natchez Indians—
 Wars, 1716
 Pequot War, 1636-
 1638
 Tuscarora Indians—
 Wars, 1711-1713
 United States—
 History—King
 William's War,
 1689-1697
 United States—
 History—Queen
 Anne's War,
 1702-1713
 United States—
 History—King

 George's War,
 1744-1748
 Wappinger Indians—
 Wars, 1655-1660
— — **1750-1815** *[E81]*
 NT Cherokee Indians—
 Wars, 1759-1761
 Dunmore's Expedition,
 1774
 Pontiac's Conspiracy,
 1763-1765
 Tippecanoe, Battle
 of, 1811
 United States—
 History—French
 and Indian War,
 1755-1763
— — **1775-1783** *[E83.775]*
 BT United States—
 History—Revolu-
 tion, 1775-1783
 NT Blue Licks, Battle of
 the, 1782
 Crawford's Indian
 Campaign, 1782
 Shawnee Indians—
 Wars, 1775-1783
 Sullivan's Indian
 Campaign, 1779
 Yuma Indians—
 Wars, 1781-1782
— — **1790-1794** *[E83.79]*
 BT Delaware Indians
 NT Harmar's Expedition,
 1790
 St. Clair's Campaign,
 1791
 Wayne's Campaign,
 1794
— — **1812-1815** *[E83.812]*
 NT Creek War, 1813-1814
 Harrison, Fort, Battle
 of, 1812
— — **1815-1875** *[E81]*
 NT Black Hawk War,
 1832
 Cheyenne Indians—
 Wars, 1857
 Comanche Indians—
 Wars, 1840
 Comanche Indians—
 Wars, 1859
 Creek War, 1836
 Mill Creek Indians—
 Wars, 1857-1865
 Pacific Coast Indians,
 Wars with,
 1847-1865
 Paiute Indians—
 Wars, 1860

Rogue River Indian
War, 1855-1856
Seminole War, 1st,
1817-1818
Seminole War, 2nd,
1835-1842
Seminole War, 3rd,
1855-1858
— — 1862-1865 *[E83.863]*
NT Birch Coulee, Battle
of, 1862
Dakota Indians—
Wars, 1862-1865
Platte Bridge, Battle
of, 1865
Powder River
Expedition, 1865
Sand Creek Massacre,
Colo., 1864
Shoshoni Indians—
Wars, 1863-1865
— — 1866-1895 *[E83.866]*
NT Apache Indians—
Wars, 1883-1886
Bannock Indians—
Wars, 1878
Black Hawk War
(Utah), 1865-1872
Butte, Battle of the,
1877
Cheyenne Indians—
Wars, 1876
Dakota Indians—
Wars, 1876
Dakota Indians—
Wars, 1890-1891
Modoc Indians—
Wars, 1873
Nez Perce Indians—
Wars, 1877
Red River War,
1874-1875
Tuuarika Indians—
Wars, 1879
Ute Indians—Wars,
1879
— — 1868-1869 *[E83.866]*
UF Washita Campaign,
1868-1869
NT Beecher Island,
Battle of, 1868
— — Veterans
BT Veterans
—Water rights
BT Indians of North
America—Legal
status, laws, etc.
—Weapons *[E98.A65]*
UF Indians of North
America—Arms
and armor

NT Tomahawks
—Weights and measures
BT Weights and measures
—Wife abuse
BT Indians of North
America—Crime
Wife abuse
—Wills *[E98.W5]*
BT Indians of North
America—Inheritance
and succession
Indians of North
America—Legal
status, laws, etc.
—Women *[E98.W8]*
UF Women, Indian
Women, Native
American
—Wood-carving *[E98.W85]*
BT Indians of North
America—Art
—Wounds and injuries
[RD93.6I53]
—Writing *[E98.W9]*
—Youth
UF Indian youth (North
America)
Youth, Indian (North
America)
BT Indians of North
America—Children
—Alabama
NT Alabama Indians
Creek Indians
Mobile Indians
Taensa Indians
— — Antiquities
—Alaska
NT Ahtena Indians
Chilkat Indians
Chimmesyan Indians
Dena'ina Indians
Eyak Indians
Haida Indians
Ingalik Indians
Koyukon Indians
Kutchin Indians
Natsitkutchin Indians
Tahltan Indians
Tanana Indians
Tlingit Indians
Tsetsaut Indians
Tsimshian Indians
Tukkuthkutchin
Indians
Vuntakutchin Indians
— — Antiquities
— — Languages
—Alberta
NT Kainah Indians
— — Antiquities

— — Reservations
NT Blood Indian Reserve
(Alta.)
— — Trading Posts
NT Nottingham House
(Alta.)
—Arizona
NT Cocopa Indians
Havasupai Indians
Hopi Indians
Hualapai Indians
Maricopa Indians
Mimbreno Indians
Mogollon Indians
Mohave Indians
Pima Indians
Piman Indians
Sobaipuri Indians
Tewa Indians
Tohono O'Odham
Indians
Western Apache Indians
Yaqui Indians
Yavapai Indians
Yuma Indians
— — Antiquities
NT Cohonina culture
— — Languages
NT Cocopa language
Keres language
— — Music
NT Chicken scratch music
— — Reservations
NT Colorado River Indian
Reservation
(Ariz. and Calif.)
Fort Apache Indian
Reservation (Ariz.)
Gila River Indian
Reservation (Ariz.)
Hualapai Indian
Reservation (Ariz.)
Salt River Indian
Reservation (Ariz.)
San Carlos Indian
Reservation (Ariz.)
Tohono O'Odham
Indian Reserva-
tion (Ariz.)
— — Trading Posts
NT Hubbell Trading Posts
National Historic
Site (Ganado, Ariz.)
— — Wars
NT Maricopa Wells
(Ariz.), Battle
of, 1857
—Arkansas
NT Quapaw Indians
Tunica Indians

Indians of North America
—**Arkansas** *(Continued)*
— — **Antiquities**
    NT Cedar Grove Site
        (Lafayette
        County, Ark.)
—**British Columbia**
    NT Bella Coola Indians
        Bellabella Indians
        Carrier Indians
        Chehalis Indians
        Chilcotin Indians
        Chilkat Indians
        Chilliwack Indians
        Chimmesyan Indians
        Clayoquot Indians
        Coast Salish Indians
        Comox Indians
        Cowichan Indians
        Eyak Indians
        Haida Indians
        Haisla Indians
        Kaska Indians
        Kitksan Indians
        Kitwancool Indians
        Kutenai Indians
        Kwakiutl Indians
        Lillooet Indians
        Lummi Indians
        Nahane Indians
        Niska Indians
        Nootka Indians
        Ntlakyapamuk Indians
        Okinagan Indians
        Oowekeeno Indians
        Sekani Indians
        Shuswap Indians
        Slave Indians
        Squawmish Indians
        Stalo Indians
        Tagish Indians
        Tahltan Indians
        Tsimshian Indians
        Wakashan Indians
— — **Antiquities**
— — **Languages**
—**California**
    UF Mission Indians of
        California
    NT Achomawi Indians
        Aguas Calientes Indians
        Atsugewi Indians
        Cahuilla Indians
        Chilula Indians
        Chimariko Indians
        Chumashan Indians
        Cocopa Indians
        Costanoan Indians
        Cupeno Indians
        Diegueno Indians
        Gabrielino Indians

Hupa Indians
Juaneno Indians
Kamia Indians
Karok Indians
Kashaya Indians
Kato Indians
Kawaiisu Indians
Keeche Indians
Kiliwa Indians
Luiseno Indians
Lutuamian Indians
Madehsi Indians
Maidu Indians
Miwok Indians
Mono Indians
Moquelumnan Indians
Nicoleno Indians
Nisenan Indians
Nomlaki Indians
Palaihnihan Indians
Patwin Indians
Pomo Indians
Saclan Indians
Salinan Indians
Serrano Indians
Shasta Indians
Shastan Indians
Sinkyone Indians
Tolowa Indians
Tubatulabal Indians
Wailaki Indians
Wappo Indians
Washo Indians
Wintu Indians
Wintun Indians
Wiyot Indians
Yana Indians
Yokayo Indians
Yokuts Indians
Yuki Indians
Yuma Indians
Yurok Indians
— — **Antiquities**
— — **Languages**
    NT Wintun languages
        Yuki language
— — **Reservations**
    NT Colorado River
        Indian Reservation
        (Ariz. and Calif.)
        Santa Ysabel Indian
        Reservation (Calif.)
        Tule River Indian
        Reservation (Calif.)
—**Canada**
    UF Indians of Canada
— — **Government relations**
    BT Indians of North
        America—Govern-
        ment relations

    NT Indians, Treatment
        of—Canada
— — **Mixed bloods**
    USE Indians of North
        America—
        Canada—Mixed
        descent
— — **Mixed descent**
    UF Indians of North
        America—
        Canada—Mixed
        bloods
    NT Metis
—**Canada, Eastern**
    NT Abnaki Indians
        Algonkin Indians
        Iroquoian Indians
        Mistassin Indians
        Woodland Indians
—**Canada, Northern**
    NT Chipewyan Indians
        Kawchottine Indians
        Kutchin Indians
—**Colorado**
    NT Jicarilla Indians
        Moache Indians
        Tabeguache Indians
        Ute Indians
        Wiminuche Indians
— — **Antiquities**
— — **Reservations**
    NT Southern Ute Indian
        Reservation (Colo.)
        Ute Mountain Indian
        Reservation
—**Connecticut**
    NT Mohegan Indians
        Nipmuc Indians
        Paugusset Indians
        Pequot Indians
        Quinnipiac Indians
        Scaticook Indians
        Siwanoy Indians
        Tunxis Indians
        Wappinger Indians
— — **Reservations**
    NT Golden Hill
        Reservation (Conn.)
—**Delaware**
    NT Assateague Indians
        Wappinger Indians
—**East (U.S.)**
    NT Iroquoian Indians
        Shawnee Indians
        Woodland Indians
—**Florida**
    NT Apalachee Indians
        Calusa Indians
        Mikasuki Indians
        Timucua Indians
        Yamassee Indians

— — Antiquities
— — Languages
    NT Timucuan languages
—Georgia
    NT Creek Indians
        Guale Indians
        Timucua Indians
        Yamassee Indians
— — Antiquities
    NT Cemochechobee
        Archaeological
        District (Ga.)
—Great Basin
    NT Paiute Indians
—Great Lakes Region
    NT Neutral Nation Indians
        Potawatomi Indians
—Great Plains
    NT Arapaho Indians
        Arikara Indians
        Brule Indians
        Cheyenne Indians
        Comanche Indians
        Crow Indians
        Dakota Indians
        Dhegiha Indians
        Hidatsa Indians
        Hunkpapa Indians
        Iowa Indians
        Kiowa Indians
        Mandan Indians
        Mill Creek Indians
        Miniconjou Indians
        Oglala Indians
        Omaha Indians
        Oneota Indians (Great
        Plains)
        Oohenonpa Indians
        Oto Indians
        Ponca Indians
        Sans Arc Indians
        Saone Indians
        Sihasapa Indians
        Siksika Indians
        Siouan Indians
        Sisseton Indians
        Teton Indians
        Yankton Indians
— — Antiquities
    NT Mill Creek culture
— — Music
    NT Siyotanka (Musical
        instrument)
—Idaho
    NT Bannock Indians
        Kalispel Indians
        Kutenai Indians
        Paloos Indians
        Salish Indians
        Skitswish Indians
        Tukuarika Indians

— — Antiquities
— — Reservations
    NT Duck Valley Indian
        Reservation
        (Idaho and Nev.)
        Lemhi Indian
        Reservation (Idaho)
—Illinois
    NT Peoria Indians
        Piankashaw Indians
— — Antiquities
—Indian Territory
    NT Five Civilized Tribes
—Indiana
    NT Wea Indians
— — Antiquities
—Iowa
— — Antiquities
    NT Mill Creek culture
— — Reservations
    NT Sac and Fox
        Reservation (Iowa)
—Kansas
    NT Kansa Indians
        Pawnee Indians
        Wichita Indians
—Louisiana
    NT Atakapa Indians
        Caddo Indians
        Chitimacha Indians
        Houma Indians
        Koasati Indians
        Taensa Indians
        Tunica Indians
— — Antiquities
    NT Tchefuncte culture
— — Languages
    NT Chitimacha language
—Maine
    NT Abnaki Indians
        Malecite Indians
        Norridgewock Indians
        Passamaquoddy Indians
        Penobscot Indians
        Pequawket Indians
        Sokoki Indians
        Wawenock Indians
— — Antiquities
—Manitoba
    NT Cree Indians
— — Antiquities
— — Reservations
    NT Fort Alexander
        Indian Reserve
        (Man.)
—Maritime Provinces
    NT Micmac Indians
—Maryland
    NT Choptank Indians
        Conoy Indians
        Nanticoke Indians

        Susquehanna Indians
—Massachusetts
    NT Dudley Indians
        Gay Head Indians
        Mashpee Indians
        Massachuset Indians
        Nauset Indians
        Nipmuc Indians
        Pocasset Indians
        Stockbridge Indians
        Wachuset Indians
        Wamesit Indians
— — Antiquities
—Michigan
    NT Fox Indians
        Menominee Indians
        Ottawa Indians
— — Antiquities
—Middle Atlantic States
    NT Conestoga Indians
        Conoy Indians
        Delaware Indians
        Erie Indians
        Moravian Indians
—Middle West
    NT Illinois Indians
        Kaskaskia Indians
        Mascouten Indians
        Miami Indians
        Potawatomi Indians
        Sauk Indians
—Minnesota
    NT Kiyuska Indians
        Mdewakanton Indians
        Wahpeton Indians
— — Reservations
    NT Fond du Lac Indian
        Reservation (Minn.)
        Leech Lake Indian
        Reservation (Minn.)
        Mille Lacs Indian
        Reservation (Minn.)
        Prairie Island Indian
        Reservation (Minn.)
        Red Lake Indian
        Reservation (Minn.)
        White Earth Indian
        Reservation (Minn.)
—Mississippi
    NT Biloxi Indians
        Chickasaw Indians
        Natchesan Indians
        Natchez Indians
        Pascagoula Indians
        Tunica Indians
— — Antiquities
—Mississippi River Valley
    NT Tonikan Indians
—Missouri
— — Antiquities

Indians of North America
(Continued)
—**Missouri River Valley**
   NT Missouri Indians
       Osage Indians
—**Montana**
   NT Atsina Indians
       Crow Indians
       Kalispel Indians
       Kutenai Indians
       Salish Indians
— — **Antiquities**
— — **Reservations**
   NT Blackfeet Indian
       Reservation (Mont.)
       Crow Indian
       Reservation (Mont.)
       Flathead Indian
       Reservation (Mont.)
       Fort Belknap Indian
       Reservation (Mont.)
       Fort Peck Indian
       Reservation (Mont.)
       Northern Cheyenne
       Indian Reservation
       (Mont.)
—**Nebraska**
   NT Pawnee Indians
       Wahpekute Indians
—**Nevada**
   NT Gosiute Indians
       Washo Indians
— — **Antiquities**
— — **Reservations**
   NT Duck Valley Indian
       Reservation
       (Idaho and Nev.)
       Pyramid Lake Indian
       Reservation (Nev.)
—**New Brunswick**
   NT Malecite Indians
       Passamaquoddy Indians
— — **Reservations**
   NT Tobique Indian
       Reserve (N.B.)
—**New England**
   NT Arosaguntacook Indians
       Brotherton Indians
       Wampanoag Indians
—**New Hampshire**
   NT Pennacook Indians
—**New Jersey**
   NT Hackensack Indians
       Minisink Indians
—**New Mexico**
   NT Acoma Indians
       Apache Indians
       Capote Indians
       Cochiti Indians
       Isleta Indians
       Jemez Indians

       Jicarilla Indians
       Keresan Indians
       Laguna Indians
       Lipan Indians
       Mescalero Indians
       Mimbreno Indians
       Moache Indians
       Mogollon Indians
       Piman Indians
       Piro Pueblo Indians
       Sia Indians
       Tanoan Indians
       Taos Indians
       Tewa Indians
       Tigua Indians
       Ute Indians
       Warm Spring Apache
       Indians
       Zuni Indians
— — **Antiquities**
— — **Languages**
   NT Keres language
— — **Reservations**
   NT Ute Mountain Indian
       Reservation
—**New York (State)**
   NT Cayuga Indians
       Esopus Indians
       Iroquois Indians
       Mahican Indians
       Manhattan Indians
       Massapequa Indians
       Mingo Indians
       Minisink Indians
       Mohawk Indians
       Montauk Indians
       Oneida Indians
       Onondaga Indians
       Scaticook Indians
       Seneca Indians
       Shinnecock Indians
       Siwanoy Indians
       Susquehanna Indians
       Tuscarora Indians
       Wappinger Indians
       Wenrohronon Indians
— — **Reservations**
   NT Allegany Indian
       Reservation (N.Y.)
       Onondaga Indian
       Reservation (N.Y.)
       Saint Regis Mohawk
       Indian Reserva-
       tion (N.Y.)
—**Newfoundland**
   NT Beothuk Indians
       Naskapi Indians
— — **Languages**
   NT Beothuk language
—**North Carolina**
   NT Cheraw Indians

       Keyauwee Indians
       Lumbee Indians
       Occoneechee Indians
       Tuscarora Indians
       Tutelo Indians
       Welsh Indians
— — **Reservations**
   NT Cherokee Indian
       Reservation (N.C.)
—**North Dakota**
   NT Yanktonai Indians
— — **Antiquities**
— — **Reservations**
   NT Fort Berthold Indian
       Reservation (N.D.)
       Fort Totten Indian
       Reservation (N.D.)
       Lake Traverse Indian
       Reservation
       (N.D. and S.D.)
       Standing Rock Indian
       Reservation
       (N.D. and S.D.)
       Turtle Mountain
       Indian Reserva-
       tion (N.D.)
— — **Trading posts**
   NT Fort Union (N.D.)
—**Northeastern States**
   NT Munsee Indians
—**Northwest, Pacific**
   NT Nez Perce Indians
       Salishan Indians
       Shahaptian Indians
—**Northwest Territories**
   NT Bearlake Indians
       Slave Indians
       Thlingchadinne Indians
       Vuntakutchin Indians
— — **Antiquities**
—**Ohio**
   NT Mingo Indians
— — **Antiquities**
—**Oklahoma**
   NT Cherokee Indians
       Five Civilized Tribes
       Kickapoo Indians
       Peoria Indians
       Piankashaw Indians
       Seminole Indians
       Tawakoni Indians
       Tonkawa Indians
       Wea Indians
       Wichita Indians
— — **Antiquities**
   NT Panhandle culture
— — **Legal status, laws, etc.**
— — **Reservations**
   NT Ponca Indian
       Reservation (Okla.)

—Ontario
NT   Abitibi Indians
       Cayuga Indians
       Cree Indians
       Huron Indians
       Iroquois Indians
       Missisauga Indians
       Mohawk Indians
       Nipissing Indians
       Oneida Indians
       Onondaga Indians
       Ottawa Indians
       Seneca Indians
       Timiskaming Indians
       Tionontati Indians
       Tuscarora Indians
— — **Antiquities**
— — **Reservations**
NT   Akwesasne Indian
       Reserve (Quebec
       and Ont.)
       Fort Hope Indian
       Reserve (Ont.)
       Grassy Narrows
       Indian Reserva-
       tion (Ont.)
       Tyendinaga Indian
       Reserve (Ont.)
       Whitefish Lake Indian
       Reservation
       No. 6 (Ont.)
—Oregon
NT   Alsea Indians
       Cayuse Indians
       Chetco Indians
       Chinook Indians
       Chinookan Indians
       Clackamas Indians
       Coos Indians
       Coquille Indians
       Kalapuya Indians
       Klamath Indians
       Kuitsh Indians
       Lutuamian Indians
       Modoc Indians
       Molala Indians
       Multnomah Indians
       Nehalem Indians
       Shasta Indians
       Shastan Indians
       Siletz Indians
       Siuslaw Indians
       Takelma Indians
       Tillamook Indians
       Tolowa Indians
       Tututni Indians
       Umatilla Indians
       Umpqua Indians
       Walla Walla Indians
       Walpapi Indians
       Wanapum Indians

       Wasco Indians
       Wyam Indians
       Yahuskin Indians
       Yakonan Indians
       Yoncalla Indians
— — **Antiquities**
— — **Reservations**
NT   Umatilla Indian
       Reservations (Or.)
       Warm Springs Indian
       Reservation (Or.)
—Pennsylvania
NT   Mingo Indians
       Susquehanna Indians
—Prairie Provinces
NT   Assiniboin Indians
       Hidatsa Indians
       Sarsi Indians
       Siksika Indians
       Slave Indians
       Tsattine Indians
—Quebec (Province)
NT   Mohawk Indians
       Montagnais Indians
       Naskapi Indians
       Oka Indians
       Tetes de Boule Indians
— — **Reservations**
NT   Akwesasne Indian
       Reserve (Quebec
       and Ont.)
       Betsiamites Indian
       Reserve (Quebec)
—Rhode Island
NT   Narraganset Indians
       Nipmuc Indians
       Pequot Indians
       Pocasset Indians
       Sakonnet Indians
—Saskatchewan
NT   Cree Indians
— — **Antiquities**
—South Carolina
NT   Catawba Indians
       Cheraw Indians
       Kusso Indians
       Santee Indians
       Waccamaw Indians
       Yamassee Indians
—South Dakota
NT   Yanktonai Indians
— — **Reservations**
NT   Cheyenne River
       Indian Reserva-
       tion (S.D.)
       Lake Traverse Indian
       Reservation
       (N.D. and S.D.)
       Pine Ridge Indian
       Reservation (S.D.)

       Rosebud Indian
       Reservation (S.D.)
       Standing Rock Indian
       Reservation (N.D.
       and S.D.)
— — **Trading posts**
NT   Fort Manuel (S.D.)
—Southeastern States
NT   Yuchi Indians
—Southern States
NT   Apalachicola Indians
       Biloxi Indians
       Cherokee Indians
       Choctaw Indians
       Koasati Indians
       Muskogean Indians
       Pascagoula Indians
       Seminole Indians
— — **Antiquities**
NT   Lamar culture
       Poverty Point culture
— — **Beverages**
NT   Black drink
— — **Languages**
NT   Mobilian trade
       language
       Uchean languages
—Southwest, New
NT   Azteco-Tanoan Indians
       Basket-Maker Indians
       Cliff-dwellers
       Comanche Indians
       Kiowa Apache Indians
       Navajo Indians
       Pueblo Indians
       Yuman Indians
— — **Antiquities**
NT   Hohokam culture
       Mogollon culture
       Panhandle culture
— — **Dances**
NT   Matachines (Dance)
— — **Languages**
— — **Textile industry and fabrics**
NT   Ojo de Dios
       (Talisman)
—Tennessee
— — **Antiquities**
—Texas
NT   Atakapa Indians
       Caddo Indians
       Coahuiltecan Indians
       Hasinai Indians
       Jumano Indians
       Karankawa Indians
       Koasati Indians
       Lipan Indians
       Mescalero Indians
       Patarabueye Indians
       Tawakoni Indians
       Tonkawa Indians

Indians of North America
—Texas *(Continued)*
    Waco Indians
— — Antiquities
    NT Panhandle culture
— — Wars
    NT Adobe Walls, Battle
        of, Tex., 1874
—United States
    USE Indians of North
        America
—Utah
    NT Gosiute Indians
        Tabeguache Indians
        Uinta Indians
        Ute Indians
        Yampa Indians
— — Antiquities
— — Reservations
    NT Ute Mountain Indian
        Reservation
—Virginia
    NT Bocootawwonauke
        Indians
        Cheraw Indians
        Manahoac Indians
        Monacan Indians
        Nottaway Indians
        Occoneechee Indians
        Pamunkey Indians
        Potomac Indians
        Powhatan Indians
        Rappahannock Indians
        Tutelo Indians
—Washington (State)
    NT Cayuse Indians
        Chinook Indians
        Chinookan Indians
        Clackamas Indians
        Clallam Indians
        Coast Salish Indians
        Colville Indians
        Cowlitz Indians
        Dwamish Indians
        Kalispel Indians
        Klikitat Indians
        Lummi Indians
        Makah Indians
        Muckleshoot Indians
        Nehalem Indians

        Nespelim Indians
        Nisqualli Indians
        Nooksack Indians
        Nootka Indians
        Okinagan Indians
        Paloos Indians
        Puyallup Indians
        Quileute Indians
        Quinault Indians
        Samish Indians
        Sanpoil Indians
        Shoto Indians
        Sinkiuse-Columbia
        Indians
        Skagit Indians
        Skitswish Indians
        Skokomish Indians
        Snohomish Indians
        Spokane Indians
        Stillaquamish Indians
        Suquamish Indians
        Swinomish Indians
        Tlakluit Indians
        Tulalip Indians
        Twana Indians
        Wakashan Indians
        Walla Walla Indians
        Wanapum Indians
        Wenatchi Indians
        Yakima Indians
— — Reservations
    NT Colville Indian
        Reservation (Wash.)
        Makah Indian
        Reservation (Wash.)
        Puyallup Indian
        Reservation (Wash.)
        Shoalwater Bay
        Indian Reserva-
        tion (Wash.)
        Spokane Indian
        Reservation (Wash.)
        Tulalip Indian
        Reservation (Wash.)
        Yakima Indian
        Reservation (Wash.)
—West (U.S.)
    NT Numic Indians
        Shoshonean Indians
        Uto-Aztecan Indians

—Wisconsin
    NT Fox Indians
        Mdewakanton Indians
        Menominee Indians
        Stockbridge Indians
        Tionontati Indians
        Winnebago Indians
— — Reservations
    NT Red Cliff Indian
        Reservation (Wis.)
—Wyoming
    NT Bannock Indians
        Crow Indians
        Tukuarika Indians
— — Antiquities
    NT Colby Mammoth Site
        (Wyo.)
— — Reservations
    NT Wind River Indian
        Reservation (Wyo.)
—Yukon Territory
    NT Eyak Indians
        Ingalik Indians
        Kaska Indians
        Nahane Indians
        Tagish Indians
        Tukkuthkutchin Indians
        Tutchone Indians
        Vuntakutchin Indians
— — Antiquities
Indians of North America,
    Treatment of
    USE Indians, Treatment of—
        North America
Indians of North America as
    seamen
    BT Indians of North America—
        Wars
    SA *subdivision* Participation,
        Indian *under individual*
        wars
    NT United States. Navy—
        Indians
Indians of North America as
    soldiers
    USE United States—Armed
        Forces—Indians
Indians of North America in art
    USE Indians of North America—
        Pictorial works

AUTHOR/TITLE INDEX

Generally, the numbers in this index refer to entries. References to page numbers are preceded by "p." References to authors, titles, associations, publishers, and computer vendors within the annotation are followed by "(n)".

SUBJECT INDEX

Generally, the numbers in this index refer to entries. References to page numbers are preceded by "p." References to subjects within an annotation are followed by "(n)."